Rent Adjustment and Tenant Default
in English and German Commercial Property Leases

Jan Matauschek

Rent Adjustment and Tenant Default in English and German Commercial Property Leases

An Economic and Legal Analysis

PETER LANG
Frankfurt am Main · Berlin · Bern · Bruxelles · New York · Oxford · Wien

Bibliographic Information published by the Deutsche Nationalbibliothek
The Deutsche Nationalbibliothek lists this publication in the Deutsche Nationalbibliografie; detailed bibliographic data is available in the internet at http://dnb.d-nb.de.

Univermerk: Zugl.: Hamburg, Univ., Diss., 2010

Cover Design:
Olaf Glöckler, Atelier Platen, Friedberg

D 18
ISBN 978-3-631-60949-1

www.peterlang.de

Acknowledgements

This book is the result of my doctoral research at the Institute of Law and Economics at the University of Hamburg. While writing a dissertation is largely a solitary task, I am grateful to many people who helped and supported me.

First and foremost, I wish to thank my supervisor, Professor Dr. Thomas Eger. He was always available to discuss my proposals and was a patient and interested listener. I am also grateful to Professor Dr. Heribert Hirte for being the second examiner of the thesis, and Professor Dr. Michael Adams for chairing the examination board.

The staff of the Universities of Hamburg, Bournemouth, Cambridge and London equipped me with the skills necessary to complete a doctoral thesis, for which I am profoundly grateful. Here I would especially like to mention Bernard Smales of Bournemouth University, who has not merely been my teacher but also a friend, and Professor John Glascock, then at the University of Cambridge, whose lucid thinking shaped my understanding of real estate economics. I was also inspired to conduct research in real estate economics and law by Dr. Shaun Bond, Professor Tony Ciochetti, Dr. Martin Dixon, Professor Gerwyn Griffiths, Barry Moore, Dr. Kanak Patel and Professor Dogan Tirtiroglu.

Utz Schlicht has been a friend and mentor and I am grateful to him for his friendship, advice and support.

I would especially like to thank Marcus Marschall for sharing his insights into the functioning of real estate markets and invaluable spreadsheet and financial modelling skills with me.

Many thanks also go to Conrad B.R. Herrmann, Arnd Reifenrath, Dr. Rolf Seebauer, Ralph Siebald and Christoph Zimmer of ICME Management Consultants for providing me with the opportunity to apply strategy consulting and real estate management in practice. I would also like to thank the many clients we advised, as every project is a learning process also for the consultant.

Above all, I am grateful to my late father and my mother. I can always count on my mother's support and owe everything to her.

Jan Matauschek

Contents

Exhibits

Tables

English Cases

Part 1: Business leases in Britain & Germany

1 Property investment in a borderless world

Property investment has undergone significant changes in recent years. The property industry has witnessed an unprecedented internationalisation and globalisation. These trends originate in the United States and have by now, via the UK property and investment landscape, reached the German market.

The globalisation of property markets is fuelled by several causes: The invention of new property vehicles and financing structures, such as Commercial Mortgage-Backed Securities (CMBS), and the globalisation of mortgage and investment markets in general allow for the financing of much larger transactions than seen in the past. At the same time, advances in data processing and computer technology enable property investors to manage much larger portfolios than previously feasible. In recent years financial markets have furthermore witnessed a high degree of liquidity, fuelled by until recently very low interest rates and increasing investments from emerging economies. This led to rising pressure on asset managers to identify attractive investments and to diversify with the aim of achieving an acceptable balance of risks and returns.

Within the European Union, the free movement of capital is furthermore guaranteed under the Treaty on the Functioning of the European Union (TFEU).[1] European harmonisation favours cross-border investments and enables investors to choose legal entities and tax structures that optimise their pan-European investments.

In 2005 commercial real estate investment in Europe reached a new record, topping US-$ 190 billion, representing an increase of over 20% vis-à-vis 2004 (Jones Lang LaSalle, 2006, p. 12). Cross-border capital flows increased by 43% compared to 2004. These cross-border capital flows accounted for more than half of total investment (59%; Jones Lang LaSalle, 2006, p. 12).

These large volumes can be explained by the occurrence of large-scale portfolio transactions. The sellers are often large industrial conglomerates that seek to focus on their core businesses and public institutions; the buyers are

1 Art. 26 (2) TFEU; (ex 14 (2) EC Treaty), detailed in Art. 63-66 TFEU.

mostly international (Anglo-American) investment groups. Unlike conventional conveyances, these transactions are characterised by large-scale due diligences assisted by investment banks, external consultants and law firms and by the use of innovative financial structures. The table below gives an overview of major deals in Germany in 2006/07:

Table 1-1: Selected transactions in Germany by opportunity/private equity funds 2006/07

Year	Seller	Buyer	Name	Property type	Purchase price in € bn
2007	DEGI	Whitehall Fund (Goldman Sachs)	Spring Portfolio	Office	€ 2,45 bn
2007	Union Investment Real Estate	Morgan Stanley	Part of Pegasus Portfolio	Mixed use	€ 1,36 bn
2007	Dieter Becken	Morgan Stanley	-	-	€ 0,67 bn
2007	ThyssenKrupp	Deutsche Bank, Herder & Partner	-	Office, industrial	€ 0,25 bn
2006	KarstadtQuelle	Whitehall Fund (Goldman Sachs)	Karstadt Portfolio	Office, retail, parking	€ 4,50 bn
2006	City of Dresden	Fortress	Woba Dresden	Residential	€ 1,75 bn
2006	DEKA	Oaktree Capital Management	Herkules Portfolio	Office	€ 1,10 bn
2006	Commerz Grundbesitz Invest	Morgan Stanley	-	-	€ 0,53 bn
2006	DB Real Estate	Eurocastle (Fortress)	Bridge Portfolio	Office	€ 0,50 bn

Source: CorpusSireo Research (2007)

The longer term success of such transactions depends on the ability of the investor to generate stable and increasing cash flows from the properties in the portfolio. This is even more important insofar as most of these transactions are highly leveraged. The severe crisis of financial markets that has been developing since summer 2007 has for the time being halted large transactions: Access to capital was severed and interest rates hiked, partly because of an increasing awareness of the risks of certain investments and partly because of central banks' strategies to tackle increasing inflation throughout 2008. Inflation, however, ceased to be of any concern at the moment and central banks resorted to the strategy of flooding markets with liquidity, arguably already setting the foundations for a new series of highly leveraged transactions.

Regardless of size or financing of the transaction, every real estate investment depends on cash flows from rents to be profitable. The diagram shows current market rents for office space in selected European cities in the third quarter 2008 and the second quarter 2009.

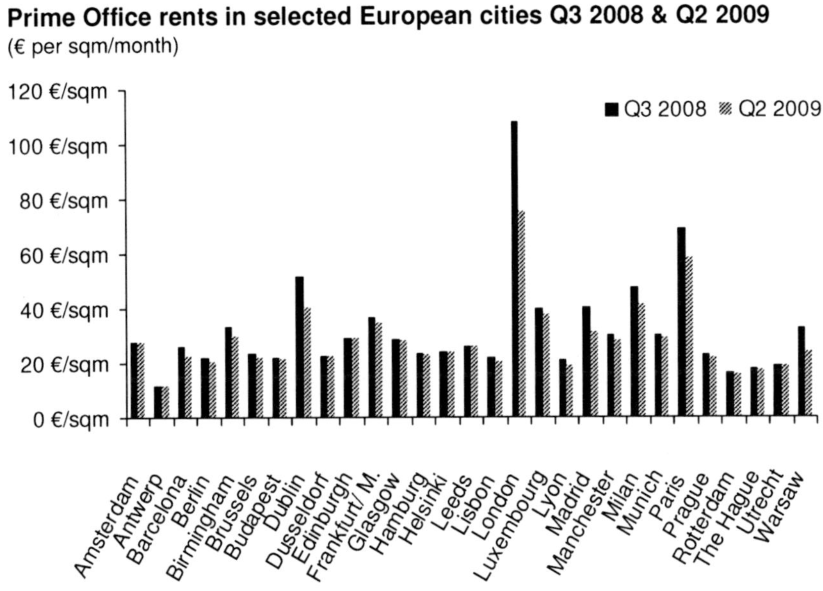

Source: Jones Lang LaSalle Research (2008 & 2009)
'Prime Rent' represents the top open-market rent that could be expected for a notional unit of the highest quality and specification in the best location in a market, as at the survey date.
Exchange rate EUR in GBP: £ 0.890 as per 15 Dec 2008

Exhibit 1-1: Prime Office rents in Europe: 2008 - 2009

The chart shows that market rents differ significantly between European office markets and that market rents can change rapidly. The short period from Q3 2008 to Q2 2009 was deliberately chosen to show how market rents react to a changing economic environment.

To take such a chart as an orientation for property investment may, however, be misleading: lease terms for commercial property may easily exceed ten years and in the UK the 25-year institutional lease is no exception (Edwards and Krendel, 2007, p. 9). Rents paid by sitting tenants therefore almost certainly differ from current market rents. If, for example, a lease contract in Hamburg was agreed on in Q3 2008 at the then market rent of 23.50 € the rent would by Q2 2009 already have fallen to 23.00 €.

As a result of changes on the property market, rents have to be adjusted over the term of the lease. The concrete methods by which rents are adjusted depend on the institutional and legal framework of the national market: Property law remains largely unaffected by harmonisation processes which took place within the European Community. This is because property law does not fall within the ambit of competences granted to the EC under the EC Treaty[2]. As a result, there are significant differences in the ways commercial lease contracts are structured in European countries.

In this respect real estate differs significantly from other asset classes: shares and fixed-income securities are traded on institutionalised exchanges that are subject to fairly harmonised regulations. Furthermore, the underlying economic drivers of stocks and bonds are very comparable between countries because of, for example, ratings provided by internationally operating rating agencies and the harmonisation of accounting standards through IFRS and US-GAAP.

International property investors therefore have to cope with a somewhat unbalanced situation: while investment strategies are formulated globally and cross-border investments are the norm, the lease contracts that form the underlying economic drivers of investment are very heterogeneous.

The author seeks to analyse lease contracts from the perspective of a real estate investor, such as a pension fund or an insurance company. It should be borne in mind that such investors can invest in four generic groups of assets. Real estate has quite distinct properties when compared to the other available assets. The following table sets out the characterising features of available asset classes and points out how real estate differs.

---

2 The free movement of capital does of course promote cross-border investment, but does not affect contractual structures as such.

Overview of asset classes

Asset classes	Stocks	Bonds (Government& Corporate)	Real Estate	Cash / Money Market
Role in an investment portfolio	Speculative element in portfolio	Typically largest part of portfolio, should warrant steady income	Depending on portfolio strategy, often as an inflation hedge	Only to "park" funds before other investment
Risk-return profile	High risks but highest potential returns	Ratings questionable, but traditionally moderate risks	Depends on entry in life-cycle (e.g. development)	Low risks, but often return <= inflation
Revenue planning & monitoring	Equity research & Key Performance Indicators	Mostly through Key Performance Indicators	Revenue influenceable through marketing, tenant improvements	Market screening to reduce spreads
Role of asset management	Monitoring of portfolio	Monitoring of portfolio	Active role, more akin to an entrepreneur	Monitoring of target returns
Source of cash flows	Dividends & gains in share prices	Interest payments & changes in bond prices	Rents (depending on contract) and value appreciation	Interest payments

Not included in table: derivative forms of investment (options, certificates etc.)

Exhibit 1-2: Overview of asset classes

Two significant differences between real estate and other asset classes are the roles of asset management and the sources of cash flows. For stocks, bonds (and investments in the money market) asset management mostly takes place in the form of monitoring the assets held in a portfolio and comparing actual performance with the benchmarks defined in the portfolio's investment strategy. Asset management for real estate takes a very different form. As a physical asset is held, the asset manager's role is more akin to that of an entrepreneur who has to market and maintain the assets.

The more entrepreneurial, proactive role of the real estate asset manager also means that – to a certain extent and of course always taking the general market into account – the asset manager is able to influence cash flows from individual real estate assets. This is so because cash flows stem from an individually negotiated lease. Asset managers of stocks and bonds have, on the other hand, no effective means of influencing cash flows, e.g. dividends, which are generated by an asset.

The present work therefore seeks to analyse commercial lease contracts in England (and Wales) and Germany as the main source of income from commercial property[3]. The focus of the work is the economic efficiency of either

3 The return from commercial property is actually a combination of cash flows from letting and value appreciation realised by an eventual sale. The sales price, however, is directly related to the rental income of the property as sales prices are mostly quoted as a multiple of yearly rents or in the form of an exit yield (e.g. the market requires a yield of 5% for office properties, meaning that a building

jurisdiction. England and Germany are chosen for two reasons: First of all, England and Germany are the most important commercial real estate markets in Europe, Germany being the biggest market, and England being the second biggest with the special role of London as the European financial centre. In 2005, the UK accounted for 36% of all European cross-border investments (rank 1) and Germany accounted for 21% of these investments, placing the country on the second rank (Jones Lang LaSalle, 2006, p. 12).

Secondly, both countries have developed quite distinct rules of regulating real estate. In Germany, a commercial lease contract is first and foremost a regular contract governed by the German civil code, the *Bürgerliches Gesetzbuch* (BGB). In England, on the other hand, lease contracts combine elements of the law of contract and of property law. Property law has, for historic reasons, developed as a separate branch of law, and is governed by quite different and for the Continental reader seemingly archaic rules.

As the objective of this work is to compare the economic efficiency of the overall regulation of real estate leasing in the two countries, both the legal framework and prevailing market practices have to be analysed.

The study proceeds as follows: First of all, relevant background information on the property markets in England and Germany is provided. Institutional differences and characteristics of the markets are pointed out. Second, the economic methodology to be used for the analysis is briefly described: The theory of long-term contracts.

It is clearly impossible to compare all aspects of business leases. The topic is too wide to cover all issues. The author therefore had to decide upon a selection. The criterion applied to identify suitable sub-topics was the impact on cash flows from real estate. As this work focuses on real estate held as an investment, rental cash flows are the most relevant figure to compare properties.

Two topics were identified as having the strongest impact on cash flows from a lease: Rent adjustments over the term of the lease and the treatment of tenant default.

In order to secure investment returns, adapt to changing economic environments and maintain incentives, rent adjustment is quintessential especially for long-term leases. The author looks at the prevalence of certain types of rent adjustments in England and Germany and evaluates their legal regulation and economic impact. Particular attention is placed on the economic incentives provided by different lease adjustment models.

---

currently generating a rental income of € 100,000 is expected to have a sales price of € 2,000,000).

The second topic to be examined is tenant default. The enforcement of rent payments is a sensitive issue. The law has to strive for a balance between the interests of tenants who are in financial difficulties and landlords' commercial interests. The law must take into account public policy arguments and must protect businesses from too fast and simple eviction. The situation is further complicated by the heterogeneity of tenants, some of whom are rogues who intentionally do not fulfil their obligations, while other tenants genuinely face difficulties. As commercial tenants are typically companies, the position of an insolvent corporate tenant and his landlord are also examined.

The question is how the legal regimes in England and Germany enable landlords to enforce rent payments and how tenants are protected. The author draws conclusions from the literature on the economic analysis of insolvency law. In a final chapter, conclusions will be drawn as to the efficiency of both legal systems.

The work continues with a characterisation of the countries' property markets.

2 Market parameters

2.1 Structure of the UK property market

The following PESTEL framework[4] offers an analysis of the macro-environmental influences which affect a company or industry (Johnson and Scholes, 2002, p. 102). The table below displays the framework for the UK property industry:

Table 2-1: PESTEL UK property industry

Political - Generally investor friendly climate - Open economy with high foreign investments	**Economic Factors** - Economic growth has in recent years to a great extent been fuelled by property industry - Current downturn and "credit crunch" hitting industry hard (high integration of property and financial markets)
Socio-cultural factors - Historically grown property profession with high level of self-regulation - Property industry highly esteemed by population	**Technological** - Highly developed financial markets allow for innovative property investments such as derivatives
Environmental - Recently increasing importance of sustainability issues regarding property	**Legal** - Liberal regulation of financial markets - Legal framework generally characterised as "landlord-friendly", but to be scrutinised

Because of its long history of professional property management and a generally liberal regulation of markets, the UK property market has proved to be very attractive to both domestic and international investors.

4 PESTEL: Political, economical, sociological, ecological, legal.

The structure and size of the UK property market has been the subject of substantial research commissioned by the Investment Property Forum (IPF, 2005).[5] By the end of 2003, the estimated total capital value of the UK commercial property stock was estimated to be £ 489 bn. The capital value of commercial property held as an investment was £ 254 bn, i.e. 52% of the commercial property stock were used for investment purposes while the remaining 48% were held by owner-occupiers (IPF, 2005, pp. 34-35).

The chart below breaks down the main types of property investors (according to IPF, 2005, p. 34):

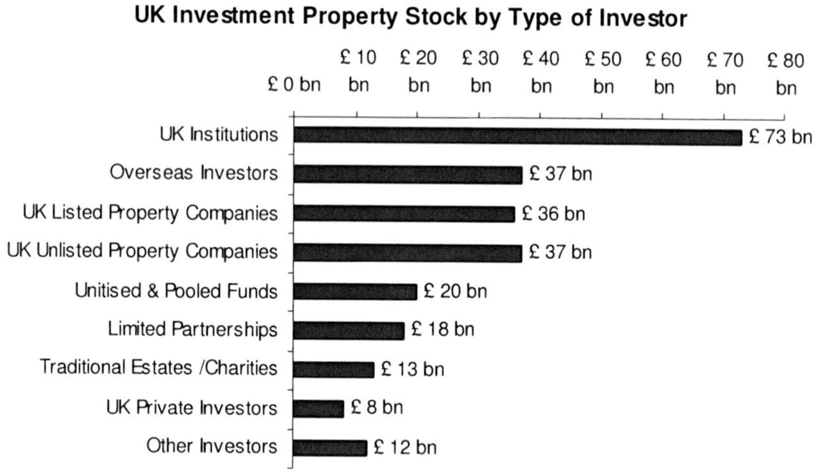

Exhibit 2-1: UK property investors

UK institutions are the largest single group on the investment market. These institutions are insurance companies and pension funds that invest in real estate to meet future liabilities. Their direct investments amount to £ 73 bn. In addition, institutional investors hold around 50% of Limited Partnerships and 90% of Pooled Funds so that their total market exposure amounts to £ 100 bn. Remarkably, investors from overseas hold property worth £ 37 bn which means that they hold the same share of the market as UK Listed and Unlisted Property Companies. The IPF (2005, p. 37) reports that the invested stock by overseas

5 The IPF, founded in 1988, is one of the leading property industry bodies with more than 1,900 members, which have an investment property background. IPF's stated central objective is "to advance the knowledge and understanding of property as an investment" (http://www.ipf.org.uk/MainWebSite/GeneralContent8ffa20e881efb5fc43dfbd5b.aspx?Map=65AD683EC539CB0BBB08C3C7A8330E6B; accessed on 27 July 2008).

investors has increased by 83% from 1998 to 2003. This is not only a reaction to the positive economic climate in the UK by that time but reveals the dramatic internationalisation of property investment. The strong presence of listed property companies is another defining element of the UK property market. There are currently 32 property companies listed on the main LSE exchange. Property companies have a long tradition in the UK and auditing and accountancy standards favour listed property companies: there is no depreciation of real property but a yearly valuation of properties to their market value. Six main companies dominate the market with a combined investment portfolio of £ 32 bn. This group of companies thus holds 80% of the property held by UK listed property companies. The companies are: Land Securities, British Land, Liberty, Hammerson, Slough and Brixton (IPF, 2005, p. 31). Finally, the degree of professionalism of the UK market is revealed by the small share of private investors. This group is made up of non-professional investors who invest through a variety of forms including direct investments, limited partnerships and so on. The total investments held by this group only amount to £ 8 bn, showing that the UK property market is a market for professional investors.

Another important characteristic of the UK property market is the concentration of investments in Greater London. This applies in particular to office and industrial properties while the retail investment stock is more evenly distributed across the country. For example, almost 80% of office stock by capital value in London is held as an investment compared to only around 15% in Wales (IPF, 2005, p. 40).

2.2 Structure of the German property market

As a general introduction, the following PESTEL-framework seeks to characterise the German commercial property market:

Table 2-2: PESTEL German property industry

Political	Economic Factors
- Some political resistance against foreign investments, particularly hedge funds - No unanimous backing of free market economy by the political elite	- After several years of stagnation, the German economy has recovered and enjoyed a growth period since 2005. Recession puts pressure on rents - No property market bubble as in US, UK and other European countries.

	Economic Factors (contd.) - German institutions in general not as severely affected by credit crunch as UK competitors (exceptions: Hypo Real Estate, *Landesbanken*)
Socio-cultural factors - No tradition of a property profession, therefore little institutionalised property education at universities etc. - Drive towards professionalism in recent years, pushed by foreign investors - Often semi-professional management not familiar with international real estate standards - Property industry does not enjoy best reputation	**Technological** - Market for innovative property investments not developed, e.g. no property derivatives - No country-wide real estate indices with broad coverage
Environmental - Traditionally strong emphasis on environmental protection and widespread support of "green" issues	**Legal** - Some tendencies to restrict investment, e.g. no residential property in G-REITs (Real Estate Investment Trusts – tax-neutral property investment vehicles) - Legal framework generally characterised as "tenant-friendly", but to be scrutinised

The German property market is characterised by two fundamental differences to the UK market: First of all, the markets are decentralised. Because of Germany's history – unification under one German state only in 1871 – and a strong emphasis on federal structures and decentralised decision making, several major cities developed. For example, Frankfurt is the financial centre, Hamburg the largest port and an important location for the media industry, Munich is home to many high-tech industries and also a strong financial sector. Cologne and Düsseldorf are the centres of the densely populated Rhine-Ruhr area with around 11,800,000 inhabitants[6]. Berlin is the capital and the largest city in the

6 http://www.megacities.uni-koeln.de/documentation/, accessed on 8 August 2008.

country, but for historical reasons does not have a strong economy. For investment purposes, property consultants typically focus on the so-called "Big 6", the six most important cities in terms of size and economic importance: Berlin, Düsseldorf, Frankfurt, Hamburg, Munich and Stuttgart. The international real estate consultancy Jones Lang LaSalle observed that in the first quarter of 2008 around 30% of property transactions (by capital values) took place in these big cities, resulting in a transaction turnover of around € 2.3 bn (Jones Lang LaSalle, 2008, p. 2). This figure reveals just how fragmented the German market is: the six most important cities account for only 30% of transactions. It also points out an ongoing tendency to invest in smaller cities because of expected higher returns. These cities are sometimes referred to as "B-cities" and include, among many others, Hanover, Leipzig, Dresden, Nuremberg and Essen.

The decentralised structure of Germany shaped its property market. Decentralisation is disadvantageous for the development of a property industry working to commonly accepted standards (see below). Markets are regionalised and often follow individual patterns. The property industry has traditionally been viewed as a regional industry and many people associate property investment with local, colourful *Immobilienbarone* ("real estate barons"), private investors who made their fortunes by using special knowledge of a local market and probably not always the most transparent methods in dealing with public authorities.

On the upside, the decentralisation of the German property market makes it an attractive opportunity for private equity funds. Fairly incomplete market information offers the chance for returns above the market average via arbitrage. As local market knowledge and extensive research are a pre-condition to spot such opportunities, some private equity investors, e.g. Lone Star, have set up regional offices across Germany while other US/UK investors that maintained only a HQ in Germany or steered all their operations from abroad partly failed to identify market opportunities.

In the UK and the United States financial markets and real estate have already been integrated for a long time in the form of real estate investment banking whereby investment banks either act as finance brokers or principal investors and real estate investments and investment banking are very much aligned throughout the real estate life-cycle.

In Germany, this combined approach is not yet as advanced and together with the decentralised structure of the country's property market it may be the reason why Germany is not as severely affected by the real estate crash and "credit crunch" that has been shaking most financial markets since the second half of 2007. German real estate is usually more conservatively funded and because markets are more regionalised, they are affected by the current crisis only to a lesser degree[7]. For these reasons, Ernst and Young's real estate consultancy has voted Germany to be the most attractive country for real estate investors in 2008.[8] However, pressure on rents and prices is also observable on the German real estate market, on the one hand because of the pessimistic economic outlook for the next few years but also because most large transactions in the past were carried out by international investors.

In the author's opinion, lack of transparency is, together with the decentralised structure, the major factor that distinguishes the German and UK property markets. The next section will therefore examine transparency-related issues.

2.3 Transparency

Because of the heterogeneous nature of real property, each asset being different because of location, building quality, and so on, real estate markets will always remain less transparent than markets for homogeneous and more fungible assets such as equities. The following exhibit summarises the main reasons for the real estate market being an imperfect market (adopted from Gondring, 2009, p. 25).

Sources of imperfection of real estate markets

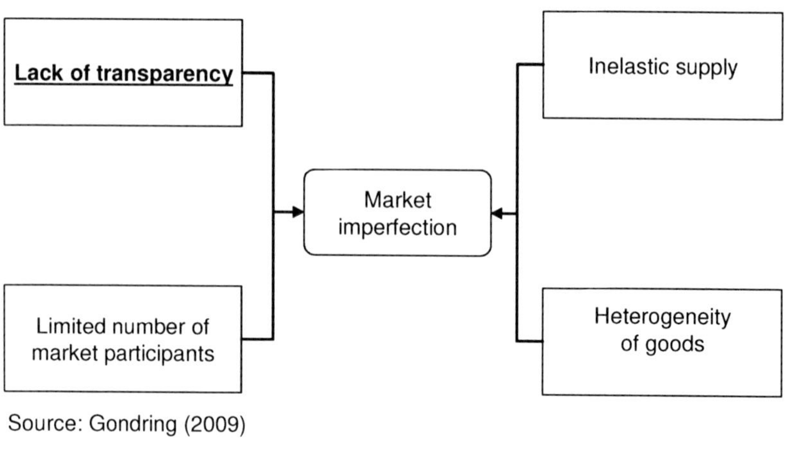

Source: Gondring (2009)

Exhibit 2-2: Imperfection of real estate markets

7 It should be highlighted that this statement refers to real estate markets only, not to German (real estate) banks which were also very much exposed to US asset-backed securities that caused the current crisis.

8 *Frankfurter Allgemeine Zeitung* of 29 February 2008, p. 45.

It is desirable for real estate markets to enhance transparency and thus reduce market imperfections. As observed by Schulte et al. (2005, pp. 90-91), transparency refers to equivalency of information between parties. A market that lacks transparency is characterised by information asymmetries. The authors find, by comparing the availability of market information through databases and publications as well as changes in corporate governance and real estate training and education that transparency on the German market has significantly improved over the past 15 years.[9]

The international real estate consultancy Jones Lang LaSalle has published a transparency index of global real estate markets in regular intervals since 1999.[10] It is found that compared to the real estate markets in the US and the UK the German market still lacks transparency.

In the 2006 report the United Kingdom attains rank 5 which positions the country in the tier with the most transparent markets.[11] Germany misses the top-tier and is ranked on place 12. The evaluation criteria are the typical requirements of cross-border property investors:

- Accurate market and financial information;
- Reliable performance benchmarks;
- Enforceable contracts and property rights;
- Clarity regarding the taxation and regulation of real estate;
- Fair treatment in the transaction process;
- Ethical standards among professionals hired to transact business.

A market is considered to have a low degree of transparency, on the other hand, where some or all of the following apply:

- Absence of benchmarks for financial performance;
- Lack of historical and current market statistics on demand, supply or rents;

9 Schulte et al. (2005, pp. 92-93) attribute a substantial part of improvements of transparency to the emergence of the internet: through the use of property websites and quick distribution of information by e-mail, market information is more readily available than in the past.

10 Jones Lang LaSalle (2006) *Real Estate Transparency Index*. The research is conducted by the firm's international research staff.

11 The other countries in the top-ten were: 1) Australia and the United States; 2) New Zealand; 3) Canada; 4) N/A; 5) UK; 6) Hong Kong; 7) Netherlands; 8) Sweden; 9) France; 10) Singapore.

- Financial statements of listed vehicles do not meet International Accounting Standards (IAS);
- Real estate tax procedures, building and zoning codes are not published or selectively enforced;
- Lack of title records or title insurance;
- Government or public utilities acquiring private property for necessary public uses give short notice or do not fairly compensate the owner.

Accordingly, the Jones Lang LaSalle researchers composed sub-indices based on the above criteria on the basis of which an overall transparency index is computed. The sub-indices are computed for "investment performance", "market data", "disclosure and governance", "regulatory and legal framework" and "professional standards and transaction process".

It should be noted that Germany attained a top-tier ranking in several categories. The overall ranking was, however, tainted by deficiencies in terms of financial statements and accountability. Jones Lang LaSalle criticised that accountancy practices relating to German open-ended funds[12] were lacking transparency as valuation of properties was not reflecting market values. The authors of the study also refer to the collapse of two such funds that shook up the German real estate investment landscape.[13]

German listed property companies[14] are also criticised for a lack of transparency. The rating agency Feri analysed the annual reports of German, Austrian and Swiss listed real estate companies with market capitalisations exceeding € 50 million. With the exception of a short property share boom in 2006, German property shares generally belong to the weak performers on the stock market. In particular, these shares trade at a significant discount to their Net Asset Value (NAV), i.e. the value of their assets minus debts.[15] The average discount in 2007 for the 29 analysed companies was 17%.[16] Feri Research

12 *Offene Immobilienfonds.*

13 The events referred to are now known as the Black Tuesday of open-ended funds because on Tuesday, 13 December 2005, Deutsche Bank had to close one of its funds because the fund's value had to be significantly corrected. Only about a month later a second fund by KanAm had to be closed because of liquidity problems following massive withdrawals of funds because of problems with one of the firm's asset management partners (*Frankfurter Allgemeine Zeitung*, 18 January 2006, p. 19).

14 Referred to as *Immobilien-AGs* because they are, unlike the newly introduced G-REITs, regular listed companies (*Aktiengesellschaften*).

15 Discounts to NAV can also be observed in other markets but in Germany the discount is quite significant.

16 Feri Research, cited in by Reichel in the *Handelsblatt*, 16 July 2008.

concluded that the discounts are based on analysts' lack of trust in the valuation of properties. In particular, the companies' annual reports failed to address the future potential of their portfolios both in terms of qualitative criteria, such as location, and quantitative criteria such as rent growth.

Jones Lang La Salle point out that transparency and reporting deficiencies of German property vehicles could be mitigated by the introduction of G-REITs: As REITs are traded at the stock exchange as any other stock, irregularities in accounting/reporting would immediately be punished by dramatic declines in share prices, thus disciplining management. Furthermore, G-REITs must comply with all accounting and reporting standards applying to publicly traded companies, in addition to the specific REIT-regulation. Because of turmoil in the financial markets, most German property companies have, however, suspended their planned conversions to G-REITs.[17] In the author's opinion, the G-REIT regulation is furthermore unattractive to investors because residential properties are excluded from G-REIT conversion[18] and secondly because financial gearing is strictly limited to 55%[19]. Property investment without high gearing, however, almost always results in low returns on equity, thus making these investments less attractive.

Another aspect where Germany and, indeed, the whole Continent lag behind developments in the UK is the availability of property indices. Jones Lang LaSalle (2006, pp. 12-13) observe that the IPD UK Annual Index is used as a basis of property derivatives. Because IPD indices are not so well developed on other markets, however, it would take some time before these innovative financial products are introduced to Continental property markets. It should nevertheless be noted that the study by Jones Lang LaSalle may partly return too harsh a verdict on the German property market. The study is largely written by London-based authors who are familiar with the highly centralised UK property market and may not fully recognise the challenges posed by the fragmented German market.[20]

---

17 Hamburg-based ALSTRIA Office Reit is one of a few successful example of a conversion from a "regular" listed company to a G-REIT. The REIT invests predominantly in office space across Germany. A substantial part of its portfolio is comprised of properties formerly owned and now rented back by the City of Hamburg. The company, however, struggles to maintain its REIT-status because of high debts.

18 s. 1 (1) 1a. G-REIT Act (*Gesetz über deutsche Immobilien-Aktiengesellschaften mit börsennotierten Anteilen – REIT-Gesetz*). It is noteworthy that German lawmakers decided to use the term REIT – Real Estate Investment Trust – instead of a German term.

19 s. 15 G-REIT Act.

20 Shortly before going to press of this book, Jones Lang LaSalle released preliminary results of the 2010 transparency study where Germany is now ranked

The transparency of a real estate market would appear to be closely related to the degree of centrality of the market. It was stated above that the UK market is characterised by a strong bias of investors to invest in or around London. It therefore comes as no surprise that the London property market is also the best researched property market in Europe and that the UK attains a top-position in the Jones Lang LaSalle transparency ranking.

The density and quality of market information will, all other things being equal, be lower where the market is characterised by decentralised structures. The dispersed structure of the German market means that less market data, both in quantitative and qualitative terms, is available for the different regional markets. Ludwig (2005, p. 13) quotes a survey among German real estate firms and research bodies investigating their collecting of market data. The institutions responded as follows:

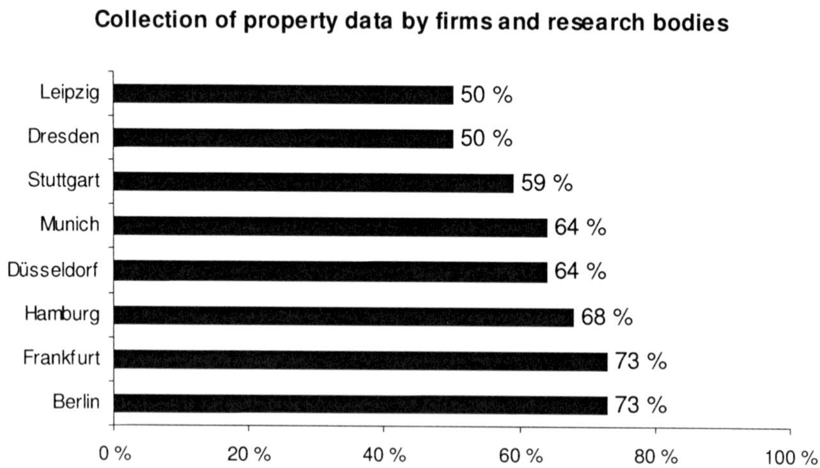

Exhibit 2-3: Collection of data for major German markets

The survey reveals the percentages of respondents who collect data for given regional markets. Frankfurt and Berlin are thus covered most widely, with 73% of respondents collecting market data on the cities. For Stuttgart, after all a "Big 6"-location, only 59% of respondents collect data and even less for the two East

---

10th, thus attaining the group of most transparent markets. A quoted reason for this improvement is an enhanced availability of market data. Nevertheless, limited transparency of financing structures and regional differences continue to be a concern (IZ Aktuell Newsletter, 22 June 2010). The above remarks on the German market thus remain valid.

German cities of Leipzig and Dresden. It is remarkable that there is no particular market for which all respondents collect data. Given that Frankfurt is the capital of the financial services and banking industries it is quite surprising that 27% of respondents do not seem to find it necessary to collect data. Ludwig (2005, p. 13) also points out that even less data is collected for other large regions such as Cologne, Nuremberg and Hanover and that are also many other smaller and medium-sized cities that, taken together, have a large stock of commercial property with a very low density of available data. Ludwig (2005, p. 14) recognises that availability of market data facilitates market entry by non-local investors but also acknowledges that the costs associated with market research are only justified where the market has a certain size and promises adequate returns.

2.3.1 Property market data in this study

The differences in availability of property market data also have implications for the discussion of specific issues in the second part of this study. Property market data is used to support theoretical observations of the property market.

Different types of data are used for UK and German leases, which is partly because of different degrees the countries' property markets are institutionalised and partly because of the availability of data because of the author's professional work.

2.3.2 UK lease-data

The empirical data on UK leases is sourced from the major property database, the IPD (Investment Property Databank) and partly also the data collected by the Valuation Office Agency.

The IPD states that: "at the end of 2006, the 12,137 properties covered by the Annual Index were valued at £192 billion - equivalent to 49% of the UK investment market."[21] The data used for this study is taken from the Report to the Deputy Prime Minister on the 2002 Code of Practice for Commercial Leases (Crosby et al., 2005). For this government-commissioned study IPD provided much more data than is normally made available to its subscribers from within the property industry.

---

21 http://www.ipd.com/GlobalNetwork/IPDinEurope/UnitedKingdom/tabid/470/Default.aspx (accessed on 10 May 2008); IPD also provides information on the German market from its office in Wiesbaden, yet the German IPD data does not cover the market as comprehensively as its UK parent company. The total value of properties covered by IPD Germany per Dec 2007 was € 44.5 bn.

The Valuation Office Agency is a public body that collects property data for taxation purposes (under English tax law, there are stamp duties on certain leases and council taxes, a major source of funding for local communities, are based on property values).

2.3.3 German lease-data

The data provided by databanks such as IPD gives insights on general market trends and, in case of IPD in the United Kingdom, also informs about certain clauses within the leases (e.g. types of rent review). Because of the highly institutionalised and centralised UK property market, such databases can, moreover, comprehensively depict the overall market.

The fragmented and less institutionalised German market is more difficult to represent within a database. IPD in Germany thus has less extensive market coverage than in the UK. The market leader for research on German property is Munich-based BulwienGesa AG. The firm's focus is, however, on predicting trends for local (sub-) markets and collecting and interpreting macro-economic data. BulwienGesa's main research output is the RIWIS database. It contains property market data for 125 locations in Germany. Around 70 performance indicators are available on topics such as rents for different types of use, vacancy rates and yields. RIWIS also provides macro-economic data with relevance to the property market (e.g. population growth) for a further 440 towns and counties (BulwienGesa, 2009). Nevertheless, RIWIS does not provide data on contractual clauses in leases.

In a paper written before international investors entered the German market in a larger scale, Thomas (1995, p. 73) reports that open-ended funds are the only publicly available source of real estate performance on the German market. This is so because open-ended funds have to publish annual reports.[22] Thomas (1995) also made a first attempt to create an index of property performance based on these open-ended funds performance reports. From 1996 onwards there is the *Deutscher Immobilien Index* (German Property Index) which offers investors insights into market returns generated by German investment properties. This index represents around 20% of the German institutional property market (Turner and Thomas, 2001b, p. 298).[23] The German Property Index is the only

22 Closed funds, which are organised as private companies with limited liability, are on the other hand not obliged to publish financial results.

23 Further indices are produced by a number of property consultants but they cover only certain markets or types of use (Turner and Thomas, 2001b, pp. 297-298). The figure of 20% for the German market can be contrasted with IPD's much wider coverage of 49% for the UK market (Crosby et al., 2005). Bobka (2009, p. 19) finds that now there are more than 100 German property indices on various

portfolio-based index for the German market. In a portfolio-based index actual property data is used for the calculation of the index. Notional indices, on the other hand, use market rents for the index calculation so that these indices produce higher returns than what would be achievable by actual investors (Turner and Thomas, 2001b, p. 297).

A general study on lease structures in Europe that also describes German lease structures was conducted by Lofstedt and Baum (1993). The study is more than 15 years old but confirms the leasing structures that are described in the chapter on rent adjustment.

IPD Germany today also offers the service "IPD Lease Intelligence", which is a database with multinational lease data for 1,500 cities in 11 countries.[24]

Insofar as fragmented, polycentric markets with a relatively low degree of institutionalisation are concerned, actual contracts do, however, provide the best insights into pressing issues within the property industry.

Actual contracts for larger-scale leases are mostly kept confidentially between landlord and tenant. Standard-form contracts for smaller leases are provided by industry associations or can be bought at stationery shops.[25] Such contracts are obviously only used for smaller leases and should be characterised by a lesser degree of sophistication.

The author has, however, gained access to a set of six large-scale commercial leases in a major German city.[26] These leases cover a wide set of industries (retail, office, hotel, commercial). The leases were negotiated between major players on the German property market and parties were advised by leading law firms and property consultants. These leases therefore represent the current industry standard of lease contracting in Germany.

It is particularly fortunate that the relatively small set of lease represents the most common property types and industries. As it will be discussed later on,

---

market segments using varied methodologies. She claims that the German market nevertheless lacks an index that covers the overall market as a leading index. German real estate professionals see this limited market coverage as a main reason why currently available indices are not widely employed in decision making (pp. 24-25).

24 http://www.ipd.com/LinkClick.aspx?link=downloads%2fprodukter%2fLease +Flyer+klein+Sept+2009.pdf&tabid=1089&mid=7479, accessed on 8 May 2010.

25 Consult, for example, standard lease contracts/ guidelines provided by the following Chambers of Commerce: *Industrie- und Handelskammer Frankfurt/Main (2007)* and *Industrie- und Handelskammer Nürnberg für Mittelfranken (2002).*

26 To keep confidentiality, no information can be given on the contracting parties, the exact location of the properties and the rents.

different industries should theoretically have varying requirements as to their leases. Whether this holds true in practice will be assessed by comparing the actual lease covenants to the theoretical findings.

The tables below summarise the major features of the six leases as they relate to the issues to be discussed:

Table 2-3: German lease data - case studies

No	Type of premises	Tenant's business	Let area sqm (approx.)	Lease term	Options (renewal or break)
1	Retail	Supermarket	1,700 sqm	10	3 renewal options for 5 years each
2	Commercial/ Office	Car rental station	125 sqm + 60 parking lots	10	2 renewal options for 5 years each
3	Retail	Fashion retailer	2,000 sqm	12	1 renewal option for 5 years (renewal option only valid if turnover rent was paid in the three years preceeding renewal)
4	Office	Regional headquarters (electronic goods manufacturer)	13,000 sqm + 120 parking lots and misc. areas (loading zones etc.)	10 years for 9,000 sqm and 5 years for up to 4,500 sqm	2 renewal options for 5 years each; tenant's break option after 5 years (with additional financial covenants
5	Hotel	Hotel chain	200 hotel rooms + 80 parking lots+ 350 sqm common area (lobby, reception etc.)	25 years	1 renewal option for 5 years
6	Commercial	Car service station	1,670 sqm + 80 parking lots	15 years	3 renewal options for 5 years each

(Table continues on following pages)

German lease data - case studies (continued: 2/5)

No	Rent adjustment mechanism	Landlord's repair obligations	Tenant's repair obligations	Security deposits & guarantees
1	Combination of turnover rent (3.9%) and minimum rent	Structural repairs ("Dach und Fach"), e.g. roofs and walls	Decorative repairs within the rented premises	Security deposit; tenant's bank also has to act as a guarantor for tenant's liabilities
2	CPI-dependent rent with upwards/downwards adjustment; triggered by notice of either party upon change of CPI by 4% or more	Structural Repairs ("Dach und Fach") and installations such as A/C	Decorative repairs within the premises (painting, carpets etc.). Upkeep only if costs do not exceed 150 € per individual repair or 3% of yearly rent	Bank guarantee only required from new tenant in case of assignment
3	Base rent: yearly adjustment according to CPI (upwards/downwards)	Structural Repairs ("Dach und Fach")	Upkeep and decorative repairs within the premises (painting, carpets etc.); no cap on costs	3 monthly rents (gross, including VAT and service charges); bank guarantee also required

German lease data - case studies (continued: 3/5)

No	Rent adjustment mechanism	Landlord's repair obligations	Tenant's repair obligations	Security deposits & guarantees
4	Simple indexation of 1.9% p.a.	Structural Repairs ("Dach und Fach")	Decorative repairs within the premises (painting, carpets etc.). Upkeep only if costs do not exceed 380 € per individual repair or 5% of yearly rent	Unlimited guarantee of tenant's international parent company ad bank guarantee of € 3m required
5	Yearly adjustment according to CPI: rent increase/ decrease by 65% of CPI increase/ decrease; each party may trigger review	Structural Repairs ("Dach und Fach")	Decorative repairs within the premises (painting, carpets etc.) and upkeep. For the first 2 years of lease performed by landlord but charged to tenant.	Tenant's parent company covenants to assume tenant's obligations under the lease if lease with original tenant is terminated for breach of covenant ("Mieteintritts-verpflichtung")
6	Adjustment according to CPI: either party may trigger review when CPI has changed by more than 5% since last adjustment (up/down)	Structural Repairs ("Dach und Fach") and installations such as ventilation systems	Decorative repairs within the premises (appliances in workshop etc.). Upkeep only if costs do not exceed 380 € per individual repair or 5% of yearly rent	Guarantee by tenant's parent company to meet tenant's liabilities

German lease data - case studies (continued: 4/5)

No	Penalties for late payment	Automatic forfeiture upon tenant's insolvency	Subletting & assignment	Other interesting clauses	Length of document (A4 pages)
1	Interest of 8% above ECB reference rate payable for delayed rents; right to sue for damages reserved		General permission to sub-let to members of the tenant's group of firms; in other cases security premium of up to 20% on current rent	- lease stipulates certain pricing strategies to maintain up-market image of location	35 pages
2	Interest of 8% above ECB reference rate payable for delayed rents; right to sue for damages reserved	Forfeiture upon opening of insolvency procedures or rejection of application for insolvency proceedings	Subletting only to be refused for important reasons. Tenant has principle right to assign the lease. Landlord may refuse assignment because of assignee's economic position / nature of his business	- Landlord covenants protection from competition (no letting of other premises to comparable businesses)	49 pages
3	Interest of 8% above ECB reference rate payable for delayed rents; right to sue for damages reserved	Not explicitly included in lease	Subletting of up to 15% of let area should not be refused but landlord may ask for rent premium on sub-let space of up to 20%	- type and quality of products specified in lease by reference to brand names (e.g. boss); for internal fitting tenant receives	36 pages

German lease data - case studies (continued: 5/5)

No	Penalties for late payment	Automatic forfeiture upon tenant's insolvency	Subletting & assignment	Other interesting clauses	Length of document (A4 pages)
4	Interest of 8% above ECB reference rate payable for delayed rents; right to sue for damages reserved	Forfeiture upon opening of insolvency procedures or rejection of application for insolvency proceedings	Principle right to sub-let, landlord's consent must not be unreasonably withheld		30 pages + annexes
5	Interest on delayed payments of rent at statutory rate; landlord may prove and charge higher costs	Forfeiture upon opening of insolvency procedures or rejection of application for insolvency proceedings	Landlord's consent to sub-letting must not be unreasonably withheld but depends on sub-tenant credit worthiness and business. Tenant assumes liability for sub-tenants	- required standard of 'Hotel' specified by reference to other 'Hotel' of the same chain; tenant to receive	203 pages (including annexes)
6	Interest on delayed payments of rent at statutory rate; landlord may prove and charge higher costs	Forfeiture upon opening of insolvency procedures or rejection of application for insolvency proceedings	Principle right to sub-let, landlord's consent must not be unreasonably withheld (clause fairly tenant-friendly); after 5 years tenant may propose assignee. Lease should be continued with assignee on same conditions as with tenant if tenant characteristics comparable		38 pages + 110 pages of annexes

The link between transparency and professionalism of a market is evident, but the role of the valuation profession in a country also has a significant impact on transparency. This relationship is discussed in the following section.

2.4 Development and role of the real estate professions in the UK and Germany

A major difference between the British and German property markets lies in the significantly different roles of real estate professionals. The UK property market is characterised by the dominant influence of Chartered Surveyors, real estate experts whose training and conduct is governed by their professional body, the Royal Institution of Chartered Surveyors (RICS). RICS was founded in 1868 and is now, with more than 140,000 members in 131 countries, the largest association of real estate professionals worldwide (Gondring, 2009, p. 879). Chartered Surveyors undergo significant training in all aspects of the real estate industry but mostly focus on valuation. They play an important role in advising landlords and tenants on lease contracts, rents and all other aspects related to the leasing of business premises. It is important to recognise that the role and standing of valuation professionals in Germany ("*vereidigte Sachverständige*", or "sworn valuers") is not comparable to that of Chartered Surveyors. To discover the reasons for these differences it is necessary to briefly review the different historical developments of the real estate professions in both countries (following Morgan, 1998).

Britain has been a capitalist society for much longer than Germany and a *laissez-faire* approach regarding business conduct and regulation has characterised the economy on the British Isles for centuries. This also impacted on the regulation of professions. Unlike in Germany, the professions in Britain have enjoyed and continue to enjoy wide-ranging freedoms in regulating their own affairs such as admission to the profession, training and disciplinary measures. Professional bodies were formed by industry professionals themselves and this bottom-up approach has traditionally resulted in the British professions being much closer to current market developments and trends.

In Germany, industrialisation and the development of a capitalist society set in later, fostered by the founding of the German empire in 1871. The German approach to the regulation of professions is much more characterised by a top-down approach. The state determines the conduct and training of professions and access to a profession is via university education rather than the joining of a professional body as an apprentice. The scope of self-regulation by professional bodies in Germany is fairly limited compared to Britain.[27] As one possible consequence, German professions cannot quickly re-adapt to changing market demands by altering standards or codes of conduct; they are in some way, detached from the market. Regarding real estate valuation, German valuation methods are prescribed by the *Baugesetzbuch* (*Building & Construction Act*) and the *WertV* (*Wertermittlungsverordnung*)[28], detailed in the *WertR* (*Wertermittlungsrichtlinien*). These are statutory valuation manuals prescribing which valuation techniques are acceptable under which circumstances and what has to be taken into account for a valuation (Gondring, 2009, p. 887). The focus of German valuers' work is often of a technical and architectural rather than commercial nature.

In contrast, the main focus of the work of Chartered Surveyors is commercial valuation with the aim of identifying market prices of properties. It will be shown later in the chapter on rent adjustment mechanisms that this institutional difference allowed the UK property market to develop its own mechanism (known as "rent review") to value properties and rents with close contact to the market. German sworn valuers, on the other hand, do not have close contact to real estate agencies and may have difficulties in obtaining current market information (Morgan, 1998, p. 198).

The strong influence of Chartered Surveyors means that UK lease transactions are often negotiated not by landlords and tenants directly but by their respective surveyors acting as their advocates.

Another comparative weakness of the German system is that entry examinations for sworn valuers are set by local Chambers of Commerce and that examination standards are not uniform (McParland et al., 2002, pp. 131-132). While the examinations aim to test only local property market knowledge, sworn valuers are nevertheless authorised to carry out valuations throughout the

---

27 An example may illustrate the difference: The German Lawyers' Associations (*Rechtsanwaltskammern*) monitor admission and conduct of their members but this is based on Federal statutes. In particular, their influence on legal education is limited to a vague consultative role. In contrast, the Law Society and the Bar Council regulate admission and conduct based on their own rules. The state's influence is reduced to a fairly recent statutory confirmation that such regulations are the sole affair of the respective professional bodies. Training for solicitors and barristers is also organised by their organisations and virtually free from state intervention.

28 On 1 July 2010, the new *Immobilienwertermittlungsverordnung (ImmoWertV)* takes effect, replacing the *WertV* and partly modifying valuation guidelines. The new *ImmoWertV* also aims to internationalise German valuation practices. The modifications are, however, of a gradual nature; in particular, a DCF-method is not introduced so that the changes triggered by the new regulation are likely to be limited (Ernst & Young, 2010, pp. 4-5).

country (McParland et al., 2002, p. 132). Morgan (1998, pp. 196-198) concludes that the title "sworn valuer" does not in itself guarantee the client a dependable degree of professionalism, independence and qualification.

Gondring (2009, pp. 943-944) moreover criticises that the title "real estate expert" (*Sachverständiger*) is not legally protected in Germany. The German Federal Court ruled that an expert merely has to prove that he possesses the necessary skills and professional expertise and has to demonstrate how he acquired the required knowledge[29]. Uniform standards are therefore not guaranteed. Gondring (2009, p. 945) thus also points out the need for better training of real estate professionals and more involvement of universities in providing appropriate degree programmes.

The lack of a strong valuation profession in Germany has also been identified as one of the reasons for the crisis of German open-ended funds in 2005/06. A study commissioned by the IPF (2007b) found several weaknesses of the valuation practices for these important investment vehicles. It is revealed that the properties of German funds are not valued in response to market fluctuations but a "sustainable long-term value" model is used that results in a volatility smoothing effect. As a consequence, assets tend to be overvalued in bearish markets and undervalued in bullish periods (IPF, 2007b, pp. 6-7). A problem relating directly to the valuation profession is that open-ended funds do not use international valuation firms (e.g. Jones Lang LaSalle, CBRE, DTZ) on their valuation committees. Instead, independent sworn valuers of the above-described group are used. A significant amount of the business of each of these valuers is likely to come from one client so that there is a clear risk of valuation in favour of fund management (IPF, 2007b, p. 6).

2.5 Lease contracts

While here the word "lease" is used to describe business tenancies in both England and Germany, the concept of leasing and its role within the legal system differs significantly between the two countries.

2.5.1 Leases in Germany

German law views leases as a sub-section of the law of contracts. It is paramount to point out that the German civil code (*Bürgerliches Gesetzbuch*), which regulates the major elements of private law, characterises leases only as a part of contract law but not as a part of property law. Consequently, the legal rules applying to leases are those of the law of contract and not those of property

29 German Federal Court decision of 6 February 1999.

law. The German civil code specifies general rules that apply to all contracts (such as offer and acceptance, misrepresentation, rescission of contracts and so on). Furthermore, the civil code characterises several types of contracts, one of which being the lease. The German lease is more akin to what English law would characterise as a licence. Instead of creating a property right, most rules on German leases apply also to leases of movables (cars, machinery etc.).

The main obligation of the lessor is to provide the let object in a condition fit to fulfil the objective of the contract and to maintain this condition through the term of the lease (s. 535 I BGB).[30] The main obligation of the lessee is to pay the contractually agreed rent (s. 535 II BGB). The comparison to English law will show that German lease law is characterised by a tacit understanding that the lease does not merely provide a right to occupy premises but rather that the lessor has to continuously provide a range of services to the lessee.

The formalities for creating a valid lease are also part of the law of contract. A German lease does not create a property right. Only ownership of land creates a property right (s. 873; 925 BGB). As a consequence, the lessee cannot resort to remedies that are available to holders of a property right.[31] Lease contracts are not entered on the land registry.[32]

The civil code specifies a number of remedies that are available exclusively to parties of a lease. The lessee may lower the rent if the let object/premises are defective.[33] The lessor has to guarantee that the premises are free from defects at the commencement of the lease. This is a strict liability rule (s. 536 a BGB), i.e. the lessor is responsible for the premises being free from defects irrespective of his fault. The lessee may not rescind from the contract because of defects but he has the right to terminate the lease.[34]

---

30 For example, if a car is rented the lessor has to ensure that the car is roadworthy and he has to maintain the condition of the car for the term of the lease.

31 Foremost s. 985: Claim for surrender; the owner can require the possessor to surrender the corporeal object. Translation obtained from: http://www.iuscomp.org/gla/statutes/BGBrest.htm, accessed on 4 August 2008.

32 In England, all leases for a term of more than seven years have to be registered at the Land Registry: s. 4 (1) (c) Land Registration Act 2002. Leases for a term of more than three but less than seven years have to be made by deed, a special form of contract attested by witnesses and subject to certain other formalities. For leases of less than three years a "normal" contract is sufficient.

33 This is referred to as *Mietminderung*, s. 536 BGB.

34 The main difference being the liability for payment of rent to the point of termination, s. 542 BGB.

2.5.2 Leases in England

English law characterises leases in a much different way. A lease is not merely a contractual agreement but creates a property right.

English property law dates back to the days of the Norman Conquest in 1066 and has thus preserved some archaic traits. All land in England is in principle owned by the Crown, which is referred to as *allodium*, or prerogatival ownership (Gray and Gray, 2006, p. 17).[35] Historically, the monarch granted rights to use land to aristocrats who would then grant rights to the peasants as was typical of a feudal society. The term "landlord" did not develop by coincidence. Various forms of granting rights in land were developed over time. These rights to use land are known as "estates in land".

The doctrine of estates in land states that a landholder does not own the land itself but a "slice of time in the land" (Gray and Gray, 2006, p. 17).

Today, two main estates in land are in use: the "fee simple absolute in possession", also referred to as "freehold", and the "term of years absolute", more commonly known as "leasehold". A freehold is, in practical terms, identical to ownership as it grants the right to use the land for an unlimited time.[36] The leasehold estate, on the other hand, is defined by reference to a fixed term of land use. Commercial leases are leasehold estates. While a statutory definition of freehold and leasehold estates was introduced with the Law of Property Act 1925, it was left to the courts how a lease is characterised. These characterising elements of a lease where defined fairly recently in Street v Mountford [1985] AC 809. In the House of Lords it was suggested by Lord Templeman that for there to be a lease, the tenant needs to have 1) exclusive possession of the premises, 2) it must be for a fixed or periodic term certain, and 3) there must be periodic payments or payment of a lump sum. The term "exclusive possession" merely describes that the tenant has the right to exclude everyone else, including the landlord, from the premises. It also underlines that the lease grants a property right. This power to exclude others is the main feature of estates in land. Lord Templeman described the tenant as an "owner *pro tempore*".

---

35 Powers and rights of the monarch that are not limited by statute are known as Royal Prerogative.

36 An example of an ancient form of estate in land that disappeared is the "fee tail": here the estate in land exists as long as the original grantee or any of his lineal descendants are alive. This form of estate was used as a method to retain land within an (aristocratic) dynasty (Gray and Gray, 2006, p. 18).

German leases are more akin to what English law defines as a "licence": a licence grants personal rights and does not entail the right to exclusive possession (Gray and Gray, 2006, pp. 180-182).[37]

The English landlord is not normally expected to maintain the let premises in a condition fit for the purposes for which they are let. This flows logically from the idea that granting a leasehold estate is a conveyance of a property right. A famous quote underlining this view was given by Erle CJ: "fraud apart, there is no law against letting a tumble-down house".[38] The paradigm of *laissez-faire* also dominates the current view of the courts. The condition of the premises is a question of negotiation between the parties. The law should not intervene in commercial bargaining processes. Schiemann LJ stated the principle that if a tenant "wants more he should bargain for it and be prepared to pay the extra rent".[39] There is an implied covenant for quiet enjoyment, meaning that the landlord must not interfere with the tenant's use of the property. This covenant covers only the rare cases where the landlord harasses the tenant, removes the tenant's belongings, and so on. The covenant does not imply an obligation to repair beyond what was previously agreed. Neither is the landlord obliged to repair premises that were already defective at the commencement of the lease (Gray and Gray, 2006, pp. 515-516). Finally, the landlord can discharge his obligations by exercising reasonable precaution to avoid disturbances. There is no strict liability, i.e. the landlord is only liable for defects where he has violated an express covenant or has failed to exercise reasonable precaution.

It would go beyond the scope of an introductory chapter to produce a comprehensive comparison of English and German lease law. The aspects discussed above already show that the concepts of leasing differ significantly between the two countries. German law implies a comprehensive set of obligations on the landlord and parties may contract out of these obligations. English law, on the other hand, provides almost no default rules and the general rule is that there will be no obligation unless expressly covenanted in the lease contract.

The English property industry, through its industry associations, recognises that this almost complete freedom to contract is not free from disadvantages. Contracts necessarily have to be lengthy to enunciate obligations and duties of the parties, transaction costs are high as a consequence, and the property market is characterised by a strong heterogeneity of contracts. As a response to this

37 Licences are, for example, used for students' accommodation because the university retains ultimate control and has a right to enter the rooms. The student-occupier cannot exclude university staff from his room and he cannot transfer his interest in the room as he enjoys a merely personal right.

38 Robbins v Jones (1863) 15 CBNS 221, 143 ER 768.

39 Southwark London Borough Council v Mills [2001] Ch 1, CA.

situation, a voluntary Code of Practice was launched in 1995. The Code for Leasing Business Premises is published by a joint working group of several industry bodies, government agencies and the Law Society and is now available in its 2007 edition (see The Joint Working Group on Commercial Leases, 2007, for a list of the contributors). The aim of the Code of Practice is to make leasing more transparent and especially to raise awareness of leasing among small businesses. The Lease Code suggests a number of best-practice approaches to drafting lease contracts and seeks to function as guidance for both landlords and tenants. Following a review of the previous edition of the Code, the Government recognised that the Code of Practice has been so far let to mixed results and that awareness among small businesses remains a major concern.[40]

40 Communiqué by Yvette Cooper, Parliamentary Under-Secretary of State, Office of the Deputy Prime Minister, 15 March 2005.

3 The business lease as a long-term contract

It is the aim of this part of the introductory chapter to establish the economic framework that is to be used to analyse commercial leases: the theory of long-term contracts. It will be explained what characterises long-term contracts, why parties enter such agreements and, in particular, which problems are commonly associated with this form of contractual relationship.

Parties to a contract can basically choose between two extreme types of agreement[41]: on the one hand, there are spot-market transactions which are characterised by a simultaneous fulfilment of obligations by both parties.[42] It is typical of such a spot-market transaction that there is no further relationship between seller and buyer. On the other extreme, there is vertical integration, i.e. both parties to a contract become part of the same economic entity.[43] Long-term contracts fall between these two extremes. Eger (1995, p. 20) lists two defining properties of long-term contracts: 1) There is a time lag between the conclusion of the contract and the fulfilment of contractual obligations and 2) parties face costs of moving when seeking to exit the agreement.

As the image below shows, obligations under a lease contract have to be fulfilled throughout the term of the lease, but the negotiation of these obligations has to take place at the outset of the contract.

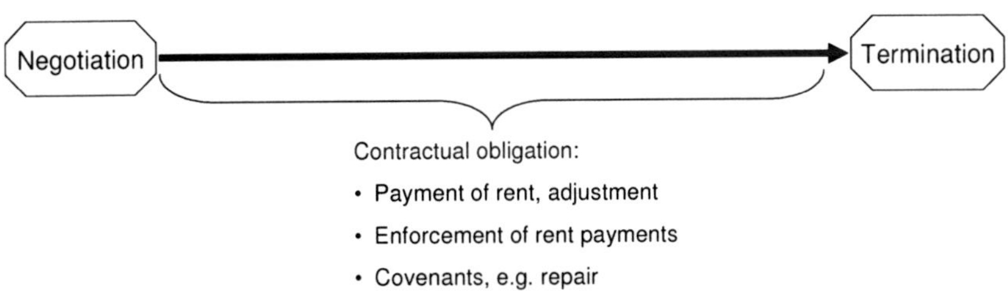

Exhibit 3-1: Characteristics of obligations under a lease

41 Following Eger (1995, p. 19).

42 At the stock market, for example, transfer of ownership of shares and payment take place almost simultaneously.

43 An often quoted example is that of a steel producer purchasing a coal mine and thus vertically integrating it, whilst the steel producer would otherwise have to buy the coal from the mine.

Hviid (1999) thus observes that for such contracts there is "the dilemma of, on the one hand, offering a means of commitment and, on the other, allowing for sufficient flexibility to adjust to changes in the environment" (p. 46). This flexibility is of paramount importance for commercial leases, which can have term of up to 25 years:[44] over such an extended period the cyclical property market will witness slumps and booms. Baird (1990) puts it as follows: "This tension between the need to fix responsibilities at the outset and the need to readjust them over time permeates the long-term contractual relationship" (p. 586).

In an (economically) ideal world, parties to a long-term contract would be able to fully identify all these needs for readjustment in advance; the contract would specify the parties' obligations for all these potential states of the world: the contract would be complete. Salanié (1997) defines a complete contract as follows: "[a contract is complete if] all variables that may have an impact on the conditions of the contractual relationship during its whole duration have been taken into account when negotiating and signing the contract" (p. 150). That such a contract can exist only in an idealised world is mainly because of the pre-condition that parties are able to foresee all future developments so that "there will never be a need for the parties to revise or renegotiate the contract as the future unfolds" (Hart, 1995, p. 22). This assumption becomes more unrealistic with an increasing term of the contract and/or increasing complexity of the economic environment. Eger (1995, p.39) identifies three pre-conditions that would need to be fulfilled for the conclusion of a fully specified long-term contract: 1) Parties would have to identify, *ex ante*, the possible states of the world that could occur over the term of the contract; 2) for each such states of the world an optimal performance of contractual obligations and associated payments would have to be identified. This means that there is an appropriate distribution of contractual rents. 3) Parties would need to be able to observe *ex post* which state of the world has occurred and whether the parties performed their contractual obligations corresponding with the occurred state of the world. Only then could their rights be enforced. In the real world, however, these conditions are not met.

Two aspects that are particularly unforeseeable in the real world were chosen as the subjects of this work: the change of market conditions (and thus contractual rents) during the term of the lease and the probability of tenant default. As market rents are difficult to predict even in the short run (Geltner and Miller, 2001, pp. 243-244), it is unrealistic to assume that a lease could correctly determine rents *ex ante* once the term of lease exceeds a certain threshold. Likewise, it is impossible to determine whether a tenant will default on his

---

44 The so-called "institutional leases" on the UK market (compare Edwards and Krendel, 2007).

obligations under a lease. Tenant default furthermore poses the problem of observing states of the world and enforcing rights.

These two aspects furthermore play an important role in real estate risk management. A study committed by the Investment Property Forum (IPF, 2007a, p. 13) identifies the three sources of risk to the income stream from commercial property:

Table 3-1: Sources of risk from commercial property

Leasing process	Functional usefulness	Change to physical fabric
-Rent reviews -Breaks -Lease expiries -Tenant default	-Legal, technological and aesthetic changes -Infrastructure changes -Physical deterioration	-Refurbishment -Redevelopment

The first source of risk, risk from the leasing process, is the subject of this investigation. It clearly is the domain of property management and lawyers while the other two categories rather fall within the professional ambit of engineers and architects.

Risks from the leasing process are closely related to lease contracts as all the sources of risks listed in the table above (rent reviews, breaks, etc.) are agreed upon in the lease.

This work will look closely at rent reviews and tenant default. Breaks and lease expiries are considered because of their interplay with rent review. A fully specified contract could theoretically provide for contractual solutions to all these risks associated with the leasing process.

However, the two aspects that confine fully specified long-term contracts to the theory are bounded rationality of contracting parties and prohibitive transaction costs. Any lease contract encountered in the real world will hence be a deviation from the theoretical ideal.

Landlords and tenants nevertheless agree to enter such agreements. In spite of difficulties in negotiating a long-term contract it may offer advantages vis-à-vis a series of short term contracts as well as compared to vertical integration.

3.1 Why do businesses lease their premises?

At first sight, leasing seems to be clearly inferior to a purchase of property. A business leasing its premises acquires only the temporary rights of use to a property but does not benefit from an appreciation of capital value. Furthermore, leasing limits the firm's ability to do with the premises what it thinks fit at any given time. Nevertheless, the majority of businesses lease their premises. The following diagram reveals that 65% of businesses in Britain lease their premises (while owner-occupation is very common for residential property in Britain)

Proportion of rented and owned property in the UK

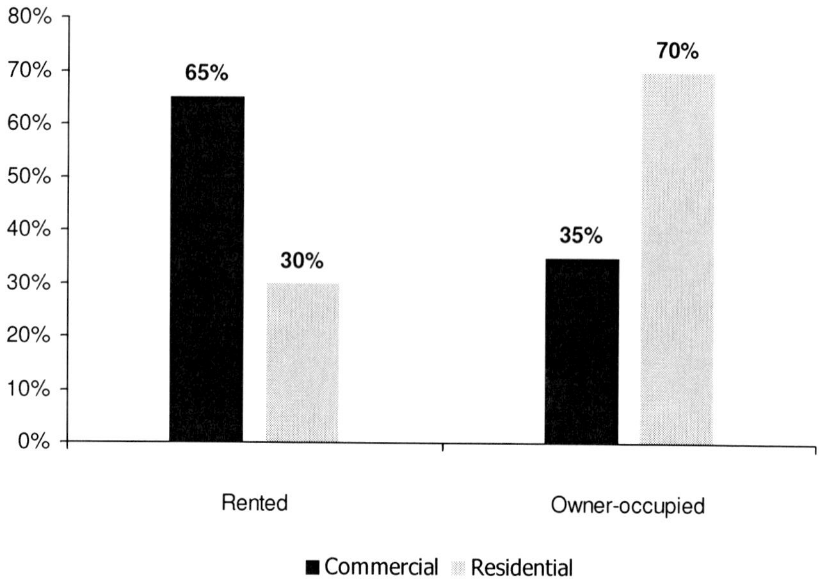

Source: Property Industry Alliance (2009)

Data compiled by Paul Mitchell Real Estate Consultancy

Exhibit 3-2: Proportion of rented and owned property in the UK

Bright and Gilbert (1995, p. 8) claim that flexibility is to be seen as the main motivation for leasing. It would seem, however, that flexibility alone is not sufficient to explain a firm's motivation for leasing its premises. The purpose of this section is to systematically discuss a firm's motivations for leasing. These reasons for leasing influence leasing policy, in particular the methods of rent adjustment which are the focus of this work.

The following issues that influence a firm's decision whether to buy or to lease property can be identified (Smith et al., 1985, pp. 895-901):[45]

---

45 The article by Smith et al. (1985) analyses all forms of leases, also those of machinery and other equipment. Only the aspects relating to real estate are discussed here.

1. **Specialisation in risk-bearing**: There is a trade-off between agency costs caused by the separation of ownership and control of an asset and gains from a specialisation in risk-bearing (Fama and Jensen, 1983). In many cases, the agency costs caused by renting are compensated for by the gains from the specialist knowledge of professional real estate investors. Owning real estate will not be advantageous where real estate markets and the property in question are complex and the tenant's market and real estate knowledge is low. Furthermore, issues of risk diversification would in many instances speak against owner-occupation. Particularly for a comparatively small business all real estate exposure would then be concentrated in one asset.

2. **Expected period of asset use**: Renting becomes more likely if the asset's useful life is longer than the need for the asset within one firm. This is obviously the case for most types of real property as buildings can be used for very long time periods. The tendency to rent is strengthened by high costs of ownership transfer as e.g. stamp duties and other taxes or legal fees. Flath (1980) furthermore suggests that information costs can be reduced by leasing. The risk of entering a short-term lease contract is lower than purchasing an asset so that leasing requires less investment in information.

3. **Comparative advantage in disposing of the asset**: Finally, an incentive to lease is provided by the landlord's superior ability to dispose of the asset at the end of the lease. Lewellen et al. (1976, pp. 796-797) point out that a landlord who has more experience in the property market may have a competitive advantage in dealing with the asset. The landlord's comparative advantage may stem from a reduction in search, information and transaction costs because of superior market exposure. A professional landlord may also have a specialist team of researchers, agents and so on.

4. **Sensitivity to use and maintenance decisions**: An asset's value is generally subject to use and maintenance. Smith et al. (1985, pp. 899-900) observe that leasing is less likely where the asset is very sensitive to use and maintenance and/or where monitoring is difficult. Where an asset is sensitive to use, lease rates would generally go up which would further adverse selection as lessees intending to use the asset moderately would in such cases purchase rather than lease the asset to avoid excessive rents.

5. **Firm-specific assets**: Problems with leasing may arise where an asset is highly specialised to a particular user and has a high value to him. Agency costs occur because of "additional negotiation, administration, and enforcement costs due to conflicts between lessor and lessee. These conflicts arise over the division of the value in excess of the alternative

use of the asset" (Smith et al., 1985, p. 900). It will be shown that tenants renting such specialised properties have longer leases and need to take particular care when negotiating rent adjustment mechanisms because of a lack of alternative premises.[46]

6. **Taxation**: Purchasing and leasing is usually treated differently by tax systems. While rents are a business expense, acquisition of real estate enters a firm's balance sheet and becomes an asset. The expenses for interests are tax-deductible, but principal repayments normally not (Geltner and Miller, 2001, p. 329). Leasing can thus be preferential as it reduces the tax burden. Smith et al. (1985, p. 898) point out that tax incentives may not be the main motivation for leasing as some assets are leased with a greater frequency than others while receiving the same tax-treatment.

7. **Compensation-related incentives to lease**: Management compensation may partly depend on returns on invested capital. Where bonus payment or performance measurements are related to the firm's assets, incentives to lease or not to lease may be created depending on the actual agreement. Furthermore, risk-aversion among a firm's management may inhibit the purchase of real estate as it would require an increased financial gearing of the firm. Given that firms face credit ratings and other constraints on their ability to raise debt finance, there needs to be a ranking among managers as to what projects are to be financed. As real estate does not assume a core role in most firms, it is unlikely that stakeholders of a firm would approve of massive investments in property.

It follows from the above that flexibility alone is not sufficient to explain why firms lease. While it has been shown that there are a sufficient number of reasons why firms would, from a managerial perspective, prefer leasing over ownership, the above discussion gives no insights as to the contractual arrangements under which real estate is rented. Given that a long-term contract always represents a compromise because of cognitive limits and prohibitive transaction costs, the alternative to a long-term lease could also be a series of transactions roughly equalling spot-market transactions on stock exchanges. Instead of committing to lease certain premises over, say, 10 years, parties would contract on a weekly or even daily basis. Problems with adjusting the contractual rent or with tenant default would not occur: the landlord would set prices according to the current state of the market and in case of default the

46 The tenant of a golf course, for example, has to ensure that a lease covers the (planned) duration of his business activity and rent adjustments need to be negotiated in such a way that the tenant is not threatened by opportunistic behaviour of the landlord. For such a business, vertical integration may be the preferred choice but is not always possible because of other restrictions.

landlord would simply not offer a new contract. Such a form of leasing is, however, only observed in hotels. The long-term contract offers a set of advantages compared to spot-market transactions. Eger (1995, pp. 20-27) observes two aspects that should be of a particular relevance to real estate: the protection of specific investments and protection against price fluctuations.

3.2 Advantages of long-term contracts over spot contracts

Instead of agreeing on a lease contract for a term of several years, landlords and tenants could theoretically also agree on a series of spot-market transactions. Parties could on a weekly or even daily basis negotiate new lease contracts. Such an arrangement would avoid the problems that are typically associated with a long-term contract, i.e. the parties' inability to specify all future states of the world. In practice, however, long-term lease contracts are the norm and spot transactions of the previously described type are never found. The long-term contract must therefore offer a number of properties that make it more attractive than spot contracts.

Firstly, a long-term contract may offer lower transaction costs that would otherwise result from a series of renegotiations. Given that lease contracts usually contain very detailed covenants it is fairly obvious that new contracting cannot take place within short intervals. Long-term contracts also ensure a higher degree of commitment by the contracting parties. These contracts furthermore allow income smoothing, i.e. better planning and distribution of revenue streams from the contract and avoidance of income fluctuations (see Hart and Holmström, 1987).

The most important advantage of long-term contracts over spot-market transactions is the protection of revenues from specific investments.[47] It is a typical characteristic of real estate leases that landlords and, more often, tenants make certain specific investments in relation to the lease. This could take the form of certain installations or fittings but also, more generally, the willingness to set up a business at a certain location. It will be discussed in much detail later that two elements define the need of a tenant to protect its investments; the specificity of his fittings and the ease or difficulty of moving them, and the goodwill of the business that depends on a certain location (see chapter on rent adjustment).

---

47 See e.g. Williamson (1971).

3.3 Advantages of long-term contracts over vertical integration

Another alternative to long-term contracts could be vertical integration. In case of real estate this would mean that instead of renting their premises businesses would own them. Eger (1995, pp. 28-29) notes that an advantage of vertical integration lays in the internalisation of costs and revenues that it should simplify the co-ordination of economic activities. The majority of businesses, 65% in the UK (Property Industry Alliance, 2009), nevertheless rent their premises. The disadvantages of vertical integration relating to real estate are significant. Generic private disadvantages of vertical integration are the loss of advantages stemming from specialisation, the costs of hierarchical control, and the inability to externalise damages (Eger, 1995, pp. 29-30). Because of an ongoing drive towards more professionalism within the real estate industry and increased demand for asset management (Schreiber, 2008), property and asset management increasingly require specialist knowledge covering the whole property life cycle, including development, financing, and letting, pushing firms to outsource their real estate portfolios as these skills are often not available in-house. Furthermore, investors on the stock markets penalise firms which hold large real estate portfolios that do not belong to their core business. For these reasons, specialised asset management has also emerged in Germany in recent years. Deutsche Telekom, for example, outsourced its asset management to Sireo, an asset management firm founded as a joint venture with Morgan Stanley. Deutsche Telekom and many other European telecoms have also sold substantial parts of their real estate portfolios.

After discussing general features of business leases in Germany and Britain and their properties as long-term contracts the second part is now analysing more specific problems of business leases.

Part 2: Selected problems of business leases

The purpose of the first part was to introduce general issues concerning business leases in both jurisdictions.

This part analyses more specific issues. The first element of leases that comes under scrutiny will be the provisions for adjusting the contractual rent over the term of the lease.

Finally, the issue of tenant default and landlords' and tenants' positions in case of tenant insolvency are discussed.

The criterion according to which these two topics have been selected is their relevance to the landlord's and tenant's financial positions. Each of these problems is of pre-eminent importance for the parties' cash flows.

An adjustment of rent over the term of the lease is important to maintain incentives during the term of the contract. Tenant default is a major risk to landlords, particularly to those who do not have a diversified investment portfolio. Default of a single tenant can then put the whole financial position of a landlord at risk.

Therefore an analysis of these two elements will provide a good proxy of the overall efficiency of the regulation of leases. While there are many other areas where the regulation of leases could be compared, it is believed that these two are the most important. This is particularly so because this research focuses on property for investment purposes, where the investor is ultimately not interested in the property itself (the bricks and mortar of the building, so to say) but in the property's ability to generate cash flows.

The first part of the analysis will now commence with an evaluation of the methods for adjusting rent during the contractual term.

4 Rent adjustment in business leases

4.1 The economics of rent adjustment

The value of investment properties depends on three income components (Maier, 1999, p. 44). These components are (1) cash flows from rents, (2) value appreciation or depreciation of the reversion, and (3) subsidies paid to investors by the state (also in the form of tax shelters etc).

Of these income components, cash flows from rents are the element which an investor can influence to the greatest extent.

Value appreciation of the property is normally a direct function of rental payments. Prices of commercial property are usually quoted as either a multiple of yearly rents (in Germany known as *Maklermethode* – estate agent's method) or through a required yield (Gondring, 2009, pp. 922-923)[51]. It is sometimes said that property investment means buying a lease rather than a property.

The required yield depends on the overall property market and thus cannot really be influenced by the seller. It is admitted that investments in the quality of the property, marketing skills, and a good network on the seller's part, taking the imperfections of the real estate market into account, may help to positively influence a property's value, but to the greatest extent the price is determined by rental cash flows.

State subsidies, either as taxes or direct payments, are normally considered only in a second step of investment appraisal when pre-tax profitability has been established. Moreover, the availability of certain tax benefits or liabilities may change frequently and depending on their legal form, investors may be differently affected by them.

Rental payments are therefore the only element of a property investment's value that the landlord can really influence. Importantly, a well drafted lease agreement can guarantee predictable cash flows from the property over a long term, even against the general market environment.

Almost every lease will contain some clause to adjust the rent over the term of the lease. At first sight, the reasons for such provisions seem fairly obvious, for example to protect the landlord's investment against inflation. The following

51 For example, if the market requires a yield of 5%, a property with a yearly rental income of € 50,000 is valued at € 1,000,000.

section will introduce the mechanisms that are available to parties of a lease to adjust rents.

Then the rationale behind rent adjustments will be analysed in more detail using the economic theory of long-term contracts. The framework to be established will finally be used to evaluate the methods by which rents are most commonly adjusted in England and Germany.

4.1.1 General mechanisms to adjust the contractual rent

Landlords, tenants, property investors and their legal advisors have developed several mechanisms of determining the contractual rent over the term of the lease. It will later be discussed which methods dominate in which country and which methods seem most desirable in terms of their economic efficiency.

Geltner and Miller (2001, pp. 806-807) identify five generic methods:

1) **Flat rent**: This simplest type is, strictly speaking, not a method of adjusting rent at all because the rent agreed upon in the contract will simply not change over the term of the lease.

2) **Graduated rent**: The rent is changing in certain intervals, also known as "step-ups". Both timing and the amount of rent increases are specified up front in the lease contract. The contract may, for example, specify that the rent increases by 5% each year or by € 5/sqm after the first three years of the term of the lease.

3) **Revaluated rent**: This type of lease is very typical of the UK commercial property market. Rental payments may change, but the amount of change is not specified in the contract. Instead, the contract provides for the lease to be re-valued in certain intervals by a professional real estate valuer. In the UK, this procedure is known as "rent review". The rent will usually only go up, but in recent years and under the pressure of sluggish markets the calls for downwards provisions have become more ferocious.

4) **Indexed rent**: This type of rent adjustment is common in Germany but uncommon in England. Indexed rents are adjusted according to a regularly reported index, for example the consumer price index. The alleged advantage of an indexed rent is that the development of rents would go in line with the development of the economy in general. This seems to indicate compatibility of rents and economic growth (an assumption that will later be challenged).

5) **Percentage rent**: This method, also known as "turnover rent", involves a change of rent over time partly according the success of the tenant's business. A certain percentage of his business' turnover (or another

suitable figure indicating business performance) has to be paid as rent. This could most obviously apply to retail premises and seems to create incentive compatibility between the landlord and the tenant. Turnover rents are not free from problems which will be discussed later on.

4.1.2 The economic rationale of rent adjustments

The general notion of a lease as a long-term contract has been introduced in the previous chapters. That a fully-specified contract that stipulates rights and obligations for all possible states of the world is only a theoretical ideal has already been stated, along with the reasons why this is the case. It would be bound to fail in reality. The costs of contracting would be prohibitively high (Eger, 1995, p. 40). This proposition is particularly valid for the adjustment of rents.

Eger (1995, p. 64) identifies two general categories of price adjustment mechanisms. It is possible for parties to a contract to (1) specify *ex ante* certain formulae or mechanisms according to which prices are adjusted. Alternatively, parties can agree (2) to specify certain events that trigger a revaluation of prices and decide *ex post* how the new price will be determined.

From the list above, graduated, indexed, turnover, and strictly speaking also flat rents would fall under the first category, while a rent revaluated through a rent review mechanism would rather fall under the second category. In the latter case parties also have to agree upon rules pursuant to which the revaluation is conducted. This means that someone is appointed to decide upon the revaluation (either a party to the contract or a third party) and / or that the rules of price negotiations will be determined in advance. Rent reviews provisions of UK leases usually contain all of these elements (Edwards and Krendel, 2007, pp. 67-82).

Eger (1995, p. 64) also discusses the problems associated with each of these methods. An *ex ante* determination of the first type ensures that price adjustments do not create additional costs and will take place swiftly on the basis of the previously agreed formula. The major disadvantage with this method is, however, that any formula devised by the parties will only be an imperfect proxy of the real state of the world and parties will come to an agreement on the basis of more or less obsolete information.

An *ex post* determination following the second approach will avoid such losses of efficiency, but this gain in efficiency comes at the expense of relatively high costs for determining the new price.

This categorisation of mechanisms to adjust the rent nevertheless leaves the question open as to why parties should have an interest in adjusting rents over the term of the lease. At first glance, one could be tempted to suggest that fixed rents would be more beneficial for both parties as they would give the landlord certain income and the tenant certain expenses which would help them to plan their business operations.

Eger (1995, pp. 77-78), however, reveals two reasons why flexible prices (or rents) are more efficient than fixed prices. He asserts that (1) flexibility of prices is a means of achieving an efficient risk allocation and that (2) fixed prices can create incentive problems. The following sections will introduce the elements of risk aversion and incentive problems.

4.1.2.1 The relevance of the parties' attitudes towards risk

A contracting party's attitude towards risk can be a determining factor in its decision between fixed and flexible rents.

There are three possible attitudes towards risk: risk aversion, risk neutrality and risk seeking. The latter attitude is of a rather theoretical application and will not be discussed further.

The distinction between risk aversion and risk neutrality can be described by an individual's attitude towards deciding between a certain payoff and an uncertain payoff.

A risk-neutral individual would be indifferent between receiving a certain payoff (e.g. € 500) or an uncertain payoff with an identical expected value (e.g. either € 1000 or nothing). A risk-averse individual would not be indifferent between these alternatives. A risk-averse individual would not only prefer the certain payoff, but also be willing to accept a payment of less than € 500 instead of having to take the risk of gambling. This lower amount that the individual would accept instead of having to gamble is called the certainty equivalent. The difference between the certainty equivalent and the expected value is referred to as the risk premium (Weise et al., 2002, pp. 92-93).

The author suggests that both landlords and tenants are unlikely to be risk-neutral – as risk-neutrality appears to be a rather theoretical concept – but that the degrees of risk-aversion may differ significantly between different groups of landlords and tenants.

4.1.2.1.1 Risk-aversion of tenants

Translating the concept of risk-aversion into the position of a tenant means thinking in terms of fixed rather than flexible rents rather than payoffs. A risk-averse tenant would prefer a fixed rent over a flexible rent with an equal expected value (or expected rent). The risk-averse tenant would not only prefer this fixed rent but would also be willing to pay a higher fixed rent than the expected value of the flexible rent.

A tenant's risk-aversion would seem to increase with the impact that a change in rents would have on his business activities. Businesses where rents form a substantial part of overall costs are more likely to be risk-averse. On the other hand, businesses where rents only have a small share in costs would be expected to display much less risk-averse behaviour.

The relationship between risk-aversion and the share of rents in overall costs can also be depicted graphically:

Risk-aversion of tenants

(Rent in proportion to other costs)

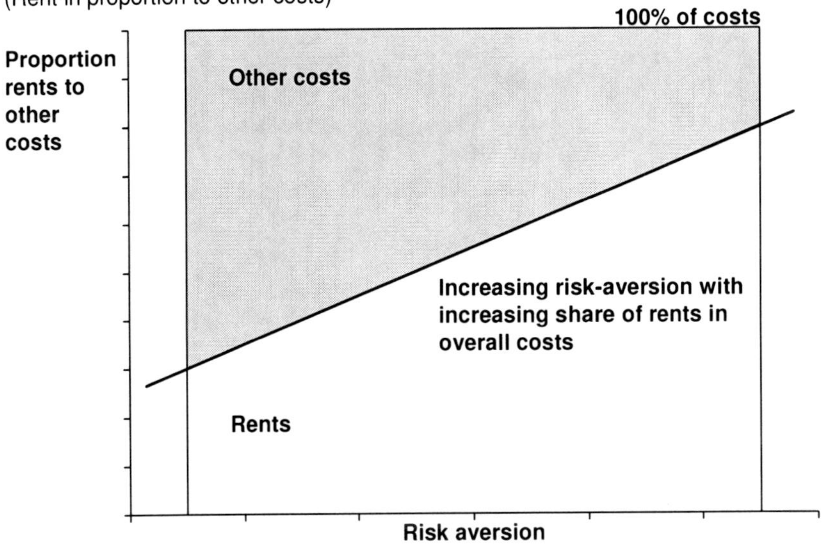

Exhibit 4-1: Risk-aversion of tenants

While the relationship between an increasing proportion of rents in overall costs and increased risk-aversion is by no means necessarily linear, the overall tendency should hold true.[52]

Schulte and Schäfers (1998, p. 40) observes that real estate occupancy costs typically range between 3% - 10% of turnover and 5% - 15% of total costs for

52 It is well conceivable that risk-aversion stays relatively flat until a certain threshold proportion of rents is reached and would then increase over-proportionally.

large corporations. In most industries real estate costs are the second largest cost group after HR costs (Cock and French, 2001, p. 4).

The relevance of rents varies between industries. Posner (1992, p. 21) reports that for professional services firms (lawyers, accountants) rents form a significant part of overall costs and that these firms face a competitive disadvantage when rents are higher than competitors' benchmarks.

For the Property Data Report 2009 (Property Industry Alliance, 2009), employment costs and rents for offices and retail premises have been compared. These two costs groups were presumably selected as they represent the most significant costs for tertiary sector enterprises.

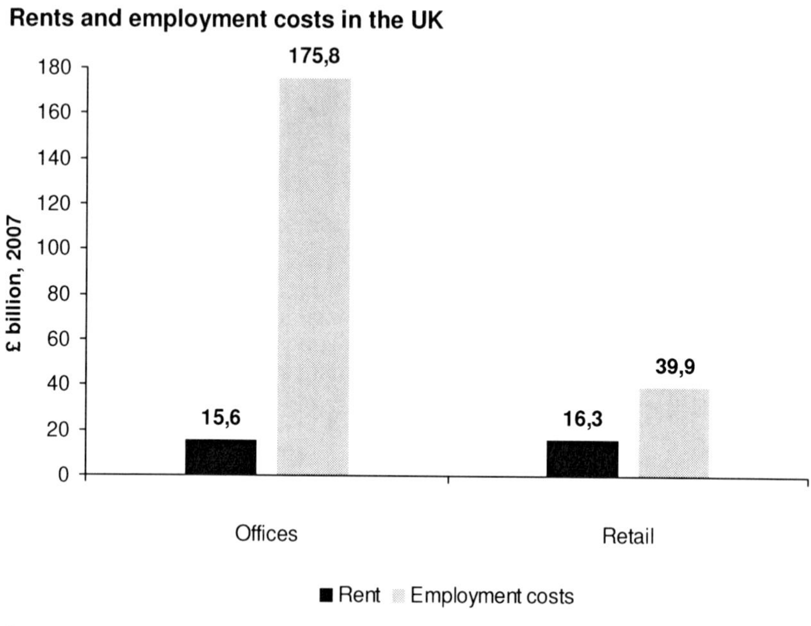

Source: Property Industry Alliance (2009)

Data compiled by Paul Mitchell Real Estate Consultancy on the basis of Valuation Office April 2005 rateable values updated for subsequent rental growth, employment costs obtained from National Statistics

Exhibit 4-2: Comparison of rents and employment costs in the UK (2007)

Lease data for this estimation was obtained from the Valuation Office, a government agency that collects property data for taxation purposes. The consultancy that conducted the study concluded that office rental costs are quite low compared to employment costs of occupiers but that in the retail sector rental costs are about two-fifths of staff costs.

Unfortunately, these estimates present aggregate numbers which do not give insights as to the relation of rents and other costs for different types of business.[53]

However, the size of a business could also influence its risk-aversion. Small businesses should generally reveal a higher degree of risk-aversion than large companies. A significant number of small businesses operate only from a single location so that they have only one lease contract (e.g. a corner shop).

Larger companies are more likely to have a diversified portfolio of leases (e.g. a chain of supermarkets). Rent increases for one particular lease in the portfolio are therefore less significant because of diversification.

The analysis of rent adjustment mechanisms will show that small tenants do indeed prefer fixed over flexible rents.

4.1.2.1.2 Risk-aversion of landlords

For discussing why landlords are unlikely to be risk-neutral one should recall some of the particularities of real estate transactions. Wüstefeld (2000, p. 95), quoting Sanders et al. (1995, p. 129), lists characteristics of real estate transactions:

1. **High costs of individual transactions**: Large sums and complex contracting are involved in each transaction (e.g. combination of contract law and property law).
2. **Limited publicly available information**: The real estate market lacks transparency compared to other asset markets because of the relatively small number of transactions (compared to bond and stock markets). Also, the publication of transactions, and particularly the publication of market prices, is quite limited.
3. **High absolute size of individual transactions**: Transactions involving legal estates in land usually require large expenditure and, associated with that, substantial financing arrangements.

---

53 The proportion of employment costs and rents may differ between enterprises for a variety of reasons including space efficiency (space per employee), type of industry (e.g. banking, consultancy) and accordingly different salary structures and headcounts, location (prime office or suburban office park). For retail premises, the type of retail business and accordingly the size and location of premises as well as number of staff are decisive.

4. **Uniqueness of each property**: While it is possible to categorise properties and quote average rents for certain property and use types, each individual property remains unique in terms of location, architecture, fittings etc.[54] This is perhaps the most significant challenge to real estate risk management and portfolio strategy.

5. **Complex types of transactions**: Real estate investors are not merely faced with a "buy or lease" decision. A variety of transactions, such as sale-and-lease-backs (SALBs) are conceivable.

6. **Differing legal frameworks depending on location**: The laws governing commercial leases vary considerable from jurisdiction to jurisdiction and create further risk.

7. **Complexity of taxation**: Differential tax treatment in different jurisdictions and for different types of transactions are another issue investors have to bear in mind.

It is evident that property investors are exposed to a variety of risks. Because of these inherent risks investors position the risk-return profile of real estate investments somewhere between stocks and bonds. The following diagram is based on a survey among investment managers of their assessment of risk-return profiles of various investments. It positions real estate between stocks and bonds.

54 In Germany, Munich-based BulwienGesa AG is the main provider of real estate market data, supplying market rents for most cities and regions. In business practice, however, rents for individual properties can differ significantly from Bulwien's data.

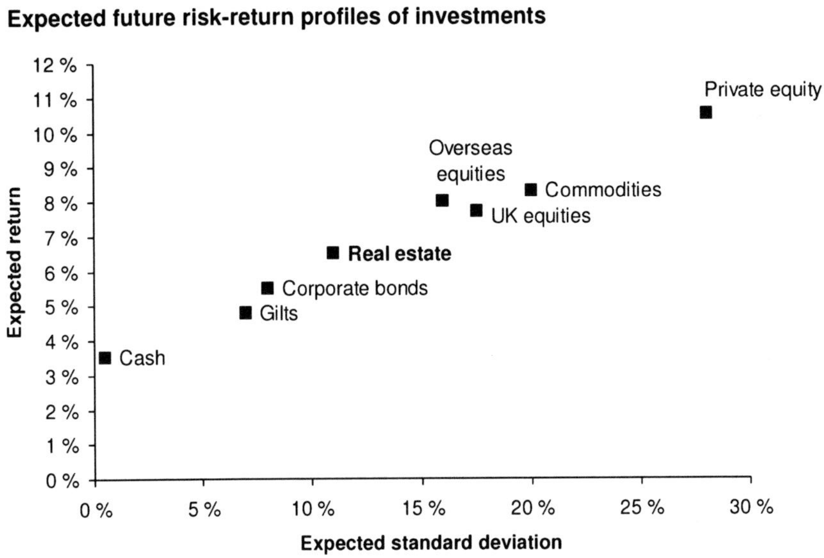

Source: Property Industry Alliance (2009)

Based on IPF Report „Multi-asset allocation in the modern world“

Exhibit 4-3: Risk-return profiles of investments

Decisive for an investor's risk-aversion is, however, not so much the risk of an individual real estate transaction but rather the effect that changes in values or rents of the property in question would have on the value of his overall portfolio.

Eger (1995, pp. 68-70) points out that a party's degree of risk aversion will depend upon its organisational form, the impact price changes will have on the party's profits from the specific contract and the impact on its overall profit and on the party's ability to protect itself against price fluctuations by way of diversification, insurance or hedging.

Analogously to the analysis of tenants' risk-aversion, landlords can be categorised as either "small" landlords or large, institutional landlords.

Taking these distinctions into account, it is proposed that the degree of risk aversion showed by a landlord will depend upon the organisational and financial structure of his business operations. While there are numerous subgroups of commercial landlords, they all fall within the extremes of institutional landlords on one side and "small" landlords on the other hand.

Institutional landlords would, for example, be property firms such as British Land and Land Securities in the UK, or IVG, Patrizia Immobilien or Colonia

Real Estate in Germany. This group would also include asset managers such as Allianz Global Investors that invest into real estate on behalf of insurance companies, pension funds or private shareholders of real estate unit trusts. "Small" landlords, on the other hand, would either be small, privately owned property firms, or individuals who own one or a few properties, e.g. because they inherited it or purchased it with a view of planning for their retirement.

The following table illustrates the major differences between the two extremes of commercial landlords and reveals why their degrees of risk aversion will necessarily differ.

Table 4-1: Differences between institutional and "small" landlords

	Institutional landlord	**"Small" landlord**
Portfolio	- Diversified in terms of types of use and locations	- Few or only one property, concentration on particular (sub-) market and type of use
Organisational form	- Diversified ownership (e.g. shareholders) - Limited liability through choice of legal form - Separation of ownership and management	- Private firm or sole proprietor - Personal (unlimited) liability - Ownership and management in one hand
Decision making	- Professional property appraisal based on research and advanced valuation techniques - Typically NPV calculation with modelling of scenarios - Individual property is seen in a general portfolio management context	- Valuation normally based on "thumb rules" - Landlord believes to "know his market" and thus may over-invest in properties - Frequently sentimental value attached to the property (long time in family ownership, inheritance etc.)
Income from properties	- Diversified tenant base - Default of individual tenant usually not a threat to the business	- Few or one property with a limited number of lease contracts - Default of one tenant may put whole business at risk

	Institutional landlord	"Small" landlord
Management	- Professional management with developed network in the industry - Access to "big", corporate tenants - Professional valuation and marketing services - Cost advantages because of economies of scale - Professional management of tenant default	- Semi-professional or part-time management or outsourcing to letting agencies - Limited network and marketing capacities - Usually no access to "big" corporate tenants with good credit risks - dependency on "smaller" tenants, usually with limited credit worthiness - Inexperienced in tenant default, no in-house legal team and dependency on external lawyers
Access to financing	- Ability to fund operations through the capital markets - Small spread between cost of lending and cost of borrowing - Economies of scale for arranging debt financing (e.g. mortgage pools, securitization) - Non-recourse loans (personal funds protected in case of default)	- Depends highly on debt financing issued by mortgage institutions or commercial banks, thus highly geared - Typically loans with recourse to landlord's personal funds

This comparison shows that the “small” landlord is normally more likely to display a relatively high degree of risk aversion. In particular, the “small” landlord is faced with a twofold risk from his operations: he has only a few or perhaps only one lease contract with a tenant. At the same time, he highly depends on debt financing and will have a highly leveraged investment. If there is uncertainty regarding his rent, his financing will also be at risk as he may then default on his mortgage. The mortgagee will most likely have recourse to the landlord’s personal funds which will be another factor favouring risk aversion. It is, moreover, quite unlikely that a “small” landlord will succeed in obtaining debt financing from a bank if he cannot present reasonably certain rental cash flows.

“Small” landlords may also be risk-averse because of a lack of professional management skills. They will normally not possess the necessary resources to cope with complex rent adjustment procedures and their valuations will not normally involve sophisticated financial analysis. Furthermore, they may be emotionally attached to their properties (perhaps because their grandparents built it, or because their family has been resident in this town for 200 years, and so on). Most certainly, they will value safety of their property much more than opportunities offered by a "gamble" on higher rents.

Institutional landlords, on the other hand, display a very different form of behaviour. Through modern investment appraisal, diversification, a financial structure that depends less heavily on debt, no recourse to personal funds and a professional crisis management, these institutional landlords will be more willing to take risks. It is, however, unlikely that they are risk neutral, as was discussed above.

On the other hand, many institutional investors on the property market are funded by other institutions or private individuals which are risk-averse themselves. This for example applies to life insurances investing in real estate on behalf of their policy holders. The chart below depicts the institutionalised market participants on the German property market by their institutional form. It can be seen that life insurances and comparable institutions play a major part on the German market.[55]

Institutional investors in Germany by funds invested

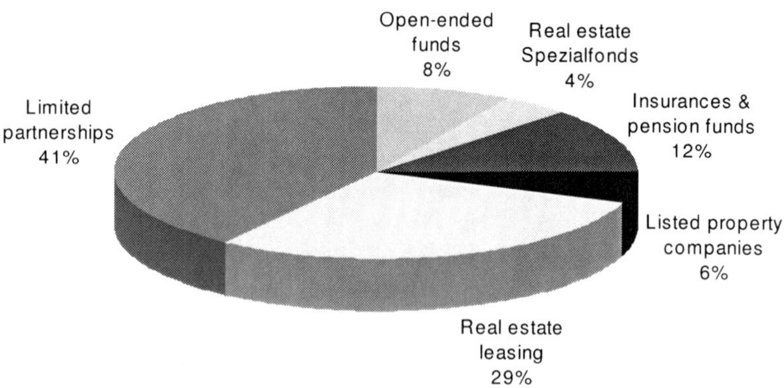

Source: BulwienGesa AG, Immobilien-Anlagevolumen institutioneller Investoren 2006

Exhibit 4-4: Institutional investors in Germany by funds invested

When considering the risk-aversion of institutional investors, organisational issues within the investment firm should not be ignored either. Many institutional real estate investors are structured as holding companies with SPVs (special purpose vehicles) that hold the properties within a certain market or industry sector. For example, *XYZ Real Estate Investment* may own the SPVs

55 The UK property market is characterised by a significantly stronger share of listed property companies.

XYZ Office Properties Hamburg, *XYZ Retail Properties Southern Germany* and so on. Each of these SPVs would, in the balance sheet, be an independent firm (German limited company or Luxembourg-based vehicle) with its own management. While it may be a valid statement that at the level of the *XYZ Real Estate Investment* umbrella decision-makers could be risk-neutral, this may not be true for the asset managers in charge of the individual SPVs. Their performance review and pay directly depend upon the performance of "their" properties and each SPV may only contain a few properties or sometimes even only one building. In such a case, it could be imagined that an asset manager working for a large institutional investor is almost as risk-averse as a "small" landlord.

4.1.2.1.3 Innovative real estate vehicles and the limits of diversification

The ability to diversify risks has been identified as one of the major drivers of risk-aversion that distinguishes "small" and institutional investors. The purpose of this section is to reveal how new, innovative investment vehicles are used to allow for further diversification of real estate investments and that there may be limitations to the ability of real estate investors to diversify their risks.

Risk-Return profiles of real estate vehicles

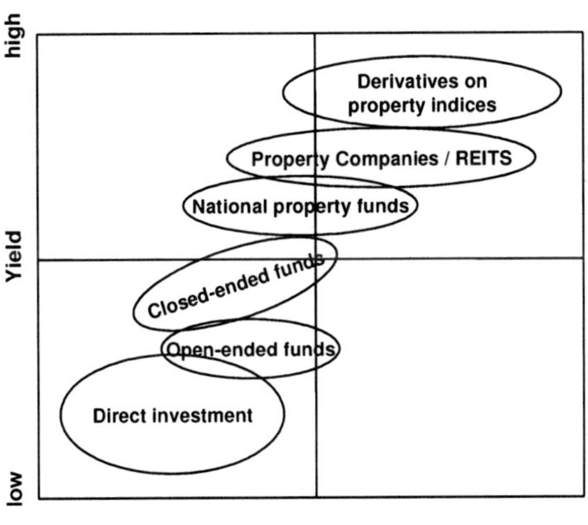

Source: ICME Management Consultants

Exhibit 4-5: Risk-return profiles of real estate investment vehicles

These new forms of real estate investment can be depicted according to their risk-return profiles. As the diagram shows, the more sophisticated instruments offer higher risk-return profiles.

One of the most important features of these innovative vehicles is to make investment in real estate more fungible. Because of complexity, relative size, its nature as a physical asset and low number of transactions, real estate is one of the least fungible investments. Property vehicles allow investing in real estate without actually holding physical properties. The investor buys shares or certificates of the investment vehicle, which – as an independent legal entity – owns and manages the assets.

The claimed advantage of these derivative property investments is that they enable a broad diversification of real estate investments also for investors with relatively small portfolios[56]. The financial crisis that has been largely caused by the collapse of the US housing market has, however, highlighted the limits of diversification and risk-reduction for real estate investors and also shown that a certain degree of risk-aversion will continue to characterise institutional real estate investors.

The crisis has demonstrated that diversification through innovative real estate vehicles may reduce specific risks of particular properties but that they do not protect against systematic risks and the collapse of overall markets.

The image below depicts the basic workings of Commercial/ Residential Mortgage-Backed Securities (CMBS or RMBS), the securities that caused a substantial part of the financial crisis and that now burden many banks as so-called "toxic assets".

56 At the expense of returns, however, as high management and administrative fees characterise the investment in most of these vehicles.

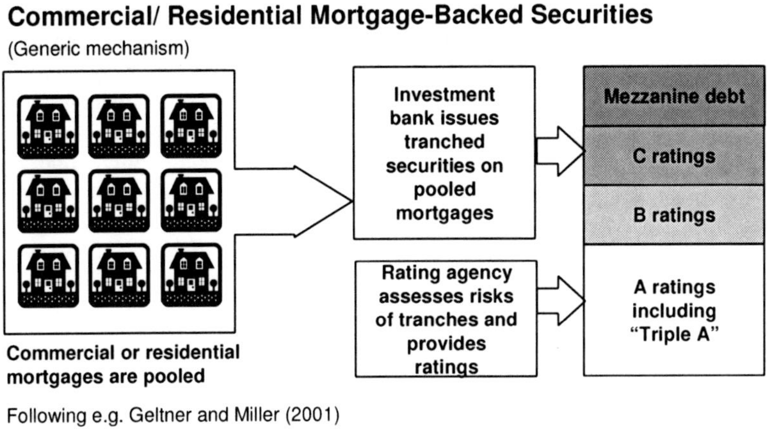

Exhibit 4-6: Commercial/ Residential Mortgage-Backed Securities

The principle of CMBS or RMBS is to pool commercial or residential mortgages in order to sell the mortgages to investors. It is decisive that the securities that are created are "tranched", i.e. that different groups of securities are issued with are characterised by different risks and accordingly with different returns. The now infamous rating agencies provide ratings for the different tranches. The different ratings express the default risks of the respective securities. When homeowners fail to pay their loans, the losses at first affect the so-called "mezzanine" (high-risk) tranch, and other tranches to a lesser extent or not at all. Should more loans default, then the C-rated tranches are affected, and so on. Using this structure, loans to homeowners with a relatively low creditworthiness or with properties in unattractive locations that – looked at individually – would carry relatively high risks, could be transformed in securities with much different risk-return structures, including securities with "triple-A" ratings that are normally awarded to government bonds of western states (the idea being that a triple-A security in a RMBS structure has a sufficient "shield" that protects it from default as defaulting loans would at first affect the junior liens with lower ratings).

Nevertheless, the mechanisms to protect investors failed when the US housing market collapsed and triggered probably the worst economic crisis since the Great Depression.

This short digression into the working of CMBS/ RMBS shows that there are limits to diversification of real estate investors even where there is a high number of underlying assets.

It could be argued that a problem of these securities was that they heavily relied on US property markets and that there should have been a further regional diversification. Business reality shows, however, that there are only a few truly international real estate investors and that most investors concentrate on a number of core markets (e.g. British Land, Land Securities, all German property companies and most German property funds): as shown above, real estate markets are characterised by relatively incomplete information and local knowledge of asset managers is crucial. The advantages from further diversification could thus be outweighed by additional asset management costs and low returns because of lacking local market knowledge. Also institutional investors should therefore display a certain degree of risk-aversion as opportunities to diversify are limited.

4.1.3 The relationship between risk-aversion and lease pricing

Risk aversion of landlords and tenants has been discussed because of its influence on lease pricing mechanisms. Depending on the relative risk aversion of parties, fixed or more flexible lease pricing mechanisms could be selected.

For each long-term contract pricing takes place within the bounds of fixed prices for the whole duration of the contract on the one hand, and spot-market pricing at the time of delivery on the other hand. Clearly, spot-market pricing would be a theoretical extreme for real estate leasing (though one could think of the prices of hotel rooms) but fixed lease prices are observable. The rent adjustment mechanisms introduced above show that most leases use a combination of fixed and flexible elements (compare Eger, 1995).

Parties would typically prefer **fixed rents** to flexible rents if, relative to the other party's risk aversion:

- The **landlord has strong valuation risks**, i.e. he would like to protect himself against fluctuations of the market rent. As discussed above, this would potentially apply to "small" landlords, or
- The **tenant faces strong cost risks**, i.e. he would like to avoid changes in rent because of high location-dependant goodwill or a high level of business-immobility.

On the other hand, parties would prefer **flexible rents** if, again relative to the other party's degree of risk aversion:

- The **landlord is confronted with strong cost risks**, which would typically exist because of flexible mortgage rates and a high level of financial gearing, or

- The **tenant's attitude towards risk is dominated by strong valuation risks**. This would apply to businesses with a low degree of location-dependant goodwill and low-level business-immobility. If the general market rent fell and a particular firm were locked into a contract with a fixed rent, this firm would be at a competitive disadvantage compared to firms with flexible rents.

In many cases, landlord and tenant are expected to have differing preferences as to flexible or fixed rents. In these cases, the relative bargaining power of parties is decisive.

These general tendencies will be used as the first part of the framework to analyse rent adjustment mechanisms. They can only be the first part, however, since if risk-aversion alone were the determining factor for choosing such mechanisms, one would expect to see a property market where parties would agree on either fully flexible or fixed rents. In practice such behaviour is not observable. Rather, lease contract typically contain a combination of flexible and fixed elements.

To explain this observation, two further issues will thus be discussed in the following sections to complete the analytical framework: A review of incentive problems associated with fixed rents and the role of transaction costs.

4.1.4 Incentive problems associated with fixed rents

The section above sought to relate rent adjustment mechanisms to the (relative) risk aversion of parties.

There are, however, other considerations that may make flexible pricing the preferred choice for risk-neutral parties. There are three general incentive problems: hold-up problems, moral hazard, and inefficient incentives to invest in information. Analyses of these incentive problems can be based on the impact that flexible prices have on the expected co-operative economic rent of parties[57]. Parties to a contract will generally prefer flexible to fixed prices if they lead to higher economic rents.

It was established above that particularly tenants will most likely be risk-averse and that also certain landlords will be rather risk-averse than risk-neutral. Nevertheless, the incentive effects identified here will also be relevant to risk-averse parties if the impact of these effects on economic rents is stronger than the parties' degrees of risk-aversion that would otherwise make them prefer fixed prices.

57 Compare Eger (1995).

4.1.4.1 Hold-up problems

A "hold-up" problem occurs if one of the parties exploits high barriers of exit of the other party. Such barriers exist if the party faces high costs when wishing to exit the agreement. This is commonly the case when a party has made specific investments from which benefits can only be derived when used in conjunction with the contractual agreement (Nagel and Eger, 2003, p. 210).

Hold-up is typically a consequence of incomplete contracts where duties, rights, and/or obligations are insufficiently specified and the party with the higher bargaining power (ie the party that does not face high exit costs) threatens the party with high exit costs to terminate the contract if there is no "agreement" on more favourable terms to the party with higher bargaining power (Nagel and Eger, 2003, pp. 210-211).

In the context of business tenancies, hold-up can be created not only by specific investments, but particularly by the high exit costs to the tenant as a consequence of two phenomena: location-dependant goodwill and the degree of business-immobility.

Generally speaking, a tenant will be less vulnerable to hold-up if he can easily move to new premises should the relationship with his current landlord deteriorate. The ability to move to new premises depends on two aspects: the importance that the location of the premises has to the business' success or the costs of moving to new premises because of logistical difficulties. The former problem will here be referred to as "location-dependant goodwill", the latter will be called "degree of business-immobility".

4.1.4.1.1 Location-dependant goodwill

The success of most businesses will to some extent depend on the location of their premises. This is here defined as "location-dependant goodwill". In accountancy literature "goodwill" would usually be defined as follows: "The amount paid for a business in excess of the fair value of its assets at the date of acquisition. It exists because a going concern business is usually worth more than the sum of the values of its separable net assets (Nobes, 1989, p90)."

The justification for paying (and charging) for goodwill is then based on "[the acquired firm's] ability to earn future profits above those of a similar newly formed company, or it may be seen as the 'goodwill' of customers, the established network of contacts, loyal staff and skilled management (Nobes, 1989, p90)."

Business goodwill can also be attached to the location of the business. A business with an established location may be able to earn future (and current) profits above those of an otherwise comparable firm in a different location. The link between location and business success differs, however, between industries.

It is assumed that location-dependant goodwill is highest for businesses with a high degree of customer/client contact. The diagram below illustrates this relationship:

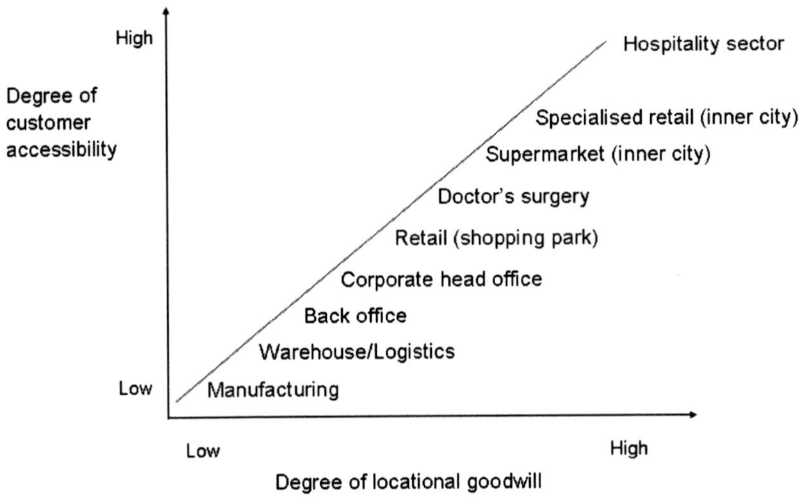

Exhibit 4-7: Location-dependant goodwill within selected industries

It is assumed that location-dependant goodwill is highest in the hospitality sector. Restaurants, hotels and bars obviously depend very much on their location as guests frequently visit these places because of location.

Corner shops, retailers and supermarkets in inner city location do also have a fairly high dependency on their location. Consumers will often visit the shop premises by walking or by public transport and may be unwilling to make a longer journey. Furthermore, the success of specialised retailers, such as fashion or book stores in city locations does not only depend on their range of products, but frequently also on whether they are located in a fashionable neighbourhood or high street.

A doctor's surgery would have a moderate dependency on location, which would however be correlated with the healthcare system and the general level of healthcare provision in a given city.

Location-dependant goodwill is certainly lower for stores and supermarkets which are located outside the city, for example in shopping parks. As customers would usually visit these premises by car, the dependency on a particular location is certainly lower than in an inner city location.

For offices, the location-dependent goodwill would not so much depend on the accessibility by customers but more on the accessibility by another important group of stakeholders: the firm's employees. Corporate head offices are usually the workplaces of the most influential management that can ultimately decide on where to locate the office. The office itself fulfils representative purposes and employees usually prefer a location that is both pleasant and easily accessible.[58] However, the success of a business will not depend on the location of its head office. The office is not income generating, as in case of retail or hospitality businesses, but merely a cost factor.

For back offices the location is even less important. They have no representative purposes, no direct customer contact, and the management is usually not as influential as that it could decide on moving. The location of back offices is usually driven by cost efficiency considerations.[59]

Warehouses and manufacturing are usually relatively independent of a particular location in terms of customer accessibility. They don not build up a specific location-dependant goodwill but are rather subject to "business-immobility", the concept introduced in the next section.

4.1.4.1.2 Degree of business-immobility

The potential costs of relocating to other premises are the second factor that should influence the tenant's sensitivity to hold-up problems. This is here referred to as "degree of business-immobility". As with location-dependant goodwill, the degree of business-immobility will vary between industries. The classification of businesses in terms of their degree of business-immobility is less straightforward than the connection between business type and its location-dependant goodwill. Therefore, business types have been grouped in three categories, businesses with a low, moderate and high degree of immobility. The diagram below illustrates which industries may particularly be affected:

---

58 One might remember the unpopularity of London's Canary Wharf when the Jubilee tube line and the Docklands Light Railway had not worked reliably. Many employees were reluctant to move from the City to the Docklands.

59 As with the many call centres in the North of England and East Germany, or Eschborn, a 1970s office suburb nearby Frankfurt. There, most major banks have their IT-operations.

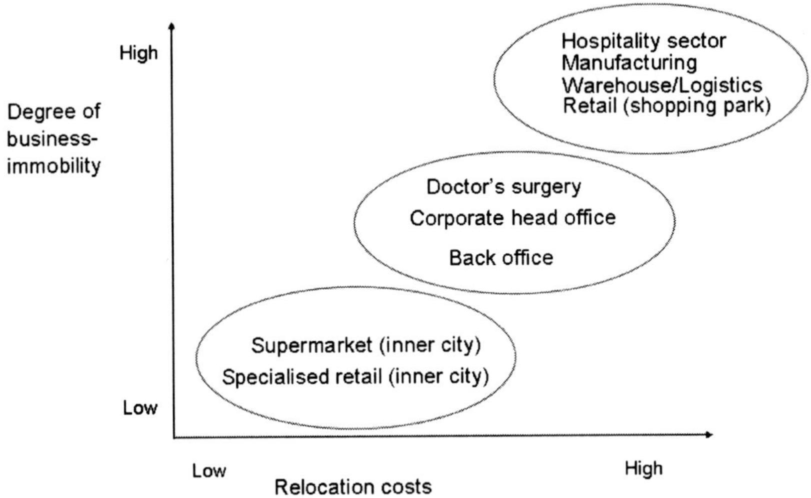

Exhibit 4-8: Business-immobility within selected industries

The degree of business-immobility is a function of the "relocation costs" of a business. On the one hand, these relocation costs depend on the obvious costs of moving, such as paying for removal companies, refitting of the property etc. Additional relocation costs are, however, imposed by the ability (or rather inability) to replicate the business in another location. This can be illustrated by looking at the cluster in the upper right section of the diagram. The hospitality sector might not suffer from large moving costs, but the ability to replicate the business in another location is low. An example was given in the case of Dolgellau Golf Club. In the case, a landlord successfully opposed the tenant's application for lease renewal under the Landlord and Tenant Act 1954, Part 2 on the ground of use of the premises for his own occupation. The premises were a golf club. It is evident that relocating a golf club is a challenging task. This is not so much because of relocation costs, after all a golf club consists mainly of a bar and an adjacent wide area of lawn. The reason why a golf club ranks in the "high business-immobility"-class is due to the inability to easily replicate the business at another location.

High business-immobility particularly applies to the manufacturing sector, warehouses, and retail premises in large shopping parks. In these sectors, business-immobility is caused by relocation costs rather than inability to replicate the business. It should be noted that in the three previously mentioned business sectors, premises are often purpose-built. If not purpose-built, they are often modified by the tenant, so that upon removal the tenant would usually incur significant costs to reinstate the premises in their original state.

In addition, moving costs in the manufacturing sector and for warehouses are high. Machinery is heavy, bulky and often customised to fit a certain location. Large retailers in out-of-town locations also use customised shop equipment which is designed to fit a certain floor plan. All these aspects push up moving costs and hence increase vulnerability at the end of the contract.

Businesses with a low degree of business-immobility are, for example, retailers in inner city locations. A drugstore, for example, could be located in a variety of different retail premises. There are no special requirements as to the design of the building, except very generic features like an appealing shop front with large windows. Hence the business model can be replicated easily at a different location. This highlights the distinction between business-immobility and location-dependent goodwill. Business-immobility refers to the ability to replicate a certain business model at another location, not its success. Location-dependent goodwill on the other hand is an expression of the link between location and business success. Whilst a drugstore could theoretically be opened almost everywhere, the ultimate success would depend on a sufficient number of potential customers within walking distance.

Moving costs for these types of businesses are also relatively low. The fittings of a drugstore for example, cash desks, shelves etc, can be moved and built up again at another location easily.

Examples of business with a moderate degree of business-immobility would include offices or doctor's surgeries. In case of a doctor's surgery, the degree of immobility would, however, vary significantly with the specialisation of the doctor. A GP can for example move easily, his relocation costs are low. Radiologists, on the other hand, use specialised equipment that requires considerable modifications of the premises and specialised removal companies in case of relocation.

A high degree of business-immobility should also be found where the operation of the business depends on licences or concessions. The radiologist, for example, will need a special permit to operate x-ray equipment in his surgery. To obtain this licence is a lengthy process (involving inspections by the local health authorities, certifications and so on). Crucially, the licence will only be valid for the current premises and will be void if the surgery is moved to another location.

If "business-immobility" is a valid concept then firms that are vulnerable to this form of hold-up would be expected to devise strategies to mitigate their risks. One such strategy is vertical integration, i.e. the purchase of real estate rather than renting. Companies where exposure to hold-up is high would thus be expected to show a higher degree of real estate ownership than companies where such risks are limited. The following diagram depicts the share of real estate assets as a percentage of total assets for a number of large German companies.

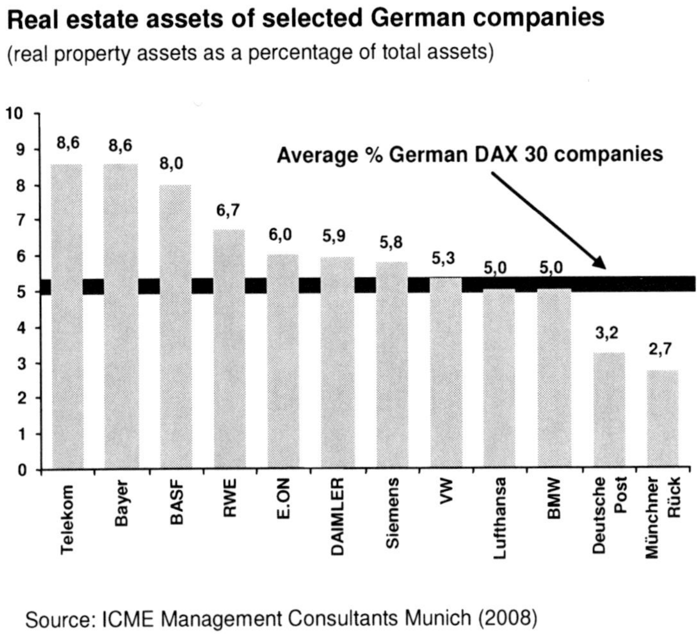

Exhibit 4-9: Real estate assets of selected German companies

At first sight it may be surprising that Deutsche Telekom has the largest share of real estate as a percentage of total assets but the company does in fact own a substantial real estate portfolio exceeding 6,000 properties. These properties are necessary to operate the fixed-line telephone network and are thus essential for Deutsche Telekom's business model.[60] Also chemicals producers Bayer and BASF have high rates of real estate ownership: their plants are certainly unique in terms of engineering, size and functionality and costs of moving would be immense. Power producers RWE and E.ON follow. Power plants would obviously also create substantial costs of moving. Property ownership of car producers is lower, partly because the manufacturing halls of car producers are

60 While glass fibre technology is on the advance, the German fixed-line telephone network is based on copper cables. For physical reasons, copper cables can only transmit signals over a distance of around seven km after which the signals have to be amplified. A network of amplifier and switchboard stations spreads over Germany, from small buildings with less than 100 sqm to large structures (such as the large Telekom building on Hamburg's *Heiligengeistfeld*).

not as unique structures as chemical plants.[61] Companies in the services sector, e.g. Munich Re, show low degrees of real estate ownership: As companies in the services sector rent almost exclusively office space, their vulnerability to hold-up is relatively low. The figures therefore indicate that companies may have realised their vulnerability to hold-up and may have reacted by vertical integration of real estate.

4.1.4.1.3 Hold-up and fluctuating prices

Hold-up problems can also occur where a long-term agreement with a fixed price is reached but (spot-) market prices of the good are subject to fluctuations (see Eger, 1995, pp. 78-81). In such cases, parties may not be able to credibly commit to fulfilling all their obligations under the contract.

Therefore, as Goldberg (1976, p.432) observed:

> The longer the anticipated relation and the more complexity and uncertainty entailed in that relation, the less significance will be placed on the price and quantity variables at the formation stage. The emphasis will instead be on establishing rules to govern the relationship; rules determining the process of adjustment to unexpected factors that arise in the course of the relationship, and rules concerning the termination of that relationship. Length and uncertainty characterise the relationship of landlord and tenant as the following examples illustrate.

The table below gives an overview of typical lease terms of commercial property:

Table 4-2: Typical lease terms of different types of use

Hotel	1 day - 1 week
Small retail	2 - 5 years
Office	3 - 10 years
Anchor retail	5 - 15 years
Industrial	5 - 20 years

(US figures, Geltner and Miller, 2001)

61 The machinery for car manufacturing can theoretically be installed in almost every hall that is sufficiently large. It should also be noted that car manufacturers outsource a substantial part of their production to external suppliers.

It is apparent that leases for certain types of use are made for considerably long terms. This is, apart from other factors, because of the tenant's vulnerability to opportunistic behaviour. It comes to no surprise that industrial leases tend to be the longest. The degree of business-immobility for industrial plants can be considerable. While the tenant's degree of risk aversion may thus make him inclined towards negotiating for a fixed rent, it seems extremely unlikely that any landlord could credibly commit to a fixed rent over a period of several years. Market rents are going to change over the term of the lease and may render the performance of the contract unattractive to the landlord. But a lease at a fixed rent could also become unattractive to tenants if the market rent falls considerably.

The next example shows that fluctuation of rents can be significant, even in markets that are considered "mature".

Offices are often believed to have the most efficient and most transparent market compared to other types of commercial property (Pretorius et al., 2003, p. 5). Office properties are relatively homogenous and – as long as they are in a similar location and have similar amenities – fairly interchangeable. One could therefore argue that the market for office properties is at least somewhat close to a spot market. The table below shows the fluctuation of prime rents for office space in Hamburg over the past years:

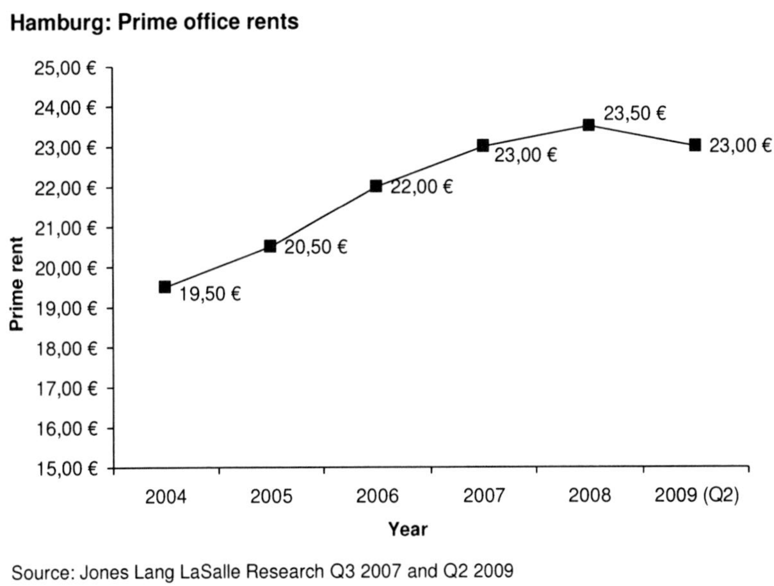

Exhibit 4-10: Prime office rents in Hamburg 2004-2009

Even though Hamburg is considered to be a relatively stable market, prime office rents fluctuated significantly. From 2004 to 2008, rents increased by 20%. Virtually no landlord could therefore commit to fixed rents over a period of several years, and anticipating an environment of falling rents, no tenant would be willing to accept a long-term, fixed rent commitment if he is not otherwise vulnerable to exploitation by the landlord. (In practice, flexibility for the tenant is often attained not by a flexibilisation of rents but by inserting break clauses in the lease.)

Hold-up creates both *ex post* and *ex ante* incentives problems for both contractual parties. Based on the research conducted by Eger (1995, pp. 78-99), these problems are applied to business leases in the following table:

Table 4-3: Fixed rents and hold-up problems

Ex post	**Landlord:** - If open market rents increase, fulfilment of contractual obligations becomes less attractive - If he has no break option, he may try to mitigate loss by reducing performance of e.g. maintenance or services associated with the lease. Tenant may be subject to harassment - Problem may be exacerbated by cost increases, in particular for mortgage payments Possible scenario: expanding national economy with rising interest rates **Tenant**: - If open market rent decreases (and moving is possible at low transaction costs), the lease becomes less attractive to the tenant - Problem may be exacerbated by lowered valuation of the lease - If he has no break option, he may overuse the premises or try to under-perform certain contractual obligations, e.g. repair, that are difficult to monitor for the landlord Possible scenario: contracting national economy with decreasing retail sales and so on
Ex ante	**Landlord and tenant**: - Both parties will anticipate at fixed prices the respective other party will not be able to make a credible commitment - Investment in the asset will thus be reduced below an efficient level

4.1.4.2 Moral hazard

In many contractual settings information asymmetry between parties exists. "Information asymmetry" means that the parties have – contrary to the economic theory on perfect competition – different levels of information regarding the transaction. "Moral hazard" consequently describes the behaviour by a party with superior information using this knowledge for its own benefit. These problems have been widely described in the context of corporate governance, particularly with regard to the information asymmetries between shareholders of a firm, and the firm's management, described as principal-agent problems (compare e.g. Jensen and Meckling, 1976).

Moral hazard problems reduce *ex ante* incentives to attain efficient levels of transaction specific investments. Similar to the behaviour in case of hold-up problems, parties that might become potential sufferers from moral hazard would be deterred from investment and overall transaction-specific investment would decline (Nagel and Eger, 2003, p. 212). Each party will have the incentive to invest below efficient levels for all investment activities for which it cannot fully capture marginal profits. Likewise, parties will tend to use such assets beyond efficient levels for the use of which they do not have to bear the full marginal costs (Eger, 1995, pp. 85-86). Most likely to be affected by such behaviour are these activities or assets that are not specified in the lease. For example, a landlord may in case of efficient investment incentives have installed new ventilation and air-conditioning systems. This system would have created a better room climate for the tenant and perhaps also have saved energy. Because investment incentives under a fixed rent contract may be inefficient, the landlord may, however, not install the system and thus the benefits of it would be lost both for the tenant and the overall economy.

4.1.4.3 Investment in information

The third inefficiency that could be created by fixed prices is investment in information at inefficient levels. The types of information in question are *ex ante*, pre-contractual investigations into the attractiveness of the intended transaction. Eger (1995, pp. 94-96) points out that the *ex ante* attractiveness of investing in information will increase (1) with decreasing costs of information and (2) increasing value of the information to the party. Incentive problems occur if the private value of information does not equal the social value of information. The social value of information is measured by the extent to which the information improves the efficiency of resource allocation and thus overall output. The private value of the information, on the other hand, is expressed through the additional contractual rent that a party can appropriate. It is thus purely redistributive, unproductive information.

If a contracting party cannot fully appropriate the social value of information, the party will not provide enough of this information. Conversely, a party may invest too much in information if the value of it exceeds its social value (Eger, 1995, p. 98).

Take the example of a landlord who intends to invest in a property and mortgage financing would be used for the acquisition. The mortgage repayments are subject to interest rate fluctuations. Assume further that, for example, because of legal regulations, only fixed rents were allowed. The landlord would then face the problem that depending on the fluctuation of interest rates the letting of the property could become unattractive. If mortgage repayments exceed a certain level, the project will have a negative NPV. The landlord would invest in research into possible interest rate fluctuations. This research would not increase the overall output but reduce it because of the costs of obtaining this information. If, instead, flexible rates were used, there would be no need to invest in this type of information.

It is easily observable that the selection of a pricing mechanism based on risk aversion and the selection of a mechanism based on incentive considerations may lead to contradicting results. This apparent conflict will be discussed later, but in the following section the final consideration for evaluating pricing mechanisms is discussed: the transaction costs associated with a method.

4.1.5 The transaction costs of adjustment mechanisms

The analytical framework for evaluating lease pricing mechanisms has so far concentrated on two elements, the role of the parties' degrees of risk-aversion and the incentive problems that can arise if fixed rents are used. One element is, however, still missing to complete the analysis: the transaction costs associated with each of the adjustment methods that will be assessed below. Transaction costs, to use the definition given by Barzel (1989, p.2) are:

> [T]he costs associated with the transfer, capture, and protection of rights.

To be more concrete, the costs that parties face when negotiating and administering a clause to adjust the contractual rent are (following Pretorius et al., 2003, p. 11):

1. **Identification and uncovering of the nature of incentive conflicts**: This includes resources spent on predicting the other party's behaviour given assumed opportunistic behaviour. As was discussed above, rents will usually be based on a combination of fixed and flexible elements to account for the conflict between parties' risk aversion and incentive problems set by fixed prices. While the incentive conflicts created by "pure" fixed rents are clearly recognisable, a semi-flexible rent will only achieve a partial set-off of incentive problems. The difficulty for parties would be to assess whether this partial compensation of incentive problems will be sufficient.
2. **Drafting complex agreements**: Contracting is costly. Costs of contracting include fees for legal advice, letting agents, surveyors and so on. It would also

include the opportunity costs of parties. One should be aware that these costs may cause a theoretically attractive mechanism to fail. When considering the costs of contracting it is also important to keep the above-made distinctions between institutional and "small" landlords and corporate and "small" tenants in mind. The costs of drafting a complex agreement may be ignorable when a long-term industrial lease is negotiated, but the costs of drafting such a contract may be prohibitive for the "small" players.

3. **Implementation, operation and dispute settlement**: Finally, parties will have to operate the clauses they negotiated. Depending on the type of method this may in itself be a considerable task, particularly so, if third parties such as independent valuers are involved. Again, mechanisms that will be perfectly suitable for one type of landlord/tenant may be prohibitively costly for another group. The potential for conflict and the method of dispute settlement are further sources of transaction costs. While some methods leave few doubts as to the calculation of the new rent, others may lead to conflicts between the parties and the costs of dispute settlement may again render certain methods prohibitively expensive for some landlords or tenants.

A reasonable assessment of transaction costs has to look at these costs not as absolute figures but requires seeing them in line with the lease in question. The term of the lease and the rental value as well as the parties' degrees of risk-aversion and vulnerability to incentive problems such as hold-up will mean that costs invoked by a certain method cannot automatically be said to be prohibitive or not. Rather, it is necessary to identify particular constellations of landlords and tenants where certain methods could be prohibitively costly.

4.1.6 Default rules

The use of default rules may assist in reducing transaction costs. Default rules are normally legal rules provided by contract or property law or quasi-legal rules provided by industry standards such as the British Code of Practice for Commercial Leases. The main feature of default rules is that parties do not have to elect to use them. A contract is automatically governed by the default rule unless parties actively contract out of the rule.

Schwartz and Scott (2003) have examined – among other issues – the way in which default rules in contract law should be drafted to promote economic efficiency. In accordance with the theory on long-term contracts (see Nagel and Eger, 2003), the authors claim that parties would generally be interested in writing complete contracts in order to avoid all the aforementioned problems. However, they are prevented from contracting because of transaction costs. Schwartz and Scott (2003) conclude that "the state may increase efficiency in cases when contracting costs prevent parties from solving contracting problems

(p. 60)." Parties would furthermore not develop rules by themselves if they have to bear the full cost of drafting the rule but would not be able to realise the full gain as other parties would free-ride on their innovation. In such a situation, the authors find that "the social gain from having a rule – a solution to a contracting problem – may exceed the social cost but parties themselves will not create the rule. There is a case, therefore, for a publicly supplied contract law that contains efficient solutions to common contracting (Schwartz and Scott, 2003, p. 60)."

Default rules can be contrasted with mandatory rules, which are in any event binding on the parties. Schwartz and Scott (2003, p. 61) champion default rules over mandatory rules. As economic transactions are heterogeneous parties should be free to diverge from defaults. Parties, they claim, would be in the best position to judge whether a default caters for their needs or whether they should rather draft their own rules.

Schwartz and Scott (2003, pp. 61-62) proceed by identifying a set of desirable properties for default rules:

- A good default should minimise contracting cost;
- It should maximise the joint surplus of the contracting parties;
- The rule will condition on few possible states of the world;
- It will have to be simple in form;
- It will be efficient for a wide variety of contract parties.

The analysis of the various rent adjustment mechanisms will also look at the default and mandatory rules provided under the laws of England and Germany. The aim of this is to assess whether these rules increase efficiency and reduce transaction costs and, if not, what changes should be made to them.

4.1.7 Overview of the analytical framework

The foregoing three issues will now be applied to the rent adjustment mechanisms that are most commonly found in German and British industry practice. The final consideration before beginning the evaluation of the actual mechanisms will be the order and the weighing of the three separate issues.

It is proposed that the analysis should begin by evaluating the method from the perspective of risk-aversion. Clearly then, methods will be more suitable for some landlord-tenant combinations than for others. Should an adjustment mechanism contain more fixed than flexible elements, it will then be evaluated whether these fixed elements are likely to create incentive problems. Finally, transaction costs for both mechanisms with dominating fixed and dominating flexible elements are discussed. Attention is again placed on the fact that the level that would make transaction costs prohibitive will vary between parties. Default rules and their actual use will also be scrutinised.

The image on the following page depicts how the analysis will proceed:

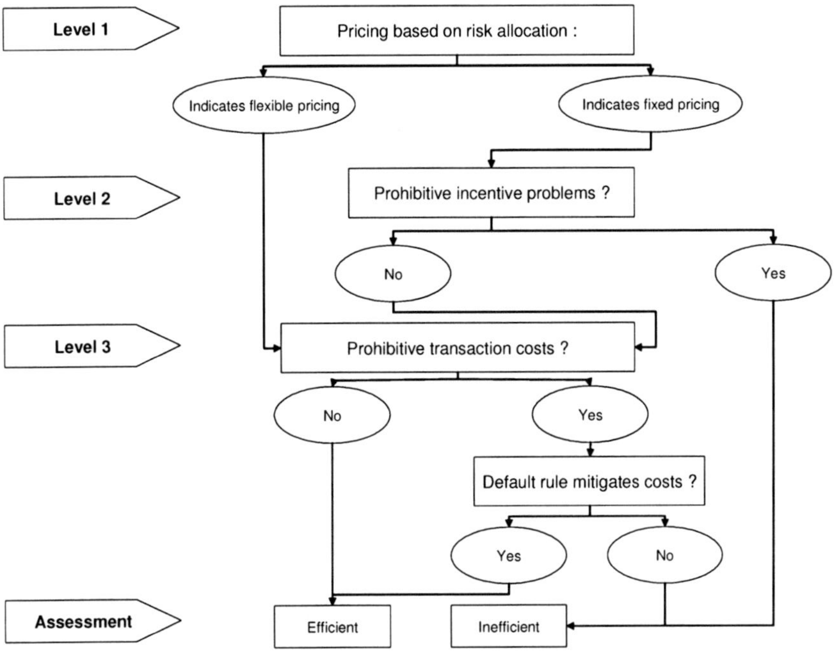

Exhibit 4-11: Overview of the analysis

4.2 Analysis of the adjustment methods observed in practice

4.2.1 Fixed rents

The first adjustment mechanism to be scrutinised is rents that are fixed over the term of the lease. Fixed rents do obviously not present a "mechanism" at all. Nevertheless, they have to be included here to aid the understanding of other adjustment mechanisms and to define the situations where no adjustment of rent may be the preferable choice for the contracting parties.

Fixed rents are indeed a popular choice: comparing the incidence of adjustment mechanisms by the number of contracts (as opposed to the volume of transactions), then contracts with fixed rents are the most common occurrence. Crosby et al. (2005, pp. 73-98) analysed data provided by the Investment Property Databank (IPD) which holds records for 10,811 individual properties at a capital value of £105bn (per 31 December 2003). The data is estimated to cover 75% of the UK institutional commercial property stock[62]. According to the IPD data, in 2003 the share of leases with fixed rents was 52.9%, compared to 36.2% of leases with a standard five-year rent review (see below). When weighted by the amount of rent, only 23.7% of leases have no review, with 60.1% having a standard five-year rent review. This indicates that fixed rents are dominant among leases at lower rents. The data also reveals that fixed rents are only found among leases with a short lease term (see detailed discussion in section on hold-up problems).

The IPD data also allows distinguishing between types of use. In 2003, 40.7% of retail leases, 60.4% of office leases, and 67.9% of industrial leases had no review. Weighted by the amount of rent, the numbers shift to 16.6% for retail leases, 25.8% for office leases and 40.4% for industrial leases. One should bear in mind that the IPD data on industrial property also includes premises used as garages, small warehouses etc. Because of the high vulnerability to opportunistic behaviour of highly specialised industrial property, vertical integration is common for key industrial properties.[63]

---

62 As discussed in the section on property data, a comparable dataset is not available for the German market. It is assumed that the general use of fixed rents is comparable.

63 This can also be seen from the annual reports of industrial concerns such as Bayer or BASF which tend to rent office properties but own their production facilities (see diagram on share of real estate assets in overall fixed assets).

4.2.1.1 *Fixed rents and risk aversion*

From a risk perspective, fixed rents suit the needs of risk-averse landlords facing demand risks and risk-averse tenants facing cost risks. It was argued above that a small tenant is more likely to be risk-averse. A small tenant typically operates his business from one location only. The rent for these premises would thus form a substantial part of his expenses. Theoretically, the small tenant should hence prefer a fixed rent. This view is confirmed by the data collected by IPD. For about 80% of IPD's lease data, the tenant can be identified as being either a "large" tenant or an SME. Crosby et al. (2005, pp. 114-115) report that two-thirds of the leases of SMEs have fixed rents and that this figure reduces to one-third for large tenants. Given that cost risks should be much more common among small tenants than valuation risks it is assumed that a majority of small tenants also has a preference for fixed rents. Apart from risk aversion, there exist few other explanations as to why fixed rents are much more common among small tenants. One other possible explanation is, however, that small tenants rent other properties than large tenants. Small tenants are more likely to rent properties in B or C locations for which demand is low so. Tenants are therefore in a better bargaining position. Also, the owners of such properties tend to be less professional than the owners of property in prime locations and transaction costs may not justify more complex adjustment mechanisms.

4.2.1.2 *Fixed rents and hold-up problems*

It was established in the section on methodology that fixed rents could lead to hold-up problems and hence inefficient incentives to invest. The principal incentive problem for landlords would be that in an environment of increasing market rents the fulfilment of contractual obligations arising from the fixed-rent lease would become more and more unattractive, especially if coupled with increases in costs. A typical scenario in the commercial property context would thus be an expanding economy with increasing interest rates. Vice versa, a tenant would find his lease increasingly unattractive if rents fell during a property recession and various other premises were available.

Such problems would exacerbate with increasing lengths of term because significant changes in relevant variables then become almost certain. Presumably, fixed rents should thus only be found in shorter leases. The IPD data confirms this hypothesis. A total of 6,697 leases were recorded in 2003, of which 3,540 had a fixed rent. None of these leases had a length of more than 9 years, 1,099 fell in a bracket of 2-4 years and 1,166 leases were for 5 years. To contrast this with leases that had a review, the longest leases were for more than 25 years and almost half of the leases with reviews were for 10 years or longer.

It seems that parties recognise that credible commitments for leases with fixed rents cannot exceed a time horizon of at most nine years. A period between 5 and 10 years would also be the time horizon that property cycles typically take. After a boom in the late 1980s, the UK property market took until the mid-1990s to recover from a recession, was buoyant till the early 2000s, has then moved sideward and again has seen some good years until it was hit fairly recently by recession. Hence it seems that landlords and tenants are willing to agree on fixed rents only for periods that, based on past experience, represent the reasonably foreseeable time horizons for property cycles.

4.2.1.3 Fixed rents and the costs of debt financing

Another aspect related to lease length and fixed rents is the importance of debt financing for real estate investment. Most real estate investments are highly leveraged. Interest rates for these mortgages are either floating or fixed for a certain period. In Germany, mortgages typically have interest rates fixed for five to ten years; the UK market is, however, dominated by floating rate mortgages. The differences in mortgage markets could also impact upon the viability of fixed rent leases. If an investment is highly geared, small changes in interest rates can have a significant impact on the investment's return. A landlord facing such risks would seek to shift them to the tenant by increasing the rent. Conversely, landlords would only agree on fixed rents if changes in interest rates do not have a significant impact on returns, meaning that the leverage ratio is low, or if interest rates are fixed or seem unlikely to change. This is also a form of risk aversion, namely the landlord's cost risk. If this is the prevailing form of risk faced by the landlord, fixed rents are not a viable option.

4.2.1.4 Investment in information

As discussed above, it is often difficult to determine what the market for certain properties is. For small industrial properties such as, say, a car garage it may be difficult to determine a market rent as in a given town there may be only few such properties. If the rent agreed upon by the parties is also comparatively low it may then be preferable not to devise an adjustment mechanism but to simply agree on a fixed rent for the term of the lease because otherwise there may be an inefficient investment in information. Whilst flexible prices would lead to efficient investments in information if (spot-) market prices can easily be determined, this may not hold true if there are significant problems in determining a market price. In such a case, the uncertainty as to the possible development of market rents, and indeed uncertainty as to whether it will be possible to fix a market rent at all, could then lead to a situation where flexible prices would lead to inefficient investment in unproductive information.

4.2.1.5 *Fixed rents and transaction costs*

The low transaction costs are an appealing element of fixed rents. Both in the drafting stage and in the monitoring stage these leases create virtually no transaction costs. Parties nevertheless have to be careful when drafting a lease without rent review, as neither German nor English law will permit later increases in rent if not so specified in the contract.[64]

Therefore, fixed rents will be appealing to small, semi-professional landlords and tenants. A reliance on external legal advice is typical of such parties and also for the monitoring of contracts they often rely on external property managers. Particularly if rents are low, fixed rents then have the advantage that parties are able to govern the lease by themselves instead.

4.2.1.6 *Institutional differences between England and Germany*

In the introductory chapter highlighting the institutional differences between the German and UK property markets, the polycentricism of German property investment was pointed out. London, the centralised business capital of the UK, has probably one of the most developed and most efficient property markets in the world. Finding market prices for properties should thus rarely be an issue. In Germany, however, and surely also in the British regions, the information depth of markets is much thinner and information on prices thus not easily obtainable. Fixed rents may therefore be efficient solutions if parties assume that market prices cannot reliably be determined.

4.2.1.7 *Evaluation*

To summarise, fixed rents can be a preferable choice to parties if the following conditions are met:

- Both parties are fairly risk-averse;
- Landlords face demand-side risks, tenants face cost risks;
- The lease length does not exceed a time horizon for which; market developments are reasonably foreseeable by the parties;

64 German law: Neuhaus (2005, p. 179) observes that if no rent review is included in the lease, parties will have to reach agreement on the date of the review and the rent increase. English law: in Street v Mountford (1985) it was ruled that a lease has to contain three key elements, one being that there is a rent. This also implies that if the parties have validly agreed on a rent and the two other components, the lease is valid and courts cannot intervene.

- It may be difficult or impossible to determine a market rent as the sub-market may be small or there are no comparable properties;
- Incentive problems are not seen as a major issue;
- The contracting parties are likely to be small and have to rely on external advice for the drafting of contracts;
- Rents for the premises are low if compared to the transaction costs that would be incurred by more complex adjustment mechanisms.

On the other hand, fixed rents will lead to an inefficient risk allocation and incentives problems if other conditions are met:

- The landlord faces cost risks but the cost risks (e.g. mortgage repayments with fluctuating interest rates);
- Incentive issues are more of a concern to the tenant than cost risks;
- The lease is for longer than approximately ten years. Parties can no longer reasonably foresee the developments of the property market and the wider economy;
- There is a functioning property market for the type of premises in question so that a new rent can easily be determined at review;
- Parties are fairly professional and experienced in drafting contracts;
- Leases have high rental values and transaction costs for drafting more complex rent adjustment mechanisms are thus fairly insignificant.

The set of six German leases reveals that fixed rents are definitely not attractive to large tenants contracting for extended time-horizons: none of the leases uses fixed rents.

4.2.2 Graduated rents

If parties agree on graduated rents then rents are set to increase in fixed intervals by a fixed amount or percentage of the previous rent (Geltner and Miller, 2001, p. 806). Graduated rents hence represent a halfway between fixed and flexible, (spot-) market pricing. Graduated rents are quite common for small leases in Germany but uncommon in the UK. In his very comprehensive handbook, Gondring (2009, p. 593) lists only graduated rents and indexation as rent adjustment mechanisms commonly used in Germany.

The UK study undertaken by Crosby et al. (2005, p. 98) found that so-called non standard review types (graduated rents and indexation) are extremely rare. In 2003, only 1.9% of leases in the IPD database had graduated rents and the percentage for indexed rents was virtually zero. In Germany, on the other hand, regional development agencies even advertise with the transparency of graduated rents for commercial leases (e.g. Luebeck Business Development Corporation, 2006).

The perceived advantages of graduated rents have been summarised by Neuhaus (2005, p. 181) as follows:

- Payable rent is clearly determined in the lease;
- Automatic increase of rents and no further formalities;
- Tenant in default without further need of notices (according to German law).

Neuhaus (2005, p. 181) also notices disadvantages of graduated rents:

- Only suitable for limited time horizons (risk of inflation); rent estimates for longer leases can be highly speculative;
- Clear formulation of clauses necessary, otherwise potential of conflicts;
- If used in combination with other clauses: risk of invalidity of complete clause also if only partially voidable (according to German law).

A major disadvantage not included in the above list, however, is that graduated rents do not take the cyclicality of the property market into consideration. Graduated rents are based on the implicit assumption that property prices are permanently on the rise. As the current meltdown of real estate markets shows, this view is highly flawed.

4.2.2.1 Graduated rents and risk-aversion

Graduated rents could be an attractive choice where the landlord is confronted with a combination of cost risks and valuation risks. A tenant accepting a graduated rent would mostly be confronted with cost risks.

Alternatively, graduated rents could also appeal where supply-side risks confront a risk-averse landlord and a risk-averse tenant is faced with demand-side risks.

As rent increases for a graduated rent are known in advance, it combines elements of fixed rents and flexible adjustment mechanisms. As long as a landlord can reasonably predict cost increases (which would thus limit the lease term for which a graduated rent could be stipulated) and as long as the landlord is reasonably certain into which direction and at what pace market rents will move, a graduated rent may put the landlord in a better position than either a fixed or a fully flexible rent. The graduated rent disadvantages the landlord where costs are higher than expected or where market rents grow faster than predicted by the landlord.

Graduated rents also provide a second-best option for tenants facing cost risks. While a fixed rent may in many cases not be negotiable, a graduated rent provides the tenant with the required certainty as to his financial obligations but at the same time a graduated rent is more acceptable to a landlord than a purely fixed rent.

4.2.2.2 Graduated rents and incentive problems

Graduated rents would be attractive to tenants with high location-dependant goodwill or high degrees of business-immobility. The certainty of future rent payments protects their otherwise vulnerable businesses from hold-up problems at least until expiry of the contract.

As in case of fixed rents, however, graduated rents can cause incentive problems where over the term of the lease a significant spread between market rents and the contractual rent arises. With market rents above contractual rents the landlord would possibly try to mitigate his losses by underperforming certain services associated with the lease (e.g. maintenance). If market rents are below the contractual rent, tenants with low hold-up costs may try to re-negotiate or exercise a break-option (if available). It would hence seem that parties only agree on graduated rents in markets where the path of market rents can be predicted with some certainty and leases do not exceed a certain length.

Another incentive problem may arise if one party to a lease is better informed and uses this information to his advantage, creating a moral hazard. A local landlord may, for example, have much better market information than a tenant trying to establish himself in a certain market and the rent increases may thus be unrealistic. Where there is a risk of such scenarios arising, rent adjustment as determined by an independent expert may be a better choice.

Related to moral hazard is inefficient investment in information where social and private information values do not correspond. The lack of flexibility of a graduated rent may result in the parties investing too much in *ex ante* efforts to research the market and estimate market movements. To avoid excessive investment in information, the lease term for which graduated rents can reasonably be negotiated is limited, or the market for the let premises is characterised by outstanding stability.

4.2.2.3 Graduated rents and transaction costs

Low transaction costs are the perhaps most appealing feature of graduated rents: drafting pitfalls are limited, rent increases take place automatically by mere lapse of time, and there is no need to involve third parties into costly re-negotiations. Furthermore, examples for drafting such clauses are readily available, e.g. from Chambers of Commerce, so that external (legal) advice is not necessarily needed for negotiating the contract.

Clauses negotiating graduated rents can be very economical in terms of verbiage. The office lease (case study no. 4) simply states:

> The monthly rent (excluding heating and operating expenses) increases [...] by 1.9% per annum (based on the initial rent).

To avoid any doubt as to the rent increases and when they are to become due, an annex to the lease sets out the rents that will be due from the beginning of each year of the lease from one to 20. This was surely inserted as a precautionary measure to avoid disputes that could arise from questions as to the correct basis for calculating the increase based on a percentage.

4.2.2.4 Case study: office lease with graduated rents

From the set of the six German leases only one, the large office lease (no. 4) uses graduated rents as an adjustment mechanism. Based on the assumptions made above that the preferred type of rent adjustment would be strongly influenced by a firm's dependency on its location and thus its vulnerability to changes in rents, this seems at first sight counter-intuitive. After all, offices can be moved easily and a firm's commercial success does not depend on the location of its offices.

In the given case, the situation is nevertheless different for two reasons: the size of the premises and the role of this tenant as an "anchor". The lease is for very large premises, 13,000 sqm, which has two implications: on a competitive property market such as Germany it is very difficult to find such a tenant, and the landlord gains significant cost advantages from having only one large tenant with good covenants rather than a multitude of smaller tenants (reduced transaction costs as less monitoring, drafting, enforcement and generally reduced administrative overheads). Also, a large tenant often acts as an "anchor" for development projects. The name and reputation of the "anchor" is thought to improve the development's overall reputation and should thus aid in attracting other tenants. In this case, the tenant is the regional headquarters of a "household-brand" electronics manufacturer.

In order to arrange the financing for larger developments, developers also often are required to have partially pre-let the development. Pre-letting means that lease contracts are concluded before the property is actually built. This provides additional safety to lenders as the risk of vacancy after completion is reduced.

These factors taken together would mean that the tenant of lease no. 4 should have been able to negotiate attractive lease terms. Indeed, the graduated rents combined with other elements of the lease provide a highly attractive arrangement to the tenant: rent increases at 1.9% per annum effectively represent merely an inflation adjustment. However, it has been shown above that rents are subject to fluctuation and may increase or decrease by much higher percentages. The tenant of lease no. 4 managed to negotiate a quite uncommon set of break options, effectively giving the tenant the opportunity to renegotiate lease conditions. The original lease term is for 10 years, but up to one third of the let area may be given back to the landlord after 5 years. There is, furthermore, a break option for the whole lease after 5 years, albeit with a penalty. The tenant is furthermore given the right to sub-let the premises. The combination of these clauses mitigates the seemingly inflexible and incentive-destroying nature of the rigid graduated rent adjustment mechanism. The rent increases may technically be fixed but in practice the tenant could negotiate a very flexible lease. If market rents plummet, the break option and the put option to give back parts of the premises provide him with a leverage to re-negotiate. If market rents rise, the tenant benefits from very moderate, barely inflation-adjusting rent increases over a ten-year horizon. The graduated rent is not a fixed agreement but ought to rather be seen as a starting point for negotiations in the future.

This, in conjunction with the rare occurrence of graduated rents on the UK market, seems to indicate that this form of rent adjustment really is unsuitable for large-scale leases. Observations from industry practice thus confirm the rather negative theoretical appraisal of graduated rents.

4.2.3 Rent review in the United Kingdom

Rent review is the prevailing adjustment mechanism for commercial leases in the UK. In a lease with a rent review provision it is stipulated that at certain intervals, normally no longer than every five years, the parties will agree on a new contractual rent that should represent the open market rent for the demised premises.

Should the parties not be able to find an agreement as to what constitutes the market rent for the premises in question, the lease will provide that an independent expert or arbitrator has the authority to determine a new lease. The independent expert will normally be a Chartered Surveyor. Appeal against the arbitrator's or expert's decision is governed either by provisions in the lease or by the Arbitration Act 1996 (Edwards and Krendel, 2007, pp. 88-89).

The common view of the function of rent review provisions held by real estate professionals and lawyers was expressed by Sir Nicholas Browne-Wilkinson V-C:[65]

> There is really no dispute that the general purpose of a provision for rent review is to enable the landlord to obtain from time to time the market rental which the premises would command if let on the same terms in the open market at the review dates. The purpose is to reflect the changes in the value of money and real increases in the value of the property during a long term.

Having the objective of pricing leases in accordance with market rents, rent review provisions would at first sight seem to be the pricing mechanisms being closest to spot markets. In line with the methodology introduced above they should thus be the preferred choice for tenants with strong valuation risks and landlords with cost risks. In addition, the fairly flexible pricing achieved by such provisions should prevent incentive problems because the landlord would have incentives to invest that would be based on the open market rent, or the perspective that his lease would in regular intervals be priced according to open market rents. The landlord could ideally be indifferent between the sitting tenant and prospective new tenants. The tenant could be indifferent between his current landlord and other offers as both would be priced at the open market rent.[66]

Rent review provisions are, however, not free from problems. The purpose of this section will thus be to analyse potential inefficiencies associated with this pricing mechanism and to discuss the types of parties for which rent review appears to be the suitable pricing mechanism.

The following issues are to be scrutinised:

The methodology introduced above would suggest that in order to emulate spot-market pricing, rents would have to be able to increase or decrease upon review. In reality, however, the vast majority of leases contain clauses known as "upward only provisions", stipulating that upon review the rent can either go up or stay at the previous level. Does this lead to incentive problems and why are leases drafted in that way?

In order to emulate spot-market pricing it is furthermore necessary that the rent determined by the independent expert closely reflects the actual market rent. Therefore, which methods are used for determining the new rent and how independent are the independent experts?

---

65 British Gas Corporation v Universities Superannuation Scheme [1986] 1 EGLR 120.

66 In reality, however, there would never be complete indifference as the tenant would face costs of moving but would, in all but the most buoyant markets, benefit from concessions or tenant improvements.

Rent review – valuation by an independent expert, possible appeal, and so on – is a fairly complex mechanism of adjusting the rent. Which role do transaction costs play and would it be desirable that government intervened by creating default rules for the rent review procedure?

The analysis will in this case commence in a slightly reverse order. First of all, the workings of rent review and the associated transaction costs will be discussed before risk-aversion and incentives are looked upon.

4.2.3.1 The workings of rent review

It should first of all be noted that rent review is an area of law that is virtually free from statutory involvement (with the exception of arbitration in case of disputes that is partly regulated by the Arbitration Act 1996). Being thus governed by common law, it will be a main focus of the discussion as to whether cumbersome processes developed over the years could be streamlined by the introduction of statutory default rules.

In essence, a rent review starts either automatically at specified dates or has to be triggered by a notice of the landlord (or, rarely, of the tenant, which is sensible only in leases with upwards/ downwards reviews). Parties will then try to agree upon a new rent.

If parties are unable to agree on a rent, an expert or arbitrator will determine the new rent for them. The lease will normally stipulate how the new lease is to be valued. Appeal to the decision of the expert or arbitrator will be possible if governed by the lease or the Arbitration Act 1996 (Edwards and Krendel, 2007, pp. 88-89). All of these issues have caused substantial litigation.

4.2.3.1.1 Review by notice

Review by notice through so-called "trigger notices" is normally no longer found in new leases but many older leases still contain notice clauses (Edwards and Krendel, 2007, pp. 68-69). Because of the lengths of institutional leases, 25 years and more, they will continue to play a role for the next years.

A "trigger notice" gives the landlord the right to initiate a rent review. The contents of these notices are not defined by statute and there has been considerable litigation on the meaning of such notices.

A trigger notice would typically specify a new rent as proposed by the landlord and state the time specified in the lease's review clause. For such clauses time is said to be "of the essence", which means that the tenant has to serve a counter-notice within the specified time. Failure to serve the counter-notice within the limitation period would mean that the proposed rent automatically becomes the new rent and all possibilities for negotiation are lost.

Less stringent clauses stipulate that the landlord's notice merely starts the time running for reaching an agreement on the new rent. The landlord's proposed rent would only take effect if no agreement were reached within the specified time, typically three months (Edwards and Krendel, 2007, p. 69). Failing agreement, reference has within this time to be made to an expert or arbitrator who is then able to set the strict limitation period aside.

Edwards and Krendel (2007, pp. 69-70) observe that rent review clauses seem to follow some trends within the industry so that rent review clauses from different periods tend to be similarly drafted. The authors warn that pre-1985 clauses require careful examination and that clauses from the 1970s and early 1980s are "often a model of conciseness, producing a clear and unambiguous directive to the valuers in less than a page, a far cry from some rent review clauses found in modern leases which sometimes extend to several pages and are unnecessarily verbose" (p. 70).

Today's leases do not normally contain time-of-the-essence clauses to avoid risks for both sides. Limitation periods are now of a consultive rather than mandatory nature. Landlords will today simply contact tenants on or before the review date and make a proposal for a new rent. Experts or arbitrators are only brought in where agreement cannot be reached (Edwards and Krendel, 2007, p. 70).

Review dates have to be specified in the lease, with the most unambiguous clauses being those which state review dates (e.g. "1 May 2015") rather than making references to the starting date (e.g. "five years from the commencement of the lease").

4.2.3.1.2 Valuation of the premises

The valuation of the premises, i.e. the determination of the new rent, is the crucial aspect of the rent review process. While the formalities surrounding rent review are a question of transaction costs, the method by which the new rent is to be determined is decisive as to whether rent review guarantees long-term incentive-compatibility between landlord and tenant.

The new rent to be established at review is called "open market rent". This open market rent is the rent at which the property is expected to be let on the open market. Crosby and Murdoch (1997) note that it is held among UK property professionals that the letting to a (hypothetical) new tenant who has no existing relationship with the landlord represents the best source of transaction evidence for determining the open market rental value of comparable properties. The precise definition of an open market rent will depend upon the definition set out in the lease in question. There is no default rule or other legally binding definition. Nevertheless, the definitions provided by lease contracts usually follow a model quoted by Crosby and Murdoch (1997):

> Open Market Rent means the best yearly rent at which the demised premises might reasonably be expected to be let at the relevant review date by a willing landlord assuming that the premises are available to let as a whole to a willing tenant with vacant possession on the open market without a fine or premium under a lease for a term of equal length to the agreed term but commencing on the relevant review date including provisions for review of rent on the review dates and otherwise on the same terms as the lease.

Furthermore, the Red Book, a pervasive valuation manual published by RICS in order to ensure "best practice" among surveyors, contains a definition of "open market rental value" to be the rent at which a new letting of an interest in property would have been completed at the date of valuation assuming:

- A willing landlord;
- That prior to the date of valuation there had been a reasonable lease-up period;
- That the state of the market, levels of values and other circumstances are the same as on the date of the valuation;
- That no account is taken of any additional bid by a prospective purchaser with a special interest;
- That both parties to the transaction had acted knowledgeably, prudently and without compulsion;
- That the property can be used for the foreseeable future only for the existing use;
- That vacant possession is provided on termination of the lease of all the property occupied by the business.

It is of paramount importance to point out again that the Red Book and other manuals provided have a pervasive influence and that therefore most professionals follow their guidance but that ultimately these are merely non-binding best practice suggestions. As a consequence, each rent review clause is different and has to be studied individually.

4.2.3.1.3 Dispute settlement

It is in the nature of rent review that landlord and tenant will not always succeed in agreeing on a new rent. For such instances the British property industry has developed two principal dispute resolution mechanisms: the referral of the matter to an independent expert or arbitration proceedings. Some authors propose that mediation may also play a role in the future, though current practice does not provide evidence for this view.

As with most other elements of rent review, dispute resolution is also a matter of self-governance and negotiation between the parties. The role of courts is fairly limited and entails only the interpretation of unclear or otherwise problematic clauses in the lease. Such matters are determined by the court before the arbitration procedure or referral to an independent expert continues. Parties are normally well advised not to refer matters to the courts because of expenses and delays. Edwards and Krendel (2007, p. 91) warn that up to a year can pass before a date for a first hearing is set. The partly incalculable costs that characterise the English civil process make resorting to the courts even less desirable.

4.2.3.1.3.1 Independent expert

The main difference between an independent expert and an arbitrator lies in their respective ranges of competence. An independent expert, typically a Chartered Surveyor, can and is expected to use his own knowledge when determining the new rent. An arbitrator, on the other hand, fulfils a quasi judicial role and can only consider the evidence that is brought before him by the parties (Edwards and Krendel, 2007, p. 88).

The lease typically stipulates that the expert should be appointed by the President of the Royal Institution of Chartered Surveyors (RICS) to avoid conflicts between landlord and tenant as to who should be the expert.

While arbitration proceedings are to some extent governed by statute, the role and powers of independent experts are governed by the terms of the lease only. The independent expert is given full authority to set the new rent, even if it is outside of the boundaries of landlord's and tenant's proposal. Traditionally, he is not required to state reasons for his decision but because tendencies to achieve greater transparency in the real estate industry, new leases now often require the expert to justify his decision. This recent development has raised concerns among independent experts because of potential negligence claims (Edwards and Krendel, 2007, p. 86).

The independent expert is under a duty to investigate all relevant facts and all the information necessary to arrive at a decision. His search would include in particular the identification of comparables as the new rent is determined by reference to comparable leases and properties.

While the expert has to base his decision primarily on his own knowledge, the lease may stipulate that parties may provide certain information relevant to his decision.

The independent expert has no powers to make costs awards unless this is specified in the lease. All decisions regarding costs have to be stipulated in the lease (Edwards and Krendel, 2007, p. 86).

4.2.3.1.3.2 Arbitration

An arbitrator fulfils a rather different role. The role of an arbitrator is more akin to that of a common law judge who is presented with evidence brought before him by the parties. Unlike independent experts, arbitrators and arbitration proceedings are partly governed by statute, currently under the Arbitration Act 1996. The arbitrator sets a new rent on the basis of submissions made by the parties. The new rent has to fall within the boundaries set by landlord's and tenant's proposals. Nevertheless, he is expected to use his own expertise to assess the quality and relevance of the evidence brought before him. Like an independent expert, the arbitrator will thus typically also be a Chartered Surveyor (Edwards and Krendel, 2007, p. 83).

The detailed procedures of arbitration are regulated in the Arbitration Act 1996 so that parties enjoy less freedom in negotiating the rent review procedure.

Two procedural powers given to the arbitrator under the Arbitration Act 1996 are worth mentioning:

1. The arbitrator has the authority to decide on the costs of the arbitration and can allocate these costs between the parties. He may, for example, decide that each party has to pay its own costs, but equally decide that one party has to pay all or a part of the other party's costs (s. 34(2)(g) Arbitration Act 1996).
2. In general, the arbitrator may only consider evidence brought before him by the parties. However, if he feels that some important information is missing, he may add this information from his own knowledge after getting consent from the parties (s. 59-65 Arbitration Act 1996). The important difference to an independent expert is that the arbitrator has to seek permission from the parties before using his own knowledge in deciding the matter.

4.2.3.1.3.3 Mediation

Mediation is not yet used in rent review proceedings. Edwards and Krendel (2007, p. 87) however claim that this form of dispute resolution has a number of advantages over other forms. Mediation is more focused on consensual outcomes and identifying options than an adversarial procedure such as arbitration.

The identified advantages include:

- Direct involvement of parties;
- No non-consensual imposition of settlements;
- Private and informal procedures;
- Wide range of (non-) legal remedies;
- Focus on continued business relationship between parties;
- Cost effectiveness.

It remains to be seen, however, whether this form of dispute resolution will make any impact on the UK property market. The author would suggest that, given the dominant position of Chartered Surveyors, they would have little interest in the emergence of more cost effective practices since this would directly affect their business revenues. Any attempt to introduce mediation as an alternative dispute resolution method would thus face strong opposition from the influential Surveyor's lobby.

4.2.3.1.4 Assessment of dispute resolution mechanisms

In a business to business context, private dispute resolution is often viewed as a superior means of adjusting long-term contracts than referral of the matter to a regular court (Eger, 1995, p. 147). Private dispute resolution is faster and less costly than regular court proceedings. Private dispute resolution also offers confidentiality as decisions are not made public. The main advantage is that the adjudicator is an expert in the given field, i.e. here a Chartered Surveyor, and not a judge who may be inexperienced in the matter.

Parties are thus in any event likely to prefer either arbitration or an independent expert over the court track. With two (or three, taking the exotic mediation route into account) available dispute resolution mechanisms, the question remains as to which of these is preferable.

Independent experts appear to be the less formal of the two mechanisms and leave a wide scope for negotiations between the parties. As the independent expert makes the rent award based on his own investigations, there is little, if any, need for parties to submit their own evidence. The lease parties have thus little influence on the determination of the new rent. This is advantageous, because transaction costs are comparatively low, but at the same time the rent award becomes a bit of a gamble: the new rent could, as explained above, take any amount the valuer thinks fit.

Arbitration is on the other hand more akin to a legal dispute in front of a court of law: parties are required to make submissions and the arbitrator decides on the basis of evidence produced by the parties. The transaction costs of such proceedings are therefore higher but at the same time parties can influence the proceedings to a greater extent: the rent award has to be within the bounds set by the parties' proposed rents and the arbitrator's award will be based on submitted evidence.

Edwards and Krendel (2007, pp. 83-84) propose a fairly pragmatic strategy for determining a dispute resolution method: from a landlord's perspective, arbitration is preferable in a falling market while determination by an independent expert is best in a rising property market. The independent expert, as a Chartered Surveyor, will keep abreast with current developments on the market. When the market is rising, he has to include his knowledge of these circumstances in the valuation.

An arbitrator, on the other hand, must not add his own knowledge when deciding on the new rent (save in particular circumstances). When the market is falling, the landlord may strategically hold back such information while the tenant may not be so aware of current developments on the market so that a better outcome may be attained by the landlord. This view has, however, to be qualified for two reasons: first of all, the method used has to be determined at the drafting stage of the lease so that market developments may not be foreseeable. Cunning solicitors advising landlords have tried to include clauses allowing the decision as to the dispute resolution method only at the time of rent review but tenants have, for good reasons, strongly objected to this drafting strategy. Secondly, it should be noted that in larger-scale arbitrations landlord and tenant do not present their evidence themselves but are normally represented by Surveyors acting on their behalf so that ignorance as to market trends should be an exception.

A more feasible approach suggested by Edwards and Krendel (2007, p. 84) is that independent experts should be chosen where the rent review of a property does not seem to pose greater difficulties, i.e. the property belongs to a clearly defined market sector and comparables are widely available. Where large amounts are at stake and/or where the property cannot be that easily classified, arbitration is the more appropriate dispute resolution method.

From the author's point of view, independent expert proceedings suffer from a lack of default rules as to procedure and costs. Eger (1995, pp. 148-149) actually points out that while harmonisation of rules lowers transaction costs there is a risk that private dispute resolution loses its informal character and thus its attractiveness to parties. He asserts that private dispute resolution mechanisms are to be seen as a last resort when all other negotiations between parties have failed but where resort to courts of law is infeasible.

Eger's arguments would speak against a harmonisation of independent expert rules. But in the author's view a set of default rules could help to make this mechanism more appealing to smaller tenants. These rules would apply where parties are unwilling or unable to draft their individual rules. Such proposals frequently attract criticisms from within the industry, particularly from RICS, officially because of the inherent heterogeneity of leases but more likely because of the loss of potential income that would be the consequence of the introduction of such default rules.

Arbitration is the more formal dispute resolution mechanism and parliament has intervened in the regulation of arbitration by way of the Arbitration Act 1996. The Arbitration Act does, however, only provide a general framework within which arbitration should take place. The Act states as a key principle: "[T]he parties should be free to agree how their disputes are resolved, subject only to such safeguards as are necessary in the public interest."[67] Notably, the Arbitration Act is composed of mandatory and default (or "non-mandatory") rules. Most rules that relate to the actual procedures of the arbitration are default rules and can thus be tailored to the needs of the parties. Rules that seek to safeguard a due process and fairness of the arbitration are, on the other hand, mandatory. These mandatory rules include: powers of court to control/remove arbitrators; general duties of arbitrators and tribunals; provisions relating to cost awards; immunity of the arbitrator.[68] The Act thus achieves to balance the need for flexibility to make arbitration attractive to businesses and the necessity of providing basic legal and procedural safeguards to parties of arbitration proceedings. Arbitration is thus the more developed of the two dispute resolution mechanisms; further, a basic legal framework would also be desirable for the use of independent experts.

The author doubts that mediation will have a great impact on the market simply because an informal mediation is already taking place between parties: the determination of a new rent by an independent expert or arbitration proceedings are just an ultimate means of settling a dispute but normally parties

---

67 s. 1(b) Arbitration Act 1996.

68 A complete list of mandatory rules is provided in Schedule 1 of the Arbitration Act 1996.

agree on a new rent informally. Eger (1995, p. 149) also observes that such dispute resolution mechanisms are to be seen as an ultimate means when all other negotiations failed, but that it should be borne in mind that usually both parties have an interest in an ongoing business relationship. In that sense, mediation is too formal to be used in lieu of the normal negotiations that would take place in any case, but mediation is at the same time too informal to be used over a more stringent dispute resolution mechanism such as arbitration.

4.2.3.2 Rent review and valuation from a behavioural perspective

The analysis has so far rested on the assumption that a valuation professional, either acting as an independent expert or advocating on behalf of a landlord or tenant, is in a position to objectively determine the open market rent for the premises in question.

A fairly recent stream of literature, termed "behavioural property research", questions this view of objective valuation. The precision of valuations directly impacts upon the ability of rent review to maintain incentives between parties. An incorrect valuation may actually distort rather than facilitate incentives. The findings of behavioural property research as it relates to the valuation profession shall thus be reviewed in the following:

Behavioural research into property was pioneered by Diaz (1990a; 1990b), expanding on the theory of human problem solving as advanced by Newell and Simon (1972) and Simon (1978).[69] Diaz (1999) asserts the relevance of behavioural research by pointing out that research into property is dominated by economic modelling and the assumption of an "infallible rational man and efficient markets" (p. 329) that fails to address key issues because "economic activity is human behaviour" (p. 327).

Diaz (1999, p. 329) observes that most publications in the behavioural property field focus on the activities of valuers. Because of the limited number of transactions on real property markets and the relative secrecy of these transactions, valuation is of major importance to provide market participants with information.[70]

---

69 Problem solving is found to occur in the short-term memory: because of limited capacity of short-term memory, humans are thought to employ "cognitive short cuts", referred to as heuristics. Whilst reducing complexity, these heuristics may produce systematic errors in cognitive processes.

70 In sharp contrast to fixed income and equity markets where publicly organised markets provide transaction data.

Diaz (1999) phrases the main research question on valuers as "do valuers do what they 'ought' to do?" (p. 329). Chartered Surveyors and all other professions concerned with property valuation have to adhere to strict rules and guidelines as to how appraisals are to be performed. These guidelines are either set by their own professional bodies (as for Chartered Surveyors) or laid down by law (as for most Continental valuation professionals). Behavioural property research investigates to what extent professionals comply with these rules and to what extent they deviate, thus potentially producing systematically incorrect valuations.

An early insight was that valuers rarely follow the guidelines set by their professional bodies. Instead of deducting results from a wide set of comparables, valuers tend to start their valuation from the property to be valued and only then search for comparables (Diaz, 1990a, pp. 11-13).[71] More concerning, Adair et al. (1996, pp. 33-34) discovered that valuers viewed certain property characteristics differently than actual market participants. With a view to rent review, this leads to the question whether a Surveyor's rent award reflects the rent that tenants would really be willing to pay.

The selection of appropriate comparables was the subject of a study by Diaz (1990b). He found that valuers have developed efficient strategies to select comparables that could, however, lead to biased results (Diaz, 1990b, pp. 539-540). This view was confirmed by Wolverton (1996) and Gallimore and Wolverton (1997). They found that knowledge of transaction prices of the property to be valued produced significantly biased results.

Timing of information and the opinion of other valuers also seem to be factors influencing the outcome of valuations.

Recent information is found to generally have a stronger influence on valuers than less recent information (Gallimore, 1994, p. 101). Gallimore (1996, p. 270) could also confirm the hypothesis that valuers typically make an early value judgement and then seek to confirm this view by finding appropriate evidence. It therefore seems that valuation manuals provided by the respective professional bodies have little impact on practitioners: good practice would be that the valuation of the property stands at the very end, not at the beginning, of the valuation process.

Valuers operating in areas unfamiliar to them are influenced in their decisions by valuations of other, anonymous valuers (Diaz and Hansz, 1997). This anchoring effect was not observed, however, where a valuer operated in an area

71 It should be noted that Diaz's research is on US property valuers. While specific valuation rules may differ, general results should hold true for all markets.

familiar to him (Diaz, 1997, p. 62).[72] This would imply that it is beneficial to select local valuers. With the majority of investment property centred in or around London, this does not appear to be a major issue in the UK.

An issue with particular relevance to rent reviews is the willingness of valuers to re-adjust their valuations. Diaz and Wolverton (1998, p. 355) observe a phenomenon called "appraisal smoothing": when comparing real estate indices that use valuation data and comparable indices that use transaction data, then it is revealed that valuers do not sufficiently update their valuations in light of actual transaction data. The authors thus find that valuers anchor to previous valuations.

Havard (1999) conducted an experiment to find out whether it is more likely that properties previously valued at a low price are valued higher at a review or whether properties previously valued at a high price are re-valued at a lower price. The study reveals that (student-) valuers have a tendency to adjust previous valuations upwards and that, other things being equal, they are less likely to adjust a previous valuation downwards (Havard, 1999, p. 372). This finding, if verified by further studies, would have a major impact on rent reviews as it would show that for behavioural reasons downward reviews are less likely.

Finally, the responsiveness of valuers to their clients was scrutinised by behavioural researchers. Ideally, a valuer should disregard the interests of his clients when valuing a lease. Only if a valuation is uninfluenced by the interests of either party will it be possible to determine a market rent that attains incentive-compatibility. Kinnard et al. (1997, p. 240) indicate that valuers in the US may respond to client pressure by changing valuations accordingly, finding that "overall, 41 per cent of the commercial appraisers [that participated in the experimental study] revised their valuation estimates, without having supportive documentation, when requested to do so by their client".

Wolverton and Gallimore (1999, pp. 428-429) claim that the aim of a valuation is strongly related to the nature and intensity of client feedback. Valuers seem to acknowledge the purposive nature of valuations, i.e. that valuation take place for the furtherance of certain objectives, and depending on the pressure received from the client, this purpose is taken into account.

The findings of behavioural research into the valuation profession raise concerns as to the validity of valuations. It would seem that valuations are not as reliable as the professional ethos of RICS would suggest. Incorrect rent awards also raise doubts as to the ability of rent reviews to provide long-term incentive-

72 In the study undertaken by Diaz (1997) appraisers from Atlanta were asked to value a parcel of land in the city.

compatibility and appropriate risk allocation between parties. Also considering the significant transaction costs of rent review, it is doubtful whether this method of rent adjustment remains at all desirable.

There are, however, some important qualifications to the findings of behavioural research that limit the relevance of the research outcomes:

1. Most behavioural studies employ experiments to test their research hypotheses. The design of the experiment and the participants are thus of major importance. The participants are very often students. Havard (1999, p. 372) notes that students may not act as qualified real estate professionals would act. The setting of the experiment may also be slightly artificial, thus producing results that would not necessarily correspond with industry practices.
2. More importantly, the author suggests that, while behavioural research can surely provide some very interesting insights, the issues raised may be attenuated by the fact that they are generally known to real estate professionals. While industry professionals generally have high professional standards (because of their status as members of a Chartered Profession), market participants are aware that all forms of valuation serve a certain purpose. If this tendency is known, market participants will adjust their behaviour accordingly. An arbitrator would, for example, know that the evidence produced to him by the Surveyors representing landlord and tenant is driven by a certain motivation.

Crosby et al. (2002) conducted a study examining problems with expert valuation witnesses in the UK. While the English reforms of the civil process (Woolf reforms) envisage that parties should agree on a single expert, it is the dominant practice that claimant and defendant bring their own experts. According to their charters, e.g. the RICS practice statement for surveyors appearing as expert witnesses, the surveyor has a "primary duty to the judicial body to whom his evidence is given" and his evidence must be "independent, objective and unbiased" (RICS Practice Statement 1997, cited in Crosby et al., 2002, p. 325). A survey among surveyors also conducted by Crosby et al. (2002, p. 333) revealed that 88% of respondents were aware of their duty to the court. When questioned on the attitude of the opponent's expert witness, 58% responded that the opponent's expert would occasionally, and 27% responded that he would usually advocate for his client and not fulfil his duty to the court. Crosby et al. (2002, pp. 337-342) also interviewed judges and solicitors. It seems that problems with such expert witnesses are well known among the legal profession.

Wright J. observed in Arab Bank plc v John D Wood Commercial Ltd [1998] EGCS 34: "The court has not been assisted by the tendency which I detected in all the expert witnesses who gave evidence before me to take upon their own shoulders the mantle of advocacy and themselves to seek to persuade the court to a desired result rather than to offer dispassionate and disinterested assistance and advice to the court to enable it to arrive at a fair and balanced view of the conflicting contentions of the parties."

One judge interviewed for the study by Crosby et al. (2002, p. 341) suggested that witnesses should actually be allowed to depart from their veil of impartiality and advocate their client's viewpoint. The judge would then have to weigh the evidence, which was now usual practice anyway.

These observations all seem to indicate that the weaknesses of valuations because of heuristic problem solving are perhaps mitigated by the common knowledge of all participants that such defects exist and are to be taken into account.

Another issue that may cause incentive problems in leases with rent review clauses is discussed next: the all-prevailing upward-only rent review.

4.2.3.3 Upward only rent reviews

The UK type of rent review would normally play out its advantages in terms of responding to the parties' degrees of risk aversion and incentives to perform only if the rents are fully flexible, that is that the outcome of the review could yield a rent higher or lower than the original rent.

However, since the widespread introduction of rent reviews in the 1960s, virtually all contracts have stipulated upward only rent reviews, known as UORRs (Edwards and Krendel, 2007, p. 79). In an upward only contract, rents never fall below the original rent. Upon review, the rents will either go up to the new open market rent determined by the surveyor, or rents will stay at the original level should the surveyor find that open-market rents are lower than the original rent. Furthermore, leases that contain multiple reviews not only protect the landlord by assuring him at least the rent of the original lease but, moreover, rents normally do not fall below the level of the previous review. This insurance against falling rents is known as "ratchet" (Sparkes, 2001, p. 658).

Over the past 20 years there has been considerable debate as to whether upward only rent reviews are justified. When this type of review was introduced to the market in the 1960s and 70s the UK business community operated in a high inflation environment. Inflation in the UK was significantly higher than in other European countries, particularly Germany (Smales, 1981, pp. 224-226). It therefore seemed a purely theoretical question as to whether rents would at some point go down. In the 1980s the market environment changed and, in particular, the market for London office properties began to show a high degree of volatility. Sparkes (2001, p. 659) observed that in times of recession upward only clauses had a "disastrous effect" on businesses. In the recession of the early 1990s many businesses became insolvent because of leases that were way above the market rents. Sparkes (2001, p. 659) also claims that ratchet clauses prevented an adjustment of the property market. There were legislative attempts to ban upwards only clauses, but the Upwards-only Rent Review Clauses (Abolition) Bill 1993 failed. The new Code of Practice suggests that parties should agree on clauses that are flexible in both directions, but application of the Code is not mandatory. Sparkes (2001, p. 659) finds that it is more realistic to combine a ratchet clause with break options than to demand upward/downward provisions, meaning that a tenant finding the new rent unjustified would have the opportunity to terminate his contract and rent new premises. This, however, can only function in a property market where alternative properties are available. In a very competitive or tight market, the tenant may not be able to find adequate new premises. The major problem with break clauses in combination with ratchets, however, is the hold-up situation. Depending on the tenant's goodwill or the degree of business-immobility, he would incur significant costs when moving. Therefore, having the opportunity to find an alternative to his old premises at a lower rent will not necessarily compensate him. Break clauses as an alternative to upward/downward clauses can therefore only be an alternative for businesses with low degrees of either goodwill or business-immobility.

Nevertheless upwards only rent reviews have continued to be the dominating form of rent adjustment for the years following the recession of the early 1990s. While the Bill to abolish these reviews had failed, a first version of the Code of Practice for Commercial Leases was introduced in December 1995 following a governmental consultation paper from 1993. One of the Code's stated objectives was to offer more flexible lease terms. After the recession, the UK economy quickly recovered and rents grew from 1996 to 1998, with 1997 showing the best letting market (Edwards and Krendel, 2007, p. 135). While a report to the DETR[73] prepared by the University of Reading showed that practitioners were open to new ideas and also believed that with an increasing number of foreign investors, foreign practices would play a greater role in the UK market, these influences did not in fact play a role for the years following the 1990s recession. Instead, lease lengths fell in many markets and ratchets remained, now often combined with break clauses. The Reading report nevertheless also highlighted a lack of awareness of alternatives to upward-only clauses, leading the then-Planning Minister Nick Raynsford to invite the working group on the Code of Practice to investigate further into the matter (DETR, 2000). Finally, a new version of the Code of Practice was released in 2002.

73 Department of the Environment, Transport and the Regions.

The new version of the Code suggests flexibility of leases in recommendation six. The recommendation reads:

> Rent reviews should generally be to the open market rent. Wherever possible, landlords should offer alternatives which are priced on a risk-adjusted basis, including alternatives to upwards only rent reviews; these might include up/down reviews to open market rent with a minimum of the initial rent, or another basis such as annual indexation. Those funding property should make every effort to avoid imposing restrictions on the length of lease and type of rent review that landlords, developers and/or investors may offer.

The proponents of a ban of upward-only rent review clauses usually base their arguments on notions of fairness.

There has, however, also been research which suggests that such a ban would have a negative effect on the property market, property investments and the economy in general. It should be noted that this research has to be approached with some caution as it has been sponsored by property industry associations so that there may be doubts as to its independence. A study by Key and Almond (2004), commissioned by the British Property Federation, investigates the impact of banning such reviews on property pricing, risk and returns, asset allocation, urban regeneration, sale & leasebacks, and investment into the UK by foreign investors which may be potential tenants.

As part of their research, the authors simulated cash flows based on historic data and market forecasts. They conclude that downward rent reviews would increase the volatility of income from property and would have reduced total income from property by up to 10 per cent in the periods worst affected by the recession in the early 1990s. It was also found that the negative impacts of downward rent reviews could largely be compensated if a so-called initial rent floor were introduced. Such a rent floor is essentially a fixed base rate. It was also found that break clauses have greater negative impacts than downward rent reviews.

In a simulation of income flows it was found that the ban of upward only reviews would reduce expected values of future rental income and increase risks of falling rental income. Assuming a fully efficient pricing of changes in income streams, the result would be an increased required rate of return on property, achieved by either rising rents or a fall in capital values[74]. Depending on the nature of particular sub-markets and negotiation strength, rents would increase where landlords have a better leverage and property values would fall in tenant-dominated markets. The authors suggest that it is doubtful that landlords would be able to charge premiums for agreeing on downward reviews. A resulting

---

74 As the required rate of return of a property (initial yield) is calculated as rent/property value, either increasing rents or falling property prices increase the rate of return.

increase of the volatility of income streams and capital value would reduce the allocation of investments by institutional investors into property by 2% to 5%. Furthermore, as volatility differs between regional sub-markets, asset allocation would move away from London and the South East to less volatile regions in Britain.

One could clearly criticise the methodology applied by the authors, using historic data and modifying it as if downward rent reviews had been implemented by that time. This methodology ignores that markets would perhaps have developed differently had these provisions been in place by that time. Nevertheless the general tendencies seem to have validity, in particular when considering the role that real estate generally plays in an investment portfolio.

Property as an asset class is characterised by moderate total returns and moderate to low risk (Geltner and Miller, 2001, pp. 140-141). In an investment portfolio, real estate is positioned between shares at one extreme (high risk, high return) and cash (very low risk, low return) at the other extreme. Real estate is particularly attractive to long-term, institutional investors because it functions as a hedge against inflation. While value appreciation of property is usually slow compared to shares, the ability to adjust cash flows from rent over time protects from inflation (Geltner and Miller, 2001, p. 141). This ought to be contrasted to corporate or government bonds where interest rates are fixed and thus no protection from inflation is provided.

Key and Almond (2004, pp. 16-18) also investigated the effects of a ban of UORRs on urban regeneration. Regeneration is of particular public interest in the UK because space constraints and partly inadequate transport links limit the ability of cities, most of all London, to spread. At the same time, many inner-city areas in London and other major UK cities attract investments and new inhabitants. It is politically desired that this "gentrification" also spread to areas that have so far not benefited from investments to make urban working and living more attractive.

The study finds that a ban of UORRs would have a severely negative impact on urban regeneration. In contrast to the acquisition of property already on the market, regeneration bears additional risks stemming from property development itself and uncertainties as to the development of the location.

Real estate development highly depends on debt financing. Key and Almond (2004, p. 17) claim that banks would be strongly disinclined to finance projects where cash flows would not be secured by UORRs. As a result of these additional risks and financing constraints, developers would either have to charge higher rents, which may be difficult in developing sub-markets, or, more likely, capital values of properties in such areas would fall.

This view is supported by another study also commissioned by the British Property Federation. Maxted and Porter (2003) investigated the potential effects of a ban of UORRs on commercial real estate lending. They interviewed professionals from 17 leading banks financing commercial property development and acquisition. It was found that, while lending activity would of course continue after a ban of UORRs, capital values would fall and banks would reduce the loan-to-value ratio (LTV ratio) up to which they would be willing to lend. Also, it is generally thought that a ban of UORRs would lead to an increase in interest rates and shorter lengths of loans, both because of shorter periods of secure income from the properties. A ban would therefore reduce borrowers' abilities to finance projects in two ways: by a reduction of the LTV ratio and by an increase in rates. In general, banks also think that a ban would lead to an increased caution among lenders to fund only prime property. This would make it more difficult for developers to obtain financing for projects in areas that are yet to benefit from regeneration.

Sale and leaseback transactions and the impact that a ban of UORRs would have upon them were also discussed by Key and Almond (2004, p. 22). Sale and leasebacks (SALBs) are large-scale transactions where companies owning real estate for their own use sell their property to an investor and at the same time lease the premises back from this investor, usually for fairly long terms of up to 25 years. While the number of SALBs is small, the volume of these transactions is high. From 1999 to 2004, SALBs have provided £1.7bn in receipts to UK businesses (Key and Almond, 2004, p. 19). The motivation for SALBs is usually the "monitization" of assets to raise capital for new, "core" investments or the reduction of debt, as several recent transactions by major European telecom concerns showed (e.g. British Telecom, Deutsche Telekom, Swisscom). It is held by Key and Almond (2004, p. 22) that a ban of UORRs would limit the ability of businesses to successfully execute SALBs. The key element of raising capital through a SALB is the seller's ability to offer the investor attractive lease covenants securing long-term, certain cash flows. Leases with a downward provision would have a negative impact on sales prices as the certainty of cash flows cannot be guaranteed anymore. The investment banks advising buyers and sellers typically model several NPV scenarios to establish a sales price. Without UORRs it would become more difficult to model prices because it would no longer be possible to establish a guaranteed minimum-NPV. As a consequence, sales prices would be negatively affected.

Finally, the research found that investment into the UK by foreign investors could be positively affected by a ban of UORRs. For this part of the study, directors of Regional Development Agencies (public agencies to promote economic growth in the regions) were interviewed. International tenants are thought to be startled by UK lease conditions. Particularly tenants from the US, who are used to more flexible lease terms, are reported to have described UK terms with words such as "horror", "shock" and "alarming". Nevertheless, it was held that lease terms would not be a deciding factor whether to establish a business in the UK, but the interviewees generally found themselves unable to quantify such effects.

One would think that in any event, tenants should prefer upward/downward provisions to UORRs. It was established above that a tenant would normally display a certain degree of risk aversion, depending, among other factors, on the relative size of rent payments compared to other expenses. Location-dependant goodwill and the degree of business-immobility would not play a role because the surveyor determining the new rent would have to ignore these elements (see above). For a tenant whose risk-aversion is determined by the relevance of rent payments to his budgeting, a lease with a UORR clause appears to be the worst choice. For a tenant with strong costs risks, a fixed rent would be preferable because it would allow him to budget his expenses for the term of the lease. A tenant that is primarily affected by valuation risks would, however, prefer fully flexible prices. One could recall the example given by Posner (1992, p. 21) of professional services firms that would face a competitive disadvantage if market rents fell and the firm were locked into a contract with a rent much above open market rents. The UORR, however, does not mitigate either type of risk. It does not assist the tenant facing valuation risks in his planning. The rent is only certain until the first review and in the following the increase in rent is uncertain. For such a tenant, a lease with pre-determined step-ups would be preferable. On the other hand, the UORR does not serve the tenant with valuation risks either, because for him it would be essential that rents could also decrease upon review. Because of the ratchet, however, he would probably find himself in a worse situation than a tenant with a fixed rent. The fact that he may be able to use a break clause upon review may not be of much assistance because of hold-up issues.

It is possible that these disadvantages for risk-averse tenants would be offset by incentive problems potentially created by a ban of UORRs. A particular attribute of real estate projects is the high reliance on debt financing and agency conflicts associated with debt financing. The hostile attitude of lenders to a ban of UORRs described by Maxted and Porter (2003) can be explained with their attitude to risk and the transaction costs associated with underwriting and monitoring loans for properties with flexible leases. Banks provide debt financing partly because of their own risk aversion. A bank could also fund operations by participating as an equity partner which would give the chance for higher returns, but the fact that lending is chosen instead is a sign that risks should be avoided as a lender has more security than an equity partner.

From a theoretical point of view, a ban of UORRs would be desirable. Nevertheless, landlords and lenders have so far successfully resisted any legislation against UORRs. In recent years property markets, particularly in the City, have enjoyed continuous growth so that rent reductions at review were not supported by comparables anyway. The current recession and collapse of the UK property market should bring this topic back on the agenda.

4.2.3.4 Rent review and the case for default rules

The previous discussion already highlighted that rent review proceedings are characterised by high transaction costs. This gives rise to two questions: 1) would default rules facilitate a reduction of such costs; and 2) if they reduced transaction costs, why have no default rules been introduced to the UK property market so far?[75]

In the introduction to this chapter the concept of default rules was established. Default rules were described as legal rules which parties may chose to use. The process of choosing takes the form of contracting around, i.e. parties to a contract are free to negotiate their own rules but where they fail to do so the default rule steps in. A role of default rules is thus to fill the gaps in contracts (Ayres and Gertner, 1989, p. 87). As discussed above, the negotiation of rent review provisions is left to the contracting parties and industry standards such as the Code of Practice are best practice recommendations only.

It is suggested that statutory intervention is desirable as it would reduce the transaction costs of drafting rent review clauses and would assist courts in filling contractual gaps. Moreover, default rules can under certain conditions induce parties to reveal socially beneficial information (Ayres and Gertner, 1989, p. 128).

Rent review clauses have produced – and continue to produce – substantial litigation. Because of the costs and unforeseeable nature of the English civil process, litigation is generally not an attractive means to fill contractual gaps. The following table provides an overview of typical disputes arising when rent reviews are due. Most of these problems could be solved with a set of default rules.

---

75 At first sight it may seem that the common law system may act as a barrier to legislative action. However, the English legislature has been active in the area of property law. Blackstone's "Statutes on property law", a students' statute book, already fills around 450 pages with property statutes. That there is no statute on rent review is therefore not explained by a general unwillingness to codify property law.

Table 4-4: Typical sources of dispute at rent review

	Issue	Key problems
Necessity of notices	- Whether it is necessary to trigger review by serving a notice and whether tenant has to serve a counter-notice objecting review	- Notices prevalent in many older leases. Missing of time-limits for serving notices can have severe consequences but no standard
Review dates	- Specification of review dates in leases (intervals, dates, notice periods)	- Problems arise as very heterogeneous definitions of review dates, either by reference to passing of time or to specific dates. Particular difficulties arise where landlord or tenant exercised break or renewal options
Treatment of VAT	- Validity of the assumption for valuation that both tenant and landlord can recover VAT in full	- Creates problems for tenants who are not able to fully recover VAT (e.g. financial institutions) which would in principle make a lower rental bid to compensate for VAT
Inclusion of disregards	- Which improvements have to be disregarded when valuing the premises for review	- Typical disregards are of occupation, goodwill and improvements, but let to negligence claims where tenant was obliged to carry out works and then improvements had been included in valuation at review. Long running debate not yet concluded
Statutory duties	- Leases typically stipulate that tenant has to carry out necessary works to comply with new statutory obligation, e.g. access for disabled persons	- No clear authority yet, particularly regarding treatment of duties arising under a non-property law statute. Best approach probably to include discount at review
Selection of comparables: particularly treatment of concessions	- When selecting comparable properties on the market for review, how should concessions (rent-free periods) be treated by the valuer	- Vast amount of case law with no definite result. Most sensible: inclusion of concession to incoming tenants granted as an incentive but no inclusion of fitting-out allowances (see separate section)

	Issue	Key problems
Displacing the "presumption of reality"	- Courts normally interpret rent review clauses "in favour of reality" (i.e. literally)	- Because of changing market environment, interpreting the clauses of (old) contracts in favour of reality may lead to results contrary to what parties had bargained for. Therefore "favour of reality" is not a mechanistic rule (Canary Wharf Investments (Three) v Telegraph Group [2003] 3 EGLR 31). Question remains when courts may depart from reality to achieve satisfactory interpretation of clauses

(based on Edwards and Krendel, 2007)

It would exceed the scope of this work to elaborate on the various issues concerning rent review clauses that have brought parties to the courts. Instead, the case for default rules is exemplified by discussing litigation on the inclusion or non-inclusion of rent-free periods in the valuation process at renewal.

4.2.3.5 Rent-free periods and their impact on rent review clauses

The treatment of rent free periods at rent reviews is an issue that has caused substantial litigation. While the courts have now settled the principal issues, it has taken years and a number of cases to establish how these rent free periods ought to be treated. This issue is therefore taken as an example to represent an array of comparable problems that have arisen with rent review and have also been litigated substantially.

Rent free periods are a common occurrence in commercial property leases. Rent-free periods allow a new tenant to occupy the premises free of rent for a certain time. There are two incentives for granting such rent-free periods: 1) tenants are sometimes granted rent-free periods in order to fit out the premises to their needs. This is common where the tenant is much better informed about his needs than the landlords. Examples include separating walls in offices or furniture for hotel rooms. German landlords are, unlike UK landlords, also quite willing to advance substantial amounts to tenants instead of granting a rent free period (two of the German leases used here as case studies contain clauses regulating such advances for fitting out). 2) In poor markets rent-free periods are used as an incentive to attract new tenants (Murdoch and Crosby, 1994, p. 43).

For the tenant, this means better liquidity at the commencement of the lease. An advantage to the landlord is the reporting of rents. Estate agents, surveyors and property consultants regularly prepare market reports with current rents. In these reports, rent-free periods are not taken into account. A lease with € 50 per square metre per month (psm) but a six months rent-free period will usually still be reported as a € 50 psm lease albeit a reduced effective rent because of the rent-free period. There is a common desire among landlords and their representatives to avoid an impression that rent levels in a certain market are falling.

It was described above that the purpose of rent reviews is to establish an open market rent for the demised premises and the treatment of such rent-free periods has caused major difficulties. The judicial treatment and litigation on this issue occupied courts for almost a decade, thus creating major uncertainties for parties to a lease. The issue first came up in 99 Bishopsgate Ltd v Prudential Assurance Co Ltd (1985) 273 EG 984. The court in Bishopsgate ruled that as the rent review clause stipulated the rent to be revalued to a rent level achievable for vacant premises on the open market, the tenant could claim all benefits that were then available to incoming tenants, including all concessions made to new tenants. Unfortunately, the court did not distinguish between rent-free periods given as an incentive to rent (the latter type describe above) and those that are granted to allow the tenant to fit out the premises according to his needs. This meant that the tenant in Bishopsgate, who rented a large office building, could at review benefit from rent-free periods granted as allowances for fitting out the premises (the former type described above). The court thus enabled the tenant to enjoy a windfall as his premises were obviously already fitted out.

While rent-free periods granted as an incentive to tenants correctly reflect current market rents, those rent-free periods granted for fitting out the premises cannot be seen to reflect the correct market rent: these rent-free periods are arrangements devised to make the premises usable by the tenant and thus would, if paid repeatedly, put the sitting tenant at an advantage compared to the incoming tenant.

The Bishopsgate decision caused advisers of landlords to draft rent review clauses seeking to exclude the consideration of rent-free periods granted for fitting-out the premises at review. Other advisers then came forward with clauses excluding all rent-free periods granted to tenants, those of the first and the second type. The drafting of clauses excluding the consideration of fitting-out allowances created surprising effects: Such clauses typically stated that at review the premises were to be treated as fitted out for the need of the hypothetical tenant. In fact this let surveyors value such premises at a premium at review because the rent review clause stated that the premises were thus to be viewed as seen in a superior state than that they actually were in when first rented[77].

Leases that sought to avoid the consideration of fitting out-allowances at rent review originally used expressions such as "[at review it is to be assumed that the premises are] fit for immediate use and occupation" (Murdoch and Crosby, 1994, p. 45). The advantages of a set of default rules were highlighted by the ruling in Pontsarn Investments v Kansalis-Osake-Pankki [1992] 22 EG 103. In this case the expression "fit for immediate use and occupation" came under scrutiny. Baker J held, probably contrary to what the parties thought the expression should mean, that "fit for immediate use" would merely mean that the premises are free from defect so that the tenant could move in. The expression does not mean, however, that the premises are already fitted out. Consequently, the tenant could claim fitting out allowances at review and the landlord could not claim an increased rent because of an alleged presumption of fitted out premises.

This result is somewhat surprising as the expression could very well be interpreted to mean that the premises are to be treated as fitted out and the author would argue that Baker J took too narrow a view when interpreting the clause. Nevertheless, in London & Leeds Estates Ltd v Paribas Ltd [1993] 30 EG 89, the Court of Appeal confirmed the meaning of the expression used in the review clause in Pontsarn Investments. The expression in London & Leeds Estates was actually more specific as it stipulated that the premises ought to be seen as "fit for immediate use and occupation and that all fitting out and other tenant's works required by such willing tenant have already been completed". Nourse LJ held that 1) the first part of the expression (as used in Pontsarn Investments) was insufficient to indicate that fitting out was already completed, 2) that the expression used in London & Leeds Estates sufficed to exclude the tenant from benefiting from a fitting out allowance at review but that 3) the landlord was nevertheless not entitled to a premium rent. This result is surprising as two experienced barristers acting as counsel in the case held the expression to be sufficient to achieve a premium rent at review.

Murdoch and Crosby (1994, p. 46) criticise this result as it makes "the task of a draftsman [to write rent review clauses] quite impossible, if wording, which appears to most to carry a clear meaning, is arbitrarily rejected by the courts".[80]

If rent review was governed by a set of default rules, such drafting problems could be avoided. The expressions in both Potsarn Investments and London &

77 Murdoch and Crosby (1994, p. 44), referring to the article "Rent reviews: back to the drawing board?" by Bell [1991] 09 EG 96.

80 Leave to appeal to the House of Lords was rejected so that this judgment is good law.

Leeds Estates were in the author's view sufficiently clear in their meaning. Default rules could fill such gaps and contracts could be much more economical in terms of verbiage and more coherent if, instead of elaborating for several pages on the inclusions and exclusions from valuation at rent review, the contracts referred to sections in the (hypothetical) Act governing rent reviews or lease contracts in general.

Such a "Commercial Leases (Rent Review) Act" could contain a fairly simple section defining when rent-free periods are to be considered at review and how they are to be valued. If parties seek to deviate from this default they would have to clearly express this in the lease contract.

The code for leasing business premises in England and Wales, shortly referred to as the Code of Practice contains a number of suggestions as to how commercial leases should be drafted.[81] The Code also contains advice on the drafting of rent review clauses. The application of the Code of Practice is voluntarily, however, and it does not set out detailed drafting rules but general proposals on how clauses should be drafted.

The English practice of individually drafted rent review provisions is particularly problematic vis-à-vis the increasing number of large-scale portfolio transactions. As pointed out in the introduction, the entry of new market participants into the UK property market, new investment vehicles and the ever-increasing capacity to process data facilitate larger real estate transactions where not only individual properties but portfolios of properties worth several billion pounds are transferred. The success of such transactions largely rests on a successful due diligence both on the side of the offeror and on the side of the bidders.

Such due diligences are usually conducted by the seller/bidder's in-house teams, external valuers, lawyers and often investment banking and consultancy teams. Key to the financial part of due diligence is a financial model using the DCF-technique and IRR calculations to establish appropriate sales/bid prices for the portfolio. A key problem of financial modelling is, however, the finding of common assumptions across the whole portfolio of properties.

The modelling of rent increases is a particularly difficult challenge if rent adjustment is regulated differently from lease to lease: for operational reasons, financial models can only process a limited number of different procedures so that a certain margin of error is inherent to modelling. The heterogeneous nature of English rent review clauses poses a significant financial risk to such portfolio transactions. Normally, real estate portfolios are offered to the market by way of a bidding process that often only takes a few weeks. During that time potential

81 The Joint Working Group on Commercial Leases (2007).

bidders can access information on the portfolio, e.g. lease contracts, technical information and so on. This so-called "data room", in the past filling hundreds of files and now mostly being provided electronically, may contain thousands of pages. The heterogeneous rent review clauses may contain legal "time bombs" that no due diligence team can discover in the limited time available. Because of a normally quite limited co-ordination between legal and financial due diligence, lawyers may actually be able to flag certain issues in the contracts but the finance team may later be unable to model these risks appropriately due to their complexity.

The reduction of transaction costs by introducing a set of default rules would thus be twofold: At a first level there would be the obvious savings at the drafting stage of individual contracts. At a second level there would, however, be the potentially much larger savings of transaction costs in case of portfolio transactions. A set of default rules could thus potentially assist in making the real estate market more efficient and transparent, thus attracting more investment and increasing overall welfare.

Rent review clauses that relate to rent-free periods granted as an inducement at the commencement of the lease have equally caused litigation: the rent review clauses challenged in court were those seeking to exclude the consideration of a rent-free period at review. A numerical example of the consequences of this distinction was provided in City Offices plc v Bryanston Insurance Co Ltd [1993] 11 EG 129: The rent review clause stated that the reviewed rent ought to be "the best yearly rent which would reasonably expected to be payable in respect of the demised premises after the expiry of any rent-free concession or fitting out period which might be given to the tenant" and that the valuer had to disregard "any notional rent-free concession or fitting out period for which allowances would or might be given to the tenant if the demised premises were let in the open market with vacant possession".

The parties to the lease had the reviewed rent determined by an arbitrator who found that, on the basis of market comparables, the premises would let at £564,327 p.a. but that a rent-free period of 12 months would have to be granted, with 3 months for fitting out and 9 months as an inducement.[83] The arbitrator found that this latter 9 months rent-free period was equivalent to a 15% discount, resulting in a rent of £479,678 p.a. The question thus brought before the court was how the wording of the review clause had to be interpreted. The landlord claimed the higher rent but the court found that the lower rent was payable. This result is surprising because it seems obvious that the clause simply sought to achieve a "day one" rent not reduced by any concession made to the

83 In 1992 the UK property market was in severe recession, thus the long rent-free period.

tenant. The landlord's mistake was the inclusion of the word "disregard" in the clause. Because of this word the first part of the clause was interpreted to refer only to rent-free periods for fitting out the premises while the second part of the clause (that had to be disregarded) was seen to refer to rent-free periods given as an inducement to new tenants. The tenant could thus benefit from a 9 month rent-free period typically given to tenants in the sluggish market in the early 1990s.[84]

There were several other cases that treated similar problems, leading Murdoch and Crosby (1994, p. 49) to conclude that rent review clauses seeking to exclude the consideration of rent-free periods will mostly prove to be unsuccessful.[85] The authors attribute this partly to deficiencies in drafting but also to a perceived unwillingness of the courts to treat the issue systematically and give a clear guidance. As a consequence, cases involving rent review clauses with rather similar wordings may lead to different outcomes and the numerical example quoted for City Offices shows that the financial consequences can be severe.

As stated above, the treatment of rent-free periods at review is used here as an example to highlight that the introduction of a set of default rules at rent review is highly desirable. Default rules can in such cases fill gaps in lease contracts much better than the courts. In addition, default rules can substantially reduce the costs of drafting leases and force parties to clearly state their intentions (Ayres and Gertner, 1989, pp. 92-95). It would be quite reasonable to assume that in several of the cases discussed above the parties were themselves not quite certain what they stipulated in the contract and how this differed from what they actually meant. Default rules would force parties to be clear on this.

That a set of defaults would be desirable cannot be questioned but it should also be asked whether it seems likely that such rules would be introduced in the UK property market.

The author is sceptical because of the institutional framework of the British property market: It was explained in the introduction that there is no strong group favouring tenants' interests but that on the other hand RICS has a very strong influence on property practice and also participates in all consultations on the regulation of leases. The voluntary Code of Practice, drafted under strong influence of RICS, does not contain default clauses. The valuation profession and the lawyers drafting contracts and representing landlords and tenants in courts actually have very little interest in such standardisation. Any form of

84 For a more detailed analysis of this complicated case see Murdoch and Crosby (1994).

85 E.g. Broadgate Square plc v Lehman Brothers Ltd [1994] 04 EG; Co-Operative Wholesale Society Ltd v National Westminster Bank plc [1994] 14 EG 130; Scottish Amicable Life Assurance Society v Middleton [1994] 10 EG 109.

default rule would have the potential to reduce their fee-income and for a contract lawyer it is financially beneficial to draft new rent review clauses rather than simply make reference to a lease code. To base contracts on governmental regulation would to some extent also go against the ethos of independence and self-regulation that characterises the Chartered Professions in Britain (Morgan, 1998, p. 189-190). As stated in the introduction, self-regulation of business conduct free from state intervention is a defining feature of the nature of British professionalism and thus stands in quite sharp contrast to the German tradition of state regulation and legislative intervention. Whilst highly desirable from an economic point of view, the introduction of default rules for the regulation of rent review is thus very likely to remain wishful thinking.

4.2.4 German rent review

Rent review as an adjustment mechanism is not exclusively known in the UK. German landlords and tenants can agree on a "German-style" rent review. Because of practical problems rent review is, however, exceptional on the German property market. In principle, three forms of rent review are to be distinguished.

4.2.4.1 Renegotiation clauses

In its crudest from, a rent review clause could simply stipulate that after passing of a certain period rents are to be renegotiated. Neuhaus (2005, p. 194) warns that such clauses are problematic because they merely state that the rent should be renegotiated but fail to prescribe what should be done when parties cannot agree on a new rent. If parties fail to reach an agreement, the court will determine what is to be seen as the "appropriate rent" for the given location.[86] From an economic perspective it is therefore not advisable to use such clauses: While they are easy to draft, the courts are ill-equipped to determine the new rent. Apart from court fees and delays, the court is unlikely to have sufficient insights into the market.

Simple renegotiation clauses ought only to be used when there are special bonds between landlord and tenant, e.g. family ties or a good reputation that would be at risk if excessive rents were demanded. Sometimes these clauses can also be found in contracts between landlords and tenants that belong to the same economic entity, e.g. where retail outlets rent properties from their head office.

---

86 Higher Appeal Court of Cologne (*OLG Köln*), judgment of 29 November 2000, 11 U 153/98, GuT 2002, 133.

4.2.4.2 *Trigger clauses*

These clauses are a hybrid of indexed rents (see below) and rent review. The initiation of rent review proceedings is triggered not by lapse of time as in the UK but by a certain change of an index or other figure used as a reference. The index used will almost exclusively be the CPI. This change, however, only triggers the actual review. Parties are fairly flexible in deciding on the basis of the review. Following Neuhaus (2005, p. 190) review may be based on:

- Market rents;
- Valuation by an independent expert;
- Determination by one of the parties (s. 315 BGB);
- Determination by a third party (s. 317 BGB);
- Reference to comparables (s. 558 BGB).

It is necessary that the clause leaves room for a certain "margin of discretion", i.e. that a change in the index that triggers the review does not necessarily lead to an increase in rents by the same percentage.[87] These trigger clauses are sometimes used for shorter leases because the use of index clauses is subject to restrictive legislation. Clauses using a "pure" indexation may only be used for tenancies of at least 10 years.[88] These trigger clauses are thus used to circumvent this legislation.

Trigger clauses combine the problems of indexation with certain institutional weaknesses of the German property market. The incentive problems that may be caused by indexation are discussed in the section on indexation clauses; here it should only be noted that the CPI does not necessarily reflect price changes of commercial real estate and should thus not be indiscriminately used as a reference for rent adjustments.

Secondly, once the rent review has been triggered, practical considerations considerably shorten the list of potential review mechanisms. Determination by one of the parties is clearly unattractive as the other party would have less influence than in case of a simple renegotiation clause. Reference to other market rents would mean that both parties have access to such information and disputes would be frequent as either party would choose comparables supporting

87 Higher Appeal Court of Hamburg (*OLG Hamburg*), judgment of 6 February 1985, 4 U 30 + 42/84, ZMR 1985, 237.

88 s. 4 Price Clauses Order; see also the section on index clauses below for a discussion of statutory intervention into the use of indexation.

their point of view.[89] All other mechanisms necessitate the involvement of a third party concerned with property valuation. The involvement of a third party, however, is stymied by the relatively small number of German "sworn valuers", by the relatively unregulated access to this profession, and by their focus on technical and architectural questions.[90]

While a UK rent review is not free from problems such as the above-discussed risk of behavioural biases in valuations or the heterogeneity of clauses, the strong advantage of the UK property market is the existence of a long-established valuation profession. A large number of surveyors, homogeneous education and an industry "best practice" developed by property professionals for property professionals ensure that valuations are conducted to a high standard.[91] In Germany, on the other hand, a standardised valuation practice cannot be expected by the parties to a lease. As a consequence, the higher costs and potential delays and risk of conflicts rarely merit the use of such trigger clauses as compared to, e.g. graduated rents or indexation.

4.2.4.3 Reference clauses

A third form of German rent reviews is found in the form of so-called *Spannungsklauseln*. These clauses define rent increases by reference to price increases of other goods or services that are "in their essential qualities equal or at least comparable" (Bartholomäi in Lindner-Figura et al., 2006, p. 307).[92] The difference between trigger clauses and *Spannungsklauseln* therefore is that review is not triggered by the change of a published index but by change of the prices of certain goods or services. In practice, these clauses are not frequently used (Bartholomäi in Lindner-Figura et al., 2006, p. 307). Neuhaus (2005, p. 193) even warns against the use of such clauses. In principle, however, *Spannungsklauseln* should be judged positively because they preserve incentives and allow parties to allocate risks based on a choice of reference good or service. Ideally, parties could decide to use price changes of the most important factors influencing business success as a reference for rent changes. For example, if the tenant is producing a certain good, price changes of this good could be used. When prices for the good are high, the rent is high, and the

---

89 For these reasons, leases with a trigger clause should also contain a dispute resolution clause stipulating determination by an independent expert in case of a non-consensual outcome of negotiations (Neuhaus, 2005, p. 192).

90 Differences between the profession of Chartered Surveyors and German *Vereidigte Sachverständige* have been discussed in the introduction.

91 Best practice is for example ensured by the RICS "Red Book" on valuation standards.

92 As defined in s. 1 (2) Price Clauses Order.

opposite. Such an agreement would suit a risk-averse tenant and would ensure that the tenant always has the incentive to fulfil his obligations under the lease.

Practical and legal issues nevertheless inhibit the use of *Spannungsklauseln* in business practice. Pursuant to s. 2 of the Price Declarations and Price Clauses Act[93] the reference used has to be "equal or at least comparable" and there have been various court decisions and academic discussions as to what is encompassed by this definition. It is argued that rents of other commercial properties fulfil the requirements of the Act.[94] Other references, however, were declared by the courts not to fulfil the criteria of sufficient comparability. These non-comparable references include: the salaries of civil servants[95], interest rates of mortgages, an index of construction costs and the value of land[96]. It is remarkable that the Federal Appeal Court also voided such clauses that made referred to figures from the real estate industry that could be well justified from an economic point of view.[97] The use of these clauses is thus handled very restrictively and parties to a lease would face the risk that at a later dispute such a clause be declared void.

Practical limitations on the use of *Spannungsklauseln* are also discussed by Neuhaus (2005, p. 193). He points out that price information may be hard to obtain as figures are unpublished. Furthermore, there is the risk that the chosen reference, e.g. another business lease, ceases to exist so that there is no further basis for rent adjustments. These clauses would thus possess desirable properties from a theoretical point of view but legal restrictions and practical difficulties make their use impossible, i.e. transaction costs are prohibitive.

It is not surprising why the German type of rent review is rarely used: There is the lack of a highly developed valuation profession that would be needed to operate such clauses effectively. Furthermore, restrictive legislation inhibits the use of clauses that would otherwise be desirable.

4.2.4.4 Rent review: the need for reform

The chapter on rent review intended to show that rent review can provide long-term incentive compatibility between parties to a lease but that the current regime operated in the UK is not free from problems. The comparison to German rent reviews also showed that statutory intervention can render rent review unattractive and force parties to resort to other adjustment mechanisms.

---

93 *Preisangaben- und Preisklauselgesetz.*
94 Schultz in Bub and Treier (1999, p. 593).
95 Federal Appeal Court (BGH), WuM 1874, 42.
96 Federal Appeal Court (BGH), NJW 1979, 1545.
97 In particular mortgage interest rates.

The UK market has the advantage of a strong, historically grown valuation profession that maintains close contact with the needs of real estate investors. As discussed, the German property market does not possess a strong valuation profession. While Chartered Surveyors are thus able to carry out rent reviews in large numbers and to a high degree of professionalism, the transaction costs remain high for small businesses and for market participants that have little access to market information.

The author therefore proposes the introduction of legislation providing a certain set of default rules regarding rent review. Commercially aware parties could still draft their own rent review clauses from scratch, but especially smaller tenants would benefit from a defined set of rules. Uncertainties and costs of drafting would be reduced. That no such proposal has so far been implemented is largely due to resistance from within the property industry, as all attempts to standardise procedures would in the end result in an overall reduction of billable hours of surveyors and solicitors.

The Code of Practice is an attempt to standardise the drafting of these clauses, but compliance with the Code is voluntary. The Code is authored by a joint working group from members of property industry groups and tenants' associations. The fact that such a working group has been set up and such a Code was drafted highlights that the need for reform has been recognised by the property industry. Nevertheless, it should be admitted that the freedom of English lease law has the advantage that well-advised parties have the ability to draft the rules that best match their interests. It is therefore important that any regulation creates default rules that make contracting easier for smaller parties but that at the same time contracting remains possible for landlords and tenants able and willing to devise their own rules.

The German legislation on rent review and rent adjustment on the other hand shows that the state should be careful when limiting contractual freedom of choice as this may inhibit the development of individually negotiated clauses that suit the economic needs and preferences of parties to a transaction.

4.2.5 Indexation

Rents of leases with indexation clauses are adjusted according to changes of a publicly reported index. The index most commonly used is the consumer price index (CPI).

Indexed rents are a widely used mechanism for adjusting rents of commercial leases in Germany.[98] They, are, however, almost never used in England. According to the study of lease patterns by Crosby et al. (2005, p. 98), so-called non standard reviews (graduated rents and indexation) are virtually non-existent on the UK property market. In 2003, the percentage for indexed rents was in the Investment Property Databank virtually zero.

In Germany, on the other hand, indexed rents are seen as a defining feature of lease structures (Klug, 2008, p. 12). Indexed rents are so common for German institutional leases that they are also used by Turner and Thomas (2001b, pp. 301-302) for the modelling of a portfolio-based property index. Indexed rents are prevalent in Continental Europe and clearly in Germany (Turner and Thomas, 2001a, p. 184).

Four of the six German case study-leases thus also use indexation clauses. It should again be pointed out that these are leases for large-scale property transactions and that contracts have been drafted by leading property consultants and law firms. In spite of the small number of leases they therefore represent a market best-practice. From the table comparing the leases it can be seen that several variations of indexation clauses are used: in the simplest form, the rent is adjusted on a yearly basis by the change of the CPI over this period. This method is used for the base rent of the fashion store (no. 3). It should be noted that rents can generally be adjusted upwards or downwards.[99] Alternatively, rents may also be adjusted only by a percentage of the change in the index. Such a clause is used for the lease of a hotel (no. 5) where the rent is adjusted by 65% of the change in the index. Finally, the rent may be adjusted once the change of the index has reached a certain threshold. The lease for the car service station (no. 6) stipulates that the rent is adjusted by the change of the CPI if the CPI has changed by more than 5% since the last rent adjustment.

---

98 Indexation is also used in many other Continental European countries (Edwards and Krendel, 2007, p. 82).

99 A downward adjustment would require deflation for a full year; a phenomenon that cannot, with the exception of Japan, normally be observed. The financial crisis and following recession have, however, caused falling prices in Europe and the United States by the mid of 2009. It is unlikely, however, that deflation for the whole year will be observed but rather that inflation will be close to zero for 2009.

4.2.5.1 Economic effects of index clauses

Indexation clauses have been scrutinised by Eger (1995, pp. 106-110). He observes that most economists and lawyers would in principle view such clauses with scepticism. Such clauses, it is alleged, were a means of exploiting weak parties, close markets for competitors or circumvent public regulation. Eger (1995, p. 107), however, points out that index clauses ought to be viewed as a means of parties to adjust contracts efficiently to changing market environments. He identifies three criteria that determine whether an index is suitable to be used as a pricing mechanism:

- The pricing of the index corresponds with the pricing of the goods or services in the contract;
- The index is easily observable (e.g. publicly reported);
- The parties cannot influence the value of the index.

Where there are no observable spot-market prices for the subject of the contract but a functioning market for a close substitute, the market price of this substitute constitutes an ideal reference for the contractual price (Eger, 1995, pp. 107-108).

Applying this more general framework to rent adjustment of commercial leases means that the following has to be considered: Commercial leases almost exclusively use the Consumer Price Index (CPI) as their reference index. This has practical as well as legal reasons. The index is publicly reported and easily observable. The public nature of the CPI assists in reducing inefficient investment in information and eliminates the potential for moral hazard on either party's side.

It should be noted that German law restricts the use of index clauses (*Wertsicherungsklauseln*) under the Price Declarations and Contract Terms Act[100], thus leaving parties to a lease with little choice as to the index. The crucial question, however, is whether the CPI can satisfactorily reflect price changes in commercial real estate.

The German CPI is composed of the consumer price indices calculated in the 16 *Länder* (federal states). These indices by state are weighed according to the state's share of the country's overall private consumption (Statistisches Bundesamt, 2006, p. 29). The heavyweights in the index are the states of North-Rhine-Westphalia (23.5%), Bavaria (15.4%) and Baden-Württemberg (13.5%), while the less populous and less economically strong states in the North and

100 *Preisangaben- und Preisklauselgesetz (PaPkG).* The rules laid down in this Act are further specified in a statutory instrument, the *Preisklauselverordnung (PrKV)*, BGBl. 1998 I, p. 3043.

East flow into the index with much lower weights (e.g. Bremen with 1% and Saxony-Anhalt with 2.7%).

The states' price indices are calculated on the basis of the consumption of a hypothetical "average" consumer. Prices of around 750 different goods and services flow into the index calculation (Statistisches Bundesamt, 2006, p. 28). The table below shows the categories of goods and services that flow into the index calculation, their weights in the index, and the price increases in the individual categories from 2000 to 2005:

Table 4-5: German CPI: composition and index change 2000-2005

Category	Weight in index	Change 2000-05
Residential rents & utilities	28,5%	+9,8%
Groceries & daily necessities	12,0%	+4,5%
Services	11,8%	+13,0%
Public transport, PGVs & fuels	9,5%	+13,2%
Clothing, shoes, jewellery & watches	5,8%	-1,6%
Hotels & restaurants	4,7%	+8,4%
Furniture	4,2%	+3,9%
Alcoholic drinks & tobacco	3,7%	+29,2%
Healthcare	3,5%	+24,3%
Electronic goods	3,3%	-25,0%
Leisure activities (toys, books etc.)	2,8%	+5,6%
Insurances	2,5%	+9,7%
Telephone charges	2,1%	-5,1%
DIY articles	2,0%	+3,3%
Package holidays	2,0%	+6,4%
Others	1,6%	+8,4%
Overall index (Weighting of base year 2000)	100,0%	+8,3%

The table reveals that price increases in the five-year period from 2000 to 2005 differed significantly between categories. Compared to the modest overall increase of 8.3%, some categories have witnessed significant increases. The costs of healthcare, for example, rose by 24.3%. The prices of electronic goods, on the other hand, fell by 25% in the same period. The crucial question, however, is whether the CPI is sufficiently connected to the development of rents for commercial premises. The author thinks that this is unlikely.

First of all, there is the regional component. It has been explained in the introduction that the German property market is characterised by regional centres and a multi-centric structure. This necessarily means that real estate prices also develop differently in different regions. Munich, for example, has witnessed steady growth in recent years, the Frankfurt office market is characterised by volatility, and the Berlin office market is fairly weak for the capital of a major industrialised nation. Indexation based on the CPI does not consider the differences between regional real estate markets. If, for example, an office rent in Bremen is indexed based on the Federal CPI, then the index is strongly influenced by the prosperous Southern states while the CPI of Bremen only carries a weight of 1% in the overall CPI. Strong growth in prosperous states may thus cause exaggerated rent increases in the economically weak state of Bremen. Incentives for tenants to fulfil their obligations under the lease may thus be distorted.

Secondly, the composition of the CPI represents the consumption of a "typical" consumer. Consumer prices and prices at the business enterprise level, e.g. wholesale prices, may, however, develop differently. The consumption portfolio of the hypothetical consumer furthermore contains various products for which price changes differ. Prices for electronic goods have, for example, dropped by 25.0% in the period from 2000 to 2005. Production costs and wholesale prices for these products, which would include computers, MP3 players and so on, have surely also dropped. Nevertheless, a significant part of these price drops can surely be attributed to competition within the fiercely competitive German retail market. Therefore, while prices for these electronic goods have dropped by 25.0%, thus putting pressure on retail margins, overall business rents with CPI indexation have increased by 8.3% over the same period. Given that for many retail outlets rent is a major cost factor and moving to different premises often not a viable alternative, CPI indexation may have an incentive distorting effect on retail businesses.

Another aspect speaking against CPI indexation is that residential rents and the costs of utilities and (public and private) transport account for around 40% of the index. Price increases in these categories are fuelled by rising energy costs (oil and gas), while price increases of other categories, such as groceries, have been very moderate. Problematically, these price increases for energy are felt by consumers and put pressure on retailers to reduce prices and/or costs as consumers may cut back expenses in these areas. At the same time, rent increases are also influenced by these rising energy costs so that retailers are in the end faced with CPI increases in two ways: by increasing rents on the one hand, and by potentially decreasing sales and compressing margins on the other hand.

Economic phenomena such as "stagflation", i.e. an economic slowdown coupled with strong inflation, also seemed to re-occur in the aftermath of the credit crunch before commodities prices also dropped and eased inflation. Stagflation would have an equally negative effect on incentives for retail tenants as sales would go down and rents go up.

Finally, it has to be noted that changes in the CPI are also influenced by changes in taxes levied at a consumer level and publicly administered prices. Increases in VAT would, for example, impact on the CPI but have no effect at a business level. Prices in the category "alcoholic drinks & tobacco" increased because of increased taxes on these products and healthcare costs have risen because the government has introduced additional fees for prescription drugs (Statistisches Bundesamt, 2006, pp. 45-46). Problematically, these price increases do not correspond with any market trend on the commercial real estate market.

The strongest argument against CPI-indexation, however, is that CPI increases and fluctuations in market rents follow very different patterns. The following chart compares the increase of the CPI from 1992 to 2007 with the market rents for prime office space in Frankfurt and Berlin:

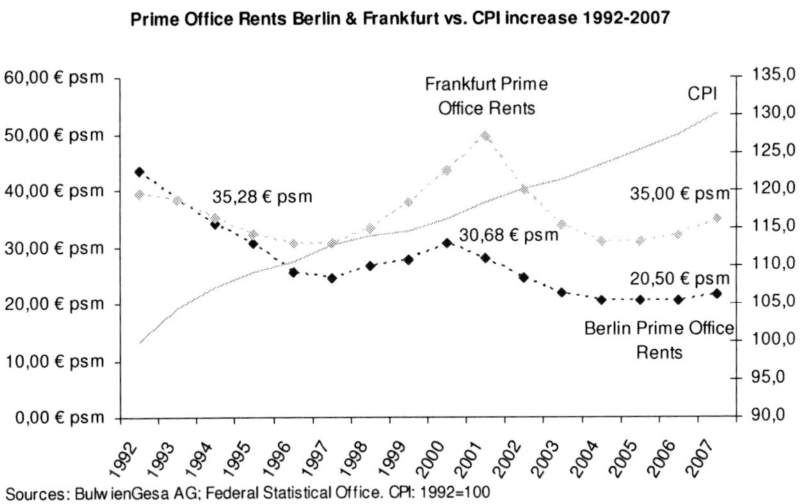

Exhibit 4-12: Prime office rents Berlin and Frankfurt vs. CPI

The inflation index is set to 100 for 1992. The index increased to 130.2 by 2007. Observing the shape of the curve it is evident that inflation has grown steadily but moderately. This is also a result of the policies of the *Bundesbank* and later the European Central Bank whose primary monetary policy objective is to control inflation.

At the same time, however, office rents both in Berlin and Frankfurt have fluctuated significantly (these cities are taken as examples because they are globally known but the figures would look very similar for any other German city). In 1994, for example, the prime office rents in Frankfurt stood at € 35.28

psm. As a result of the dot-com boom, rents peaked in the early 2000s and slumped after the bubble burst. Only recently some recovery can be observed and in 2007 rents stood at € 35.00 psm. If adjusted for inflation, real rents have thus fallen since the early 1990s. What if, however, a tenant had agreed in 1994 on a office lease with a duration of, say, 15 years, with a starting rent of € 35.28 psm and annual rent adjustment according to the CPI? In 2007, his contractual rent would have stood at € 42.82 psm – around € 7.50 psm or around 21% above current market rents. For an office of, say, 2,000 sqm the monthly overpayment compared to market rent would then amount to approximately € 15,000. It seems fair to suggest that the higher transaction costs of rent review would be justified in the light of such discrepancies.

The situation in Frankfurt is also mirrored by other markets: in Berlin, for example, prime rents fell from a peak of € 30.68 psm in the bullish year 2000 to € 20.50 psm in 2007, i.e. rents have dropped by a third. Again, a tenant who would have contracted in 2000 on a lease with CPI-linked indexation would now pay a rent that substantially exceeds current market rents. Depending on the timing, the market can of course also turn against the landlord where markets are higher than rents under a current contract. The insight from the above is that it will in almost any event be merely coincidental that inflation and market rents move in the same direction and at the same pace. Mostly, however, markets rents and inflation follow very different patterns.

These aspects show that the CPI is, in spite of its general availability and publication, not the most suitable index for adjusting the rents of commercial premises.

Somewhat ironically, the unsuitability of the CPI for the indexation of rents seems to have been implicitly recognised for residential properties in Germany. It should be noted that, unlike in Britain, the majority of German households, approximately 65%, rent their flats or houses. Most local council have set up so-called "rent mirrors" (*Mietenspiegel*) that list price ranges for residential property in a particular council.[101] Councils provide these rent mirrors as a guidance for rent increases by residential landlords. While the rent mirror is not, strictly speaking, legally binding it nevertheless has a strong persuasive influence and courts will normally follow the rents set forth in it. The methodology of setting up these rent mirrors, i.e. the use of comparables in a given area with comparable attributes reminds of UK rent reviews.

Local councils seem to have recognised that CPI indexation is not suitable for the determination of residential rents. The author would suggest that the CPI is,

---

101 The *Mietenspiegel* contains several categories of residential accommodation according to their age, size, standard and location.

because of its focus on private consumption, perhaps more suitable to the adjustment of residential rents rather than commercial rents.

Nevertheless, businesses in Germany frequently use CPI indexation and the case study-leases demonstrate how contracts are drafted to cope with the problems of CPI indexation. Reasons are the relative ease of drafting and monitoring the clauses, the frequent use of German property as an inflation hedge and also the fact that the German property market has – unlike other European markets – rarely seen strong cyclicality and the build up and burst of property "bubbles".

A common response for retail leases are turnover components that supplement a moderately high base rent that is subject to indexation. The advantages of turnover rents were discussed above. The leases for a supermarket (no. 1) and the lease for a fashion retailer (no. 3) use such turnover clauses. A turnover lease provides a close approximation between the development of the tenant's business and changes in his rent. A problem with turnover leases, however, is that such clauses can only be operated for retail premises where turnover and location of the business are clearly related to each other.

Another response by businesses is that rents are not increased by the full CPI increase. For the hotel lease (no. 5), rents increase or decrease only by 65% of the CPI increase or decrease. This solution represents a sensible compromise as price changes in the hotel sector do not necessarily correspond with overall price increases. As inflation is to a large extent fuelled by energy prices, a reduction in travelling may be the consequence. A hotel business would thus be hit by rent increases as well as sluggish occupancy. It is surprising that no turnover rent has been negotiated for the hotel, but according to an insider, the large scale of the project gave the hotel-tenant a high leverage in negotiations. The fact that indexation was used is probably because of the tenant's speculation on rather moderate inflation in Germany.

Occasionally, landlords may prefer indexed rents over turnover rents where the success of the tenant's business is uncertain or subject to strong fluctuations. This seems to be the case for lease no. 6, the car service station. The German car repair market has undergone a period of intense competition and pressure on margins. In recent months, there have been rumours in the business press that the tenant of the premises, which is owned by a US private equity group, may have to face severe changes to its business model or, in the worst case, insolvency because of declining sales.

4.2.5.2 Incentive effects

Indexation can only maintain landlords' and tenants' incentives to perform their obligations under a lease where price changes of the index and the valuation of the premises are closely connected. Where a landlord lets premises to a business with strongly growing sales and revenues, such as the emerging coffee chains in recent years, but the CPI does not reflect these changes, the landlord would prefer "eager" new tenants willing to pay a higher rent for the premises and the current lease becomes unattractive. Likewise, a tenant with declining sales in an economic environment with high general inflation would find his contract increasingly unattractive.[102] Indexation can therefore lead to inefficiencies.

The incentive problems associated with indexation are to some extent mitigated because lease terms in Germany are much shorter than in the UK. While institutional leases in the UK can have terms of up to 25 years (see for example Edwards and Krendel, 2007, p. 9), the typical German lease with institutional tenants has a term of 10 years (Thomas, 1995, p. 83). This gives the landlord the opportunity to renegotiate the lease to a market level when the lease has expired.

4.2.5.3 Transaction costs

The low transaction costs are an indisputable advantage of indexation: drafting assistance is widely available as model clauses are easily obtainable (see e.g. Neuhaus, 2005, pp. 196-199). As the use of index clauses is common practice in Germany, the courts, real estate consultants and market participants are routinely involved in this practice.

A further advantage of indexation clauses is the relatively simple modelling of cash flows from such a lease. In the section on rent review it was discussed that the modelling of periodic rent review poses a significant challenge to consultants concerned with the sale and acquisition of property portfolios. Indexation, on the other hand, is fairly simple to model because it can be uniformly applied to all properties in the portfolio and as the CPI is publicly available, historic data can be used for forecasting future inflation rates. In fact it is known to the author that major investment banks and real estate asset managers use indexation according to the CPI as a shorthand where data on actual rent adjustment mechanisms is unavailable. It would seem that in case of modelling a diversified, nationwide portfolio, CPI indexation is not as problematic as at the level of individual properties. For a large portfolio,

102 Provided that the lease constitutes a major part of his business expenditure.

distortions may be averaged out but at the level of individual properties CPI indexation may be highly flawed.

4.2.5.4 German legislation on indexation

The ability of parties to use an index that suitably mirrors changes in rents is curtailed by German law which effectively limits the choice of available indices to the CPI. According to the Price Declarations and Contract Terms Order, parties wishing to use indexation have to apply for permission to the *Bundesamt für Wirtschaft* (Federal Department for Commerce) in order to obtain an authorisation for the use of the clause[103].

An exception from this rule exists pursuant to s. 4 of the Price Declarations and Contract Terms Regulation (*Preisklauselverordnung*). According to s. 4 of the order, certain clauses are deemed acceptable, including indexations pursuant to an index of the general costs of living published by an acceptable institution (European, Federal or *Länder* statistical office). It is furthermore necessary that the lease is for at least ten years or that the tenant has the right, by using an option, to renew the lease to at least ten years.[104]

Generally non-permissible are clauses that stipulate an over-proportional rent increase following a change of the index, e.g. an increase of rent by 10% when the index increases by 10 points, as 10 points do not equal 10 percent (Neuhaus, 2005, p. 185).[105]

The legal consequences of using non-permissible clauses are not clear cut. In general, the court would seek to interpret the non-permissible clause in a way that approximates the parties' original intentions. Where such an interpretation is not possible, the contract may be void following s. 139 BGB (Neuhaus, 2005, p. 187).

The German legislation on the use of indexation in leases thus in practice makes the use of indices other than the CPI infeasible. While an application to the Federal Department of Commerce to use an alternative index is possible in theory, such application will rarely be made in practice because of uncertainties as to the Department's decision.

It is highly questionable if such regulation of index clauses is desirable. The apparent function of the Act is to protect tenants from agreeing on unfair clauses referring to ill-defined or not sufficiently publicised indices. Assuming that business tenants are sufficiently aware of the consequences of indexation and

---

103 s. 7 of the *Preisklauselverordnung*.

104 s. 4 (1) 2 of the *Preisklauselverordnung*.

105 see also s. 2 (2) No. 2 *Preisklauselverordnung*.

given that access to legal advice and information is today much more widely available than, say, 30 years ago, it should be possible for parties to a lease to agree on another index that more appropriately reflects price changes of real estate. Such indices could in particular be the sub-indices that are provided by the statistical offices reflecting price changes of certain categories only. Furthermore, indices of wholesale prices may be more appropriate for certain businesses than indices at the retail price level. This would especially apply to firms operating in a business-to-business environment.

Nevertheless, the law should, as a default rule, provide that only such indices may be used that are published by suitable authorities such as statistical offices. An approach often used to protect the potentially weaker party in English law is that the party that is deemed to have superior information has to serve a notice on the weaker party informing about the (potential) consequences of contracting out of a statutory provision.[106] The law could for example provide that where parties wish to use an index other than the CPI, the parties have to include an annex to the lease informing that both parties are aware that the selected index may develop differently than the CPI.

4.2.5.5 Why are indexed rents not used in the UK?

An indexation of rents is extremely rare in the UK. IPD data from 1997 to 2003 records the incidence of RPI (retail price index; the UK CPI) indexation at 0.0%. The number of leases with indexation is therefore close to zero (Crosby et al., 2005, p. 98).

It would seem that there are two reasons why indexation is so rarely used in the UK.

First of all, Britain has – compared to Germany – experienced a much different inflationary environment in the post-war years. The diagram below compares the inflations rates in Britain and Germany from 1950 to 1998.

106 Such an approach is for example used where parties to a lease wish to contract out from lease renewal rights under the Landlord and Tenant Act 1954, Part 2 (ODPM, 2004, p. 7).

Inflation rates UK and Germany 1950 - 1998

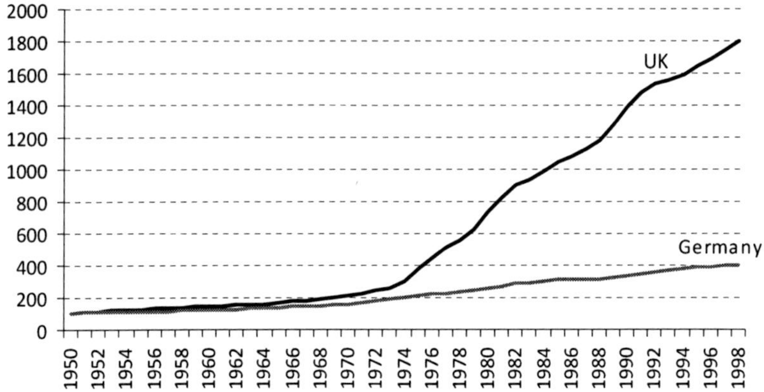

Sources: Statistisches Bundesamt, House of Commons Library (1999)

Index: 1950 = 100

Exhibit 4-13: Comparison of German and UK inflation rates

The diagram clearly shows that UK inflation has significantly outpaced German inflation since the early 1970s. Especially in the mid-1970s inflation in Britain reached record levels while inflation in Germany remained at a fairly stable level. The high UK inflation was not only because of the oil price shock that affected all industrialised nations: Britain also faced severe problems because of its mainly nationalised heavy industries, the demise of trade with former colonies and aggressive wage policies of the highly fragmented trade unions. Failed monetary policies unable to control inflation exacerbated these problems (Smales, 1981, p. 224). It is surely no coincidence that the "institutional lease" with periodic upwards-only rent review emerged in this economic climate. Because inflation, and indeed stagflation, was so high and unpredictable, neither landlords nor tenants would have found that indexation was an acceptable means of adjusting rents. In this uncertain environment, real property was seen as a safe haven and value appreciation of property outpaced inflation. Associated with this, the UK property market has also proved to be more cyclical, so that there is even less correlation between inflation and property prices.[107]

107 For example, Britain has been in an economic malaise – resulting in weak commercial property markets – for most of the 1970s while at the same time suffering from high inflation.

Secondly, the UK property market provides institutions that render indexed rents unnecessary. It was described above that indexation is to be seen as an alternative when market prices are not observable (or only observable at prohibitively high transaction costs). In Germany, indexation should be seen as a response to a highly fragmented market that was, until recently, dominated by local real estate owners using "rules of thumb" and "gut feeling" for valuation. It is described in the introduction that German "sworn valuers" are few by number and that the focus of their work is on technical issues according to a legally prescribed valuation manual rather than commercial valuation of properties. In contrast, British surveyors focus on valuation from a commercial/financial perspective and the main body, RICS, has around 140,000 members worldwide (Gondring, 2009, p. 879). The presence of a strong valuation profession with a clear focus on financial issues allows UK landlords to rely on open market valuation rather than second-best solutions such as indexation. The dominance of indexation on the German market is thus to be seen as a sign of the German property market's institutional weakness.

4.2.5.6 The German property industry's position on indexation

The analysis has thus far revealed that indexation is not free from problems. That it is nevertheless so widely used may not only be due to a lack of alternatives but may also mean that market participants see a number of advantages compared to other methods. Walter Klug, Head of Morgan Stanley Real Estate Investment Germany, underlines that the advantage of German commercial real estate is in fact indexation that provides a hedge against inflation.[108] Also from a lender's and investor's perspective indexation can be attractive because the volatility of inflation is lower than the volatility of property markets. German monetary policy has always aimed to curb inflation and has been much more successful in this than the Bank of England.

From an investor's point of view, German real estate with strong-covenant tenants may thus combine bond-like features, i.e. fairly predictable returns that are uncoupled from market volatilities, with the chance of value appreciation of the property.

The analysis of index clauses demonstrates that in spite of the ease of drafting and the publicly available CPI, these clauses can cause incentive problems as price changes of real estate and CPI changes are at best closely related at a longer-term, macro-level. For the individual business property, however, CPI indexation may lead to problematic distortions between rents paid by sitting tenants and rent levels on the open market paid by incoming tenants. The

---

108 Article in *Euro am Sonntag*, 17 August 2008.

advantages that indexation gives to a certain group of investors combined with certain institutional weaknesses of the German property market will nevertheless ensure that indexation remains the popular adjustment mechanism among German landlords.

4.2.6 Percentage rents

A percentage rent, in UK terminology more often referred to as turnover rent, is a rent that is (partially) dependant upon the success of the tenant's business. A certain percentage of the tenant's turnover is paid as rent to the landlord. Most turnover leases contain a base rent that is fixed in addition to the turnover-dependant component (Geltner and Miller, 2001, p. 807). Such turnover leases are very common for retail premises in the US and in Germany. Both retail leases in the sample of German business leases used as examples here use turnover rents. In the UK, on the other hand, turnover rents are a quite rare exception: while Eppli et al. (2000, cited in Hendershott, 2002, p. 513) found that 93% of a sample of 5,000 surveyed US retail leases contained turnover clauses, only 4% of 1998 UK retail leases in shopping centres reported in the IPD database use this form of rent adjustment. Turnover rents were never used for high street shops and could only be found in larger shopping centres (Hendershott, 2002, p. 513).

This section therefore explores the economic effects of turnover rents, their perceived advantages from a managerial perspective and why they are so rarely found on the UK property market. Furthermore, the clauses used in the two German retail leases are discussed.

4.2.6.1 Economic effects of turnover rents

A stream of literature discussed the use of so-called "share cropping" arrangements[109]. Share cropping takes places between landowners and farmers where the landowner takes a share of the harvested crops instead of a fixed payment for the use of the land. Share cropping agreements thus exhibit a machinery very much akin to percentage rents. The insights of the economic analysis of share cropping can thus be applied to this type of rent adjustment.

Eger (1995, p. 120) summarises three issues that may warrant the use of share cropping agreements: 1) risk allocation between parties; 2) reduction of efficiency losses because of moral hazard; 3) reduction of inefficient investments in information.

---

109 See summary in Eger (1995, pp. 119-128).

It should be noted that, traditionally, economists have doubted the efficiency of such arrangements, believing that the farmer's reduction in his marginal returns induces him to reduce his input of other production factors below efficient levels (Eger, 1995, p. 120; citing Marshall, 1920, "Principles of economics"). Given that variations of share cropping are widely observable in practice, it seems that this perceived inefficiency may be outweighed by other factors which are now discussed.

4.2.6.1.1 Risk aversion and percentage rents

First attempts to explain the phenomenon of such agreements have been made by Cheung (1969a, 1969b; cited in Eger, 1995, pp. 121-122). Cheung discovered that share cropping arrangements typically contain a number of covenants regulating the input of other factors so that the above mentioned inefficiencies could be compensated. The author also claimed that the sharing of risks relating to the success of the crop harvest was a major motivation for these agreements. For crops with a high variance in harvests, the risk-sharing element between landowner and farmer justifies the high transaction costs stemming from negotiating and enforcing such agreements. Cheung bases his claims on empirical observations in Taiwan. However, Reid (1977, p. 406) criticises that risk-sharing could also be achieved by other means and Rao (1971) and Allen and Lueck (1992; both cited in Eger, 1995, pp. 122-125) find other empirical results that contradict Cheung's hypotheses. Therefore, risk sharing is today largely not seen as a major motivation for share cropping.

Nevertheless, some of Cheung's observations show significant parallels to the negotiations of percentage rents.

First of all, retail leases contain a variety of covenants that specify other obligations of the tenant. These covenants seek to avoid that the tenant reduces his input of other factors. The lease for a large fashion store (no. 3 on the list) contains a variety of clauses ensuring that the tenant has to comply with a certain number of such safeguards. The lease stipulates that, among other things, the tenant is obliged:

1. To use the premises throughout the term of the lease for the purpose for which they were let [fashion store];
2. To keep the shopping premises open for the hours specified by the landlord;
3. To permanently have on offer the full range of products typically available in retail premises of this segment [in terms of prices, brands, etc.];
4. To organise end of season sales and other such events only with prior written consent of the landlord;

5. To keep shop-front windows permanently decorated in a manner attractive to prospective customers;
6. To pay a monthly fee for the advertising and marketing organised by the landlord's shopping centre management.

The lease contains a number of further clauses to the same effect and also the other retail lease for a supermarket (no. 1) contains such clauses regulating opening hours, range of products, and so on.

Secondly, the risk sharing argument in case of retail premises could be supported because of the high degree of location-dependant goodwill typical of retail premises (see above). For retail premises, the location has a decisive impact on the ability of the business to generate revenues. A good location will often be the deciding factor for success or failure of a retail business. In that sense, it is justified that landlord and tenant share a part of this risk. The landlord, by providing the premises at a certain location, already influenced the future of the retail-tenant to a large extent. This is a distinctly different feature of the retail sector that sets it apart from other types of commercial property. An office landlord has, for example, little influence on the success of the accountancy and law firms to which his premises are let.

Retail sales are also very much affected by economic cycles and shifts in consumer sentiment. It is thus more likely that retail tenants exhibit a larger degree of risk-aversion. This is particularly relevant in the groceries and white and brown goods sectors where margins are low and rents account for a significant share of business expenses.

4.2.6.1.2 Reduction of moral hazard

Share cropping can also be an attractive choice for risk-neutral parties where it can assist in reducing efficiency losses because of bilateral moral hazard (Eger, 1995, pp. 122-123). First of all, percentage rents thus provide an incentive to the tenant to fulfil repair, upkeep and other obligations under the lease.

It is no coincidence that percentage rents are most common for retail leases in shopping centres and malls that provide not only the premises as such but also a marketing concept and a certain product mix and thus create a brand of their own.[110] The landlord is thus not a mere provider of physical space but provides a whole marketing concept comparable to a franchise business where the licensor

110 A good example is the *Europa Passage* in Hamburg developed by Allianz Immobilien GmbH: the management of this shopping mall provides marketing campaigns revolving around the "Europe-theme" (tourist information, regional food events) and thus creates a brand with an international, up-market image.

provides these services. While the landlord of an office building cannot influence the success of his tenant's business, there is a clear link between business success and occupied premises in the retail sector. Retail customers often "go shopping" to certain locations rather than specific shops, especially in the upper market sector (e.g. retail customers would say they go to Oxford Street or *Kurfürstendamm*).

Eger (1995, pp. 125-126) reviewed franchise contracts and describes that they not only meticulously detail the licensee's obligations but also stipulate revenue sharing between licensor and licensee. Both parties are thought to prefer this revenue sharing to a licence granted at a fixed price because the revenue sharing helps to maintain incentives throughout the relationship between licensee and licensor: The licensor (landlord) will assure that the image of the brand is preserved because his income is dependant on the success of the licensees (tenants). The licensees (tenants) will on the other hand comply with their obligations under the agreement as their revenue will also be dependant on the success of these branding and marketing activities.[111]

4.2.6.1.3 Transaction costs of percentage rents

It appears that percentage rents, because of their incentive-aligning effects, bear a number of desirable properties. Nevertheless, they are only used for retail leases. Would it not be desirable to extend the use of percentage rents to all types of commercial properties? After all, it should theoretically be possible for all commercial properties to identify their contribution in terms of revenue or value-added to the business of the tenant. The high transaction costs of drafting and, primarily, monitoring such an agreement would, however, clearly stand against such a proposal. Retail is the only segment where the link between location and turnover can be clearly established. For other segments, rather complicated mechanisms would have to be devised to allocate a certain share of revenues to particular premises.[112] Neither landlords nor tenants would be likely to accept a turnover rent for properties other than retail premises. Another issue

---

111 The proximity of a franchise agreement and a retail lease in a shopping centre is also shown in the retail lease for the fashion store (no. 3): one clause stipulates that the tenant has to include the brand logo and name of the shopping centre on all his circulars and other advertising campaigns. The retail lease (no.1) guarantees a certain freedom from competition in that the landlord covenants not to lease other units in the centre to bakery stores, butchers or vegetable stores.

112 E.g. for a back-office there would need to be some mechanisms according to which this office's contribution to the firm's revenue is defined. Such a mechanism would, by nature, be complicated and have to use a number of assumptions. Complexity and lack of transparency would then render such a percentage rent unattractive to market participants.

would be that sensitive internal data (turnovers, revenues and so on) would have to be made available to external parties.

Even for a retail lease, the reporting of turnovers to the landlord is transaction cost intensive. The lease for the fashion store provides for a threefold reporting: the tenant has to report his turnovers in writing on a monthly basis; the tenant also has to provide the landlord with a more detailed overview of turnovers on a quarterly basis. On a yearly basis, the tenant's tax adviser or auditor has to prepare a statement summarising monthly turnovers for the past year. Furthermore, the landlord has the right to access the tenant's bookkeeping records if there are justified doubts as to the correctness of the tenant's reported figures. A further clause details which transactions are to be regarded as "turnover", a question not as obvious as it would seem at first sight. The landlord covenants to keep all such information confidential, but it is obvious that many tenants would feel uneasy if they have to provide key financial data on their business activities to a third party. These practical issues are thus also preventing the more widespread use of percentage rents.

4.2.6.1.4 Managerial considerations and effects on investment

Percentage rents also offer a number of advantages from a managerial and investment perspective.

In the previous section it was pointed out that the heterogeneity and unpredictability of rent review clauses may affect due diligences for the acquisition of property portfolios. Trends in retail sales are easier to model than changes in local property valuations. There is a significant amount of market research into consumer sentiment. Trends in retail sales would also seem to be more homogeneous on a national level than property valuations in fragmented sub-markets.

Another aspect allowing better modelling is that in the years preceding the transaction tenants would have supplied the landlord with comprehensive information on their turnovers (compare Hendershott, 2002, p. 521). These turnover figures allow for an extrapolation of trends and can provide valuable insights into the performance of retail locations, tenants' insolvency risks, and so on. In contrast, a rent review provides no information on tenants but only a market valuation subject to the various hypothetical assumptions discussed above.

A DCF-model for a nationally diversified retail property portfolio is thus able to calculate property values with more precision where percentage rents are used.

Higher transparency is, however, not always in the interest of all market participants. Several types of investors, e.g. real estate hedge funds and private equity funds, speculate on inefficiencies in the property market and search for portfolios with "upside potential". From an efficiency perspective, however, this form of investment merely represents an inefficient investment in information, leading to distributional effects only.

Hendershott (2002, p. 521) stresses that percentage rents induce co-operation between landlord and tenant. Addae-Dapaah and Yeo (1999, p. 26) describe percentage rents as a "mutually beneficial rental system", as it aligns the incentives of both parties. Shopping centre management and tenants both desire that the commercial centre succeed. This highlights once again the economic proximity of shopping centre leases and franchising.

A positive effect of turnover rents on the management, quality and upkeep of premises is indicated by Pashigian and Gould (1998, pp. 28-34): The landlord has an incentive to provide high-quality premises as his rental income depends on the tenant's commercial success.

4.2.6.2 Forms of percentage rents and their application in the UK and Germany

A reason for the limited use of percentage rents in the UK, aside from the ones indicated above, is in the author's opinion also the form in which UK clauses are drafted.

In principle, percentage rents can take three forms (McAllister, 1996, pp. 15-17):

Pure percentage rents: under this "pure" arrangement, the tenant is obliged to pay a certain percentage of his turnover as rent (from the first Euro earned). This "pure" form of percentage rent is very rare. If at all, it is only use for food courts[113] in shopping centres and specialised retail outlets (McAllister, 1996, p. 10). The rare occurrence of the pure form is not surprising: landlords agreeing on such an arrangement would need to be very well informed about the tenant's business. Otherwise, such an agreement would invite moral hazard on the part of the tenant who would be inclined not to use the premises in the most efficient way. In most cases, prohibitive transaction costs would not warrant the necessary investment in information. For a landlord showing some degree of risk aversion it is moreover preferable to have a fixed, guaranteed rental income.

113 "Food courts" are the restaurant areas in shopping centres; the tenants are mostly large fast-food chains such as McDonald's, Pizza Hut, and so on.

The limited use of "pure form" percentage rents for food courts and specialised retailers is therefore a result of reduced information asymmetries: For food courts there is a very clear link between location and business success. Above, the hospitality sector has been identified to have the highest degree of location-dependant goodwill. The landlord is therefore relatively well informed about the prospects of a business. He has detailed forecasts of customer-flows in his centre and the tenants are mostly well-known chains whose business models have been successful on the market for years. Similarly, a landlord who lets premises to specialist retailers is normally an expert in the tenant's business. In both cases, the landlord is to be seen as a business partner.

Base rent plus turnover related income: this type of rent review is prevalent on the German market. The tenant has to pay a fixed rent and an additional percentage rent. For the fashion store (lease no. 3) a fixed amount of around € 70,000 per month and a turnover rent of 7% has been negotiated. This combination of fixed and turnover-based elements seeks to avoid moral hazard issues on the side of the tenant. At the same time, the incentives of the landlord to inefficiently invest in information are reduced as a certain fixed amount is always guaranteed. However, the determination of the turnover-threshold above which a turnover rent is to be paid and the determination of the fixed component require certain insights into the market.

Another issue is the adjustment of the fixed component. For German leases, adjustment of the fixed component is mostly done by indexation or there are graduated increases. In the UK, however, the fixed component is normally subject to rent review, which gives rise to a number of valuation problems discussed below.

McAllister (1996, p. 10) observes that in the UK the turnover component for these leases only takes effect when the turnover exceeds a certain threshold, e.g. turnover rent is only payable where turnovers exceed € 500,000 p.a. There are some doubts whether this variation to the arrangement provides the appropriate incentives: it could theoretically be argued that the tenant would reduce his input once the threshold has been reached, but it seems to the author that in business practice this would have little effect.

Base rent or turnover related component: this third method is most commonly used in the UK (McAllister, 1996, p. 10). The percentage rent does, as for the second type, depend on a certain turnover threshold. The difference, however, is that the fixed base rent, and only the base rent, is payable when turnovers are below the threshold. Where the turnover threshold is exceeded, turnover rent is payable on the whole turnover, but no base rent is payable.[114] The percentage of turnover that has to be paid will depend on the type of retail business, in particular the profit margins in the retail sector (e.g. high margins in fashion retailing, low margins in groceries. Of the lease case studies, the fashion store is required to pay 7% while the supermarket pays just 3.9%).

In the author's opinion, one reason for the low acceptance of turnover rents in the UK lies in the structuring of such agreements. The German leases provide a guaranteed base rent and a percentage rent from the first Euro earned, a threshold is not generally included in the turnover clauses. The advantage of abstaining from a turnover threshold is threefold: first of all, landlord's and tenant's incentives are aligned from the very beginning. With a threshold, on the other hand, these incentive effects may be distorted as the landlord acts as a "normal" landlord for low turnovers when only the base rent is payable, and as a "partner" only once the threshold is attained. Providing incentives to the landlord would seem to be more crucial, however, where turnovers are low. The landlord's impact would seem to have more effect where the tenant is starting his business or is experiencing difficulties.

Secondly, the determination of the threshold may lead to various forms of strategic behaviour and thus cause inefficient investments in information. A tenant who is confident that he will achieve a certain turnover would probably try to negotiate a rather high threshold while a tenant insecure as to his business prospects may rather seek to negotiate a low base rent. The tenant's willingness to accept a high base rent could in the end be seen as a signal as to his confidence in his business model so that the turnover component may become less significant compared to the base rent.

Thirdly, with the turnover component decreasing in significance and risk to become an "add-on" to a base rent, the question as to how the base rent should be adjusted emerges. Under UK practice, the base rent would normally be subject to rent review (McAllister, 1996, pp. 10-11). This would then effectively combine the costs and problems associated with rent review with the additional costs and administrative effort of turnover rents so that in the end transaction costs and unpredictability of rents render this mechanism unattractive in many cases.

---

114 E.g.: a base rent of € 50,000 applies if turnover is below € 1m, otherwise 10% turnover rent. If turnover is € 800,000 the rent payable is € 50,000. If turnover is € 1,500,000 the rent is € 150,000.

4.2.6.3 Valuation of percentage leases

The literature explains the very limited presence of turnover rents on the UK market mainly with valuation difficulties (McAllister, 1996, p. 7). Several authors observe that premises let on a turnover-related basis are often valued at a discount by Surveyors (see Hawkings, 1990; Lewis, 1989; Walsh, 1988). This is attributed to a perceived higher risk of turnover rents compared to standard rent reviews. McAllister (1996) examined whether the reason for this view is purely conservatism and lack of knowledge among valuers or if turnover leases indeed exhibit a higher level of risk. McAllister (1996, pp. 22-23) concludes that while leases with turnover-related rents produce complex income streams the approach to valuation of such leases in the UK may not produce justified or logical results. The valuation practice in the UK is found to be not adequately prepared to price such premises. Valuation methods in the US based on DCF-analysis reflect these property values more accurately.[115] It would thus seem that the dominant role of Surveyors on the UK market is a major barrier to the more widespread use of turnover leases.[116]

The fact that base rents in the UK are expressed as a percentage of the premises' full rental values (usually 80% of the FRV) ensures that Surveyors continue to play an important role in the valuation of such leases. In the US and Germany, base rents are linked to the CPI or fixed so that there is no need for external valuation. A fixed base rent also has the advantage that because of inflation the turnover component will increase over time and thus turn the lease into a "purer" form of turnover lease.

The typically quite long leases are seen as another barrier to turnover rents in the UK. A poorly performing tenant could thus occupy the premises for 20-25 years (McAllister, 1996, p. 9).[117]

---

115 DCF analysis is also the valuation tool used by more sophisticated property investors in Germany. It is also used in the UK but RICS does not accept it as a valuation method but rather as a complementary, analytical tool.

116 The typical UK practice is to value a lease by reference to other leases, so-called "comparables". As there are very few comparable leases there is the risk that "circle references" are created and that the comparables selected do not provide reliable evidence of market values.

117 This argument is perhaps slightly weak as a tenant performing poorly over several years will probably go out of business. The argument would hold, however, where the tenant negotiated a high turnover threshold.

4.2.6.4 Percentage rents: the more efficient upwards-only rent review?

It was already established above that turnover rent can, for practical reasons, only be employed in a retail context. Also in this context, the UK valuation profession views turnover rents with scepticism. Retail turnovers are, it is claimed, unpredictable, subject to fluctuation, and there is the risk of fraud on behalf of the tenant and the inability to discontinue the lease with a poorly performing tenant (McAllister, 1996, p. 7). There are, nevertheless, several arguments that support the view that an intelligently drafted turnover lease can share many of the, from an investor's perspective, desirable properties of a lease with upward-only rent review, but provide these advantages at lower transaction costs.

Hendershott (2002, p. 515) points out that "traditional" rent review costs around 6% of the tenant's annual rent. If landlord and tenant fail to agree on a rent and the new rent has to be determined by arbitration, the costs of review rise to nearly 10% of the annual rent.[118] There should thus be ample incentives for both parties to reduce transaction costs. In addition to the already above mentioned advantages relating to portfolio valuation, the following aspects make turnover rents attractive:

Timing: as turnover rents are paid on a monthly or, rarely, yearly basis, rent adjustment takes place immediately. In contrast, rent review in the usual five-year intervals means that the landlord benefits much later from improving markets. Where retail sales, and thus retail rents for new leases, rise sharply, the landlord will benefit from such developments much earlier where percentage rents are used.

Market trends: opponents of turnover rents claim that they lead to unpredictable income flows as retail sales were subject to strong fluctuation. Hendershott (2002, p. 521), however, argues that in general rents and retail sales should move in the same direction. He quite convincingly argues that it is impossible for rents to go up at rent review where the retail sector is in recession. There is a clear link between the values of retail properties and consumer demand. If a rent review comes to the result that rent should go up while retail sales go down this may in fact have an adverse effect on the tenant's incentives to fulfil his obligations under the lease.

Independence from Surveyors: the fees of Surveyors are the major cost driver of rent review and the need to obtain appraisals with the potential risk of arbitration or the need to appoint an independent expert can result in delays and

118 These would mostly be the costs of valuations from external Surveyors.

spiralling costs. A percentage rent with a fixed or graduated base rent would have the advantage that it could be operated without resort to external Surveyors. As described in the introduction, in Germany there is no valuation profession comparable to Chartered Surveyors. It is thus not surprising that parties chose rent review mechanisms that can be operated without resort to external parties. One could suspect that perceived "difficulties" with valuing percentage leases in the UK are the Surveying profession's way of fending off threats to their income.

Both turnover leases and upward-only rent review clauses bear option-like properties in the sense that they contain the option to earn higher rents than what is reserved in the lease as the initial or base rent. Given that turnover rents can capture this advantage on a much less controversial but rather consensual basis, landlords should, in their own interest, promote the use of this adjustment mechanism whenever possible.

5 Tenant default

5.1 Economic analysis of tenant default

The final chapter will now turn to the regulation of tenant default. The regulation of tenant default differs in two ways from rent adjustment. Tenant default is necessarily non-consensual and parties, while attaching a certain probability to the eventuality of default, will rarely create their own detailed *ex ante* rules as to how to proceed in case of default. Secondly, lawmakers have intervened in the regulation of tenant default to a much greater extent compared to rent adjustments. While rent adjustment is predominantly left to the negotiation of the contracting parties, the landlord almost necessarily has to resort to the courts in case of default.

The analysis is again taking place from the perspective of a landlord or property investor interested in securing his rental income. Because of this investment perspective, insolvency of the landlord himself is not discussed here.

The term "tenant default" is widely defined here to include all actions or inactions by the tenant that are contrary to the covenants in the lease and that would induce the landlord to resort to remedies to either coerce compliance with the lease covenants or bring the tenancy to an end.

Thus, of the issues discussed here, tenant default best highlights the nature of a lease as a legally enforceable agreement. As Masten (2000, p. 25) puts it:

> Ultimately, what distinguishes a contract from a mere transaction is the opportunity contracts afford transactors to invoke the formal dispute resolution machinery and coercive power of the state to enforce promises.

Tenant default can take a number of forms but is always triggered by breach of an express or implied lease covenant. The most important breach of covenant will be non-payment of rent but it should be noted that there are also other breaches of covenants, such as failure to comply with repair obligations that can lead to default (Gray and Gray, 2006, pp. 522-523).

Both the English and the German legal system recognise three principle remedies that are available to the defaulting tenant's landlord: The most severe remedy is forfeiture, the non-consensual termination of the lease by way of a court order; alternatively, the landlord may sue for debt and/or for damages but the lease would continue; thirdly, in case of non-compliance with repair obligations or covenants of a similar nature, a court may also order specific performance. The actual regulation of these remedies and the courts' attitudes towards them do, however, differ significantly between the two jurisdictions. The details will be analysed below.

Before turning to this, however, it is necessary to establish an analytical framework against which the English and German rules on tenant default can be assessed.

5.1.1 A framework to analyse the regulation of tenant default

The issues facing landlords and tenants in case of default are in many ways comparable to the situation of an insolvent company and its creditors: in both cases the legal system intervenes because a party no longer fulfils its obligations. Furthermore, tenant default and insolvency will often coincide.

An economic analysis of tenant default should thus start by reviewing the literature analysing bankruptcy regulation and insolvency law.

The main similarity between bankruptcy law and the law governing tenant default lies in the similar normative objectives of both branches of law. While, however, bankruptcy law has been the subject of wide-ranging economic analysis, the law governing tenant default has so far only attracted analyses with a focus on procedural rules addressed to business professionals (see, among others, Abitz, 2004; Parsons, 2006; Bub and Treier, 1999).

The main purpose of insolvency law is to prevent a disorderly "run for assets" by individual creditors. Goode (2005, p. 5) describes this as follows:

> The primary purpose of insolvency law is to replace the free-for-all attendant upon the pursuit of individual claims by different creditors with a statutory regime in which creditors' rights and remedies are suspended, wholly or in part, and a mechanism is provided for the orderly collection and realisation of assets and the distribution of the net realisations of the assets among creditors in accordance with the statutory scheme of distribution.

Insolvency law thus sets the rules pursuant to which the claims of the creditors are satisfied. Insolvency law ought to avoid unproductive struggles between the creditors for a distribution of assets; *ex ante* insolvency law hence also reduces transaction costs if it can avoid a costly and complex contracting to protect assets in case of insolvency. Similarly, the law on tenant default should provide a means to avoid struggles over the tenant's assets between landlord and defaulting tenant. It was discussed above that the reason for tenants to enter into a long-term contract is mainly to protect specific investments and that in many instances a tenant builds up location-dependant goodwill at his premises. The rules governing tenant default have to strive for a balance between securing the tenant's specific investments and built-up goodwill and protecting the landlord's legitimate interests in his property. Furthermore, it would be unproductive if parties to a lease have to draft individual arrangements regarding the treatment of defaults.

The structure of insolvency law also creates incentive effects. It is first of all important to note that bankruptcy law creates *ex ante* and *ex post* incentives. *Ex post*, that is after the insolvency has occurred, the goal of insolvency law is to avoid a shift of risks by managers and shareholders to the creditors. *Ex ante*, insolvency law should deter managers and shareholders from the externalisation of risks on the creditors (summarising the analysis by Eger, 2001).

Eger (2001, p. 30) thus notes that:

> From an economic point of view it is of interest that the procedural and distributional rules of insolvency law create incentives which refer both to the acts before the occurrence of the insolvency (*ex ante*) as well as to acts after its occurrence (*ex post*).

Eger (2001, p. 30) points out that the rules of insolvency law determine *ex ante* how many contracts are entered upon, with whom, and which covenants are agreed upon. Insolvency law is also held to impact upon the search costs that creditors incur before entering into an agreement; monitoring costs during the term of the contract are also influenced by the workings of insolvency law. It is furthermore noted that insolvency law will influence the choice of "utilization alternatives" (Eger, 2001, p. 30) that are elected upon insolvency: is the firm liquidated, are assets transferred into a new organisation or will the existing owners be allowed to continue their operations. The private bargaining that will precede formal bankruptcy proceedings will be influenced by the financial consequences of formal proceedings.

Eger (2001, pp. 30-31) concludes that the economic objectives of insolvency law are: (1) to contribute to an efficient credit allocation by pricing credits according to their risks; (2) that credit should be used to maximise the expectation value of the enterprise and (3) that upon insolvency the use of the assets with the highest expectation value should be chosen.

In the next section the argument will be developed that a lease contract is in many ways comparable to a credit and that therefore the insights from the analysis of credits and insolvency law also apply to the relationship of landlords and tenants.

5.1.2 The lease as a credit contract

The similarities between insolvency law and the law of tenant default are most clearly visible if the lease is seen as a form of credit: the landlord grants the tenant a temporary property right, the leasehold estate, and in return the tenant undertakes to pay a premium for the enjoyment of this property right. One could imagine a situation where a tenant buys the leasehold estate from a landlord and pays him the rent for the whole term of the lease at the commencement of the lease. At the same time, the tenant arranges a credit with a bank to obtain financing for paying the rent and undertakes to pay regular instalments to the bank. Ideally, following the "golden rule" of financing, the credit will be fully paid back at the expiry of the lease. Whilst such an arrangement would seem highly unusual, it is useful to illustrate the twofold that is normally assumed by the landlord: not only does the landlord "sell" the leasehold estate; the landlord also arranges the financing for this purchase. In contrast to other forms of lease financing, leases of real property thus possess an idiosyncratic attribute. The financing of the transaction via an implied credit contract is common to all real property leases. At the same time, the costs of this financing aspect of the lease are never enunciated in the lease, while leases for equipment would more readily reveal the actual cost of financing. For leases of equipment, the costs of financing are also more easily revealed because these leased goods, e.g. cars, are also traded on open markets. The inadvertent role of landlords as brokers of financing also impacts upon their transaction costs: while banks and other organisations are typically involved in the granting of credits, landlords will be less experienced in determining credit worthiness of potential tenants. Pricing according to the risks associated with letting premises to a certain tenant will thus be almost impossible.

5.1.3 The role of security deposits

Pricing according to the individual tenant's risk profile is not observed in practice. Rather, landlords resort to shorthand-measures, most commonly deposits that have to be paid at the commencement of the lease (Allen et al., 1995, p. 272). If risk-based pricing were used it would lead to adverse selection. The intuition of risk-based pricing would be that tenants with a good credit record would pay a lower rent than tenants with a worse credit record. This would then mean, however, that high-risk tenants, typically small or newly founded enterprises, will be asked to pay rather high rents. These tenants would be the least likely to be able to afford them, however. Stiglitz and Weiss (1981, pp. 408-409) thus note that, rather than observing a clearing market, there will always be some rationing on credit markets, in the sense that banks typically lend less money than they could because of an adverse selection of possible debtors for the above-mentioned reasons. The same conclusion would hold true for lessors of real property. A differentiated calculation of security deposits has, however, been suggested as a theoretical solution to the problem and can also be observed empirically. Benjamin et al. (1992b, pp. 271-272) examined security deposits in office leases. While the focus of their research was utilisation of the property in terms of maintenance and repairs rather than default, they found that deposits present a mechanism to reduce the adverse selection of high-utilising tenants that could also reduce the adverse selection of tenants with a high probability of default. The amount of the security deposit serves as a signalling device and by committing to pay a high deposit, tenants can negotiate lower rents. The deposits reduce the risks posed by asymmetric information regarding the tenant's future behaviour. Benjamin et al. (1992a) also found similar effects for leases in the residential sector. Empirical research focussing on the role of security deposits in the residential sector was also conducted by Allen et al. (1995, pp. 281-282): Based on a data sample from the US the authors show that security deposits are set according to the property's vulnerability to damages and the tenant's likelihood to cause such damage. Nevertheless, deposits are found to have little efficacy in avoiding damages. A connection between deposits and the costs of other methods of asset protection is recognised by Smith et al. (1985, p. 903), finding that "if it is relatively inexpensive to obtain information about the lessee and also relatively inexpensive to enforce the penalty clause [or other enforcement mechanism], bonding through explicit deposits will be less frequently employed."

The function of credit securities has been investigated by Adams (1980, pp. 104-110)[119]: he points out that a distinction has to be drawn between *bona fide* debtors, who are genuinely unable to meet their financial commitments, and debtors who recklessly or deliberately fail to meet their obligations even though their financial position is otherwise sound. In the latter case, securities discipline the debtor by shifting the financial risks of judicial enforcement to him. Without security deposits debtors could defer payment to a later date and creditors would have to advance and partly bear the costs of enforcement. Adams (1980, p. 106) acknowledges that this role of securities as a measure of disciplining is an ancillary function of these instruments. The main function is the protection of creditors where the debtor is genuinely insolvent. Because repayments, or the payment of rent, will take place in the future, the creditor's position is threatened by the possibility that the debtor will not have sufficient assets to cover liabilities when payment is due. Security deposits can mitigate the creditor's vulnerability to this risk. It will be shown later on that security deposits are of particular relevance to the landlord when the tenant's business enters insolvency proceedings.

5.1.4 Hold-up costs and tenant default

The analysis of bankruptcy law by Hart (1995, chapter 5) starts with the evaluation of the quite artificial situation of a single debtor and a single creditor.

119 Deposits can be compared to credit securities as both fulfil similar economic functions.

Hart (1995) finds that in this case control of the assets shifts from the debtor to the creditor. The creditor becomes the new owner of the assets. The author concludes that the rule of bankruptcy procedures in such a case is to warrant the transfer of ownership and that the terms of the debt contract are upheld. The case of a defaulting tenant is comparable to this situation: while the landlord retains ownership of the fee simple estate of the land in a strictly legal sense, he has given up actual control of his assets. Forfeiture of the lease enables the landlord to regain this control and hence factual ownership. Nevertheless, forfeiture is seen as an *ultima ratio* by landlords and legal texts also describe it as an ultimate sanction (see e.g. Gray and Gray, 2006, p. 524). The question is thus why defaulting tenants are not immediately evicted by the landlord. Hart (1995, p. 157) gives the answer by stating that, in a one debtor-one creditor case and after gaining ownership, "the creditor should have the right to decide whether to sell off the assets, or renegotiate her debt contract with the entrepreneur, so as to keep the assets in place".

The problem of a landlord with a defaulting tenant lies in the hold-up costs created by the current and defaulting tenant. In order to regain control of the premises it is necessary to evict the tenant. The value of a property with a sitting tenant who is not meeting his financial obligations is significantly reduced. To protect the value of his property the landlord has to re-let it to another tenant. There may be situations, however, where the tenant just undergoes a temporary phase of financial constraint, or where the expectation value of the business going concern will exceed the expectation value of winding-up the tenant's business. In such a case, it would be economically efficient to continue the business (Eger, 2001, pp. 30-31).

The situation of the landlord is, however, more problematic than that of other creditors. First of all, rent arrears are likely to continue accruing while renegotiations take place. Other creditors will, upon insolvency, normally stop lending or delivering to an insolvent company. Business contacts with an insolvent company will be revived only after a settlement has been reached. Because of the special nature of real property, the landlord is not in a position to just stop supplying the tenant. Secondly, continuation of the lease may not be feasible because of the landlord's bargaining position. It is thinkable that continuation of the tenancy on existing terms is more attractive than forfeiture of the lease and re-letting of the premises. This may be the case if, for example, the lease has been negotiated when the property market was buoyant and hence favourable to the landlord but market conditions have changed since then so that market rents would be lower than they were before. Because of hold-up, the defaulting tenant may nevertheless often be in a situation to coerce the landlord to accept unfavourable terms. Such a situation can occur if three conditions are met:

1. The tenant is fairly flexible in choosing a location for his business. His business neither has a high degree of location-dependant goodwill nor a high degree of business-immobility;
2. The landlord is fairly dependant on the rental income from the property, e.g. because the tenant is large compared to other tenants in the portfolio or the property investment is highly geared, and so on;
3. The property (sub-) market is in a tenant-friendly state and alternative properties may widely be available. It is not the case that the insolvent tenant should easily be able to find alternative premises. The state of the property market rather defines the landlord's opportunity costs.

The rational landlord would then be aware that accepting a continuation of the lease under amended terms may still be a better option for the landlord than evicting the tenant and searching for a new tenant. It should be noted that in weaker property markets landlords typically incentivise prospective tenants by offering rent-free periods. (Landlords prefer rent-free periods to simple reductions of rent because nominal rents can be kept at seemingly attractive levels for reporting purposes.) The IPD data used by Crosby et al. (2005, p. 103) finds that in UK leases in 2003 rent-free periods were found in 42.0% of retail leases; 33.8% of office leases and 17.7% of industrial leases. Un-weighted, rent-free periods ranged from 5.0 months in case of retail premises to 7.2 months in the office sector. Notably, volatile markets such as the City of London office market are particularly affected by the incidence of rent-free periods. In this sub-market, the weighted average rent-free period was 28 months (9 months if un-weighted). This means that for large office properties landlords were willing to forego over two years of rent payments just to find a tenant. It is clear then, that a defaulting tenant is presented with a wide scope for negotiation if these three conditions are met.

One should note that these negotiations can take place outside of formal insolvency proceedings. The landlord would be the natural starting point for negotiations by a firm facing insolvency. Unlike suppliers of raw materials that could just suspend delivery or staff who would discontinue their work, the landlord cannot immediately stop his "supply". Equally, the general state of the property market is fairly transparent so that an informed tenant will be aware of the landlord's other options.

5.1.5 Transaction costs and tenant default

The costs of enforcing his rights are another aspect that could weaken the landlord's bargaining position. If forfeiture of the lease can only take place with a court order and if it is clear that costs of such an order are high and largely non-recoverable or if significant delays in time are involved, the tenant has more room to negotiate his obligations.

The landlord is thus disadvantaged in comparison to other creditors as he (1) cannot simply stop "lending", (2) is presented with hold-up costs created by the sitting tenant and (3) has a security that can only be utilised if the tenant is evicted.

The analysis will proceed as follows: First of all, the treatment of landlords in English and German insolvency law is reviewed. Then the remedies available to landlords are examined. The focus will be on transaction costs created by utilising the remedies. It is also discussed whether the remedies exhibit desirable properties in terms of balancing *ex ante* and *ex post* incentives.

It thus has to be noted that a legal system that provides efficient remedies does not only minimise costs that occur at default, but also reduces costs that occur *ex ante*; this would include the costs of searching for tenants and investigating their credit worthiness and also the costs of monitoring tenant's behaviour. One should also consider that security deposits, by their very nature, have to be kept in low-risk investments and attract a low yield. The opportunity costs created by not being able to invest these funds in the actual business have to be borne in mind. For small businesses the amount of security deposits may thus be a particular challenge. In extreme cases, the security deposit may even harm the tenant's financial position and thus turn the deposit that was intended to protect the landlord into a threat also to his interests.

5.1.6 *Ex ante* search costs and tenant default

Considering tenant default and search costs, the discussion of Hax's (1985) paper by Goldberg (1985) is interesting. Hax discusses the economic aspects of bankruptcy law. Goldberg (1985, p. 101) defines the costs of bankruptcy as a tax on suppliers of funds. The incidence of bankruptcy is seen as non-random, i.e. some firms are more likely to file for bankruptcy than others. When it comes to *ex ante* search costs, Goldberg (1985) elaborates on Hax's model and suggests that potential investors [or, indeed, landlords] had an incentive to spend resources to get information on the likelihood that individual firms would go bankrupt (p. 101). He claims that these expenditures will affect the likelihood of bankruptcy. It is also assumed that the rate of bankruptcy and the research skills of all investors [or landlords] are the same.

Goldberg then holds that the result will be the same as in Barzel's (1985) example of sorting oranges in a basket (Goldberg, 1985, p. 101):

> Each investor [or landlord] has a private incentive to search for higher quality securities [or tenants]. But regardless of how much searching takes place, the average quality of

> the security [the tenant] remains unchanged (by assumption). The resources expended by the investors and customers in these models are pure waste, since the expected quality for each party remains unchanged. Thus, the higher the 'bankruptcy tax' the greater the private rewards to searching for special information and the greater the social waste arising from excessive search for information.

Goldberg (1985, pp. 101-102) does, however, acknowledge that his argument could also lead to the opposite conclusion. If these searches for good risks improved the overall quality of debtors or if search reduces the rate of bankruptcy, then this type of search would not only lead to purely private benefits.

The applicability of Goldberg's (1985) suggestions to tenant default is highlighted by two much discussed idiosyncrasies of the property market: (1) The relative inefficiency of the market and (2) the strongly varying degrees of professional expertise among landlords.

To benefit the public and not only individual market participants, the results of searches for information would have to be available to other participants. Real estate markets are, however, characterised by a dominance of private information and relatively secretive transactions (see e.g. Wüstefeld, 2000, pp. 34-35). It is therefore quite unlikely that privately collected information will benefit market participants at large. The varying expertise between big and small landlords exacerbates the problem of private information. While professional landlords can investigate potential tenants more effectively and at lower costs, small landlords will have to resort to fairly crude means to assess their potential tenants' financial situations. It follows from this that privately incurred search costs lead almost exclusively to private benefits.

The so-called *Mietnomaden* ("nomad tenants") are an illustration of such phenomena and have recently attracted some media attention in Germany. These "nomads" are residential tenants that take advantage of the inability of small landlords to investigate the financial background of potential tenants and the protective nature of German residential tenancy law. A "nomad" moves into a flat and, after one or two months, discontinues rental payments. Until landlords would have obtained a court order for eviction up to a year can pass and the tenant can live "rent free" during this time. By the time eviction is imminent the "nomad" would most certainly already have rented a new flat from another ill-informed small landlord. The example highlights that unavailability of information coupled with a protective and tenant friendly law of forfeiture leads to economic inefficiencies. It is thus proposed that the criteria against which a landlord's remedies should be assessed have to be three-fold: (1) Wasteful search costs have to be minimised; (2) the role of security deposits should be reduced; (3) there have to be clear rules and a speedy process for the remedies.

A distinction has to be drawn between remedies sought for non-payment of rent and for breach of other covenants. Tenants may fail to perform their obligations under the latter type of covenants, e.g. repair covenants, for a wide range of reason. If a landlord seeks a remedy because of non-payment of rent, the tenant is, however, likely to be insolvent or faced with insolvency. The next sections will therefore illustrate the position of landlord and tenant in German and English insolvency law.

5.2 Business leases and insolvency in Germany

A reformed insolvency law came into force in Germany on 1 January 1999. In contrast to its predecessor, the stated aim of the new *Insolvenzordnung* ("Insolvency Statute", abbreviated as InsO) is the continuation of insolvent businesses wherever possible (Franken and Dahl, 2006, p. 39).

The InsO states three reasons for insolvency:

- A business is deemed unlikely to be able to meet financial obligations when they become due in the future ("imminent insolvency");[120]
- A business is already unable to satisfy its creditors;[121]
- A legal entity (e.g. a limited company) is "over-indebted".[122]

If either situation occurs, a creditor[123] or the debtors may apply to the county court[124] (*Amtsgericht*) for an opening of insolvency proceedings. In certain cases the debtor is obliged to file for insolvency.[125] Subject to meeting the necessary conditions, the court will open the proceedings and appoint a preliminary receiver.[126] The court seizes the debtor's remaining assets and creditors' claims are ranked and verified. A receiver takes control of the assets and their administration.[127] The court can equip the receiver with varying degrees of competencies. The opening of insolvency proceedings suspends all other

120 s. 18 InsO.

121 s. 17 InsO.

122 s. 19 InsO.

123 s. 14 InsO.

124 s. 2 InsO.

125 s. 13 InsO.

126 The pre-condition for opening proceedings is that the debtor's assets cover at least the costs of the proceedings (s. 26(1)1 InsO). To avoid the rejection of applications, the new insolvency law added the ground of imminent insolvency. It should be noted that the word "receiver" is here used as a translation of the German term "*Insolvenzverwalter*". However, a UK receiver and an *Insolvenzverwalter* fulfil distinctive roles.

127 s. 80 InsO.

existing legal proceedings against the debtor.[128] Landlords who have already initiated legal proceedings or started debt enforcement against a defaulting tenant are thus barred from enforcement (Franken and Dahl, 2006, pp. 42-43).

As an alternative procedure, the creditors may agree in their majority on an insolvency plan (*Insolvenzplan*).[129] Under an insolvency plan, the current management stays in place and the receiver oversees the decisions made by the firm's management. The goal of an insolvency plan is the continuation of the insolvent business; it makes a flexible restructuring of the insolvent business possible. It should be noted, however, that this flexibility does not extend to an adjustment of rents or other lease covenants against the will of the landlord (Eidenmüller, in Kirchhof, 2008, no. 111-113).

5.2.1 Administration of existing leases by the receiver

Regarding leases of real property, the receiver has wide ranging competencies while the rights of the landlord are curtailed in comparison to the old insolvency law. As the objective of the new law is the continuation of businesses, special protection is afforded to the tenant's premises as the centre of his commercial activity.

5.2.1.1 Termination of leases by the receiver

The receiver has the right to elect whether existing leases should be continued or terminated.[130] Leases can be terminated with a notice period of three months.[131]

If the lease is terminated by the receiver, the landlord has a claim for damages for the foregone earnings less the saved expenses.[132] Termination of the lease furthermore results in the release of the premises from the assets under receivership. The landlord can therefore regain control of his property.[133] All financial claims, however, including damages, will be treated as unsecured claims and receive no preferential treatment against other creditors' interests.[134]

128 s. 240 ZPO (German civil procedure rules) for lawsuits and ss. 85, 88, 89 InsO and ss. 15, 22, 146, 147a ZVG (German debt enforcement rules) for enforcement of claims.

129 Part 6 InsO.

130 s. 109 I 1 InsO.

131 s. 580 a IV BGB for new leases concluded after 1 September 2001. Older contracts are governed by the repealed s. 565 I a BGB and the notice period is only one month.

132 s. 109 (1) 3; (2) 2 InsO.

133 s. 546 (1) BGB.

134 Federal Supreme Court (BGH), decision of 5 July 2001, NZM 2001, 856.

The claim for damages that is afforded to the landlord may therefore be of little value. The landlord furthermore has the burden of proof in establishing the losses he suffered from early termination (Franken and Dahl, 2006, pp. 126-128).

Nevertheless, termination of the lease by the receiver may still put the landlord in a better position than where the receiver decides to continue the lease.

5.2.1.2 Rights of insolvent tenant's landlord under German law

Insolvency of the tenant does not give the landlord the right to terminate the lease. Once an application for the opening of insolvency proceedings has been made, the landlord loses the right to forfeit the leases because of non-payment or delayed payment of rent.[135] Clauses in the lease that purport to give the landlord the right to terminate the lease in case of tenant's insolvency are void.[136] Likewise, if an application for the opening of insolvency proceedings is rejected, a right to terminate the lease does not arise either.[137] The landlord would then have to resort again to the forfeiture procedures described later in this chapter.

The rent arrears that have accrued before insolvency proceedings have been opened will be treated in the same way as other creditors' claims.[138] Landlords thus have to be careful to have rent arrears included in the list of claims kept by the court.

5.2.2 Rent arrears accruing after the opening of insolvency proceedings

While forfeiture of the lease for rent arrears that have accrued before the opening of insolvency proceedings is not possible, the landlord can terminate the lease if arrears continue accruing after the opening of proceedings. The lease can then be forfeited if rent has not been paid for two months after the opening of proceedings.[139] It was the apparent intention of legislators that the new insolvency law should thus enable the tenant to continue its business upon the opening of insolvency proceedings but at the same time not to put too strong a burden on the landlord.

---

135 s. 112 (1) InsO.

136 s. 119 InsO; see also Hörndler in Lindner-Figura et al. (2006, p. 782).

137 Federal Supreme Court (BGH), decision of 23 January 2002, XII ZR 5/00, NZM 2002, 524.

138 s. 108 (2) InsO.

139 In line with the rules set out in s. 543 (2) 1 No. 3 BGB.

To regain possession of the premises, the landlord has to turn again to the courts because an eviction of the tenant can only be made by way of a court order. This is a weakness in insolvency law because landlords may have to resort to the courts twice. Legal proceedings initiated before the opening of insolvency proceedings because of "old" rent arrears would have been suspended; for the "new" rent arrears it is, however, necessary to initiate new proceedings to finally secure repossession of the premises.

Rent arrears that accrue after the opening of insolvency proceedings are, however, classified as so-called *Masseverbindlichkeiten* (liabilities which have priority over ordinary claims).[140] The receiver has the duty to fulfil financial obligations arising from such liabilities or, alternatively, has to terminate the lease (Neuhaus, 2005, pp. 472-474).

The duty of the receiver to meet financial obligations stemming from the lease does not extend to liability for damages to the property, however, unless these damages occurred during the receivership.[141]

5.2.3 Security deposits

Security deposits that have been paid to landlords of tenants under receivership do not have to be handed over to the receiver.[142] When the lease comes to an end, the landlord has the right to offset claims against the tenant with the deposit. The security deposit is hence classified as a *Masseverbindlichkeit* with special priority rules.[143]

5.2.4 Distress for rent

The landlord's right to seize goods belonging to the tenant in case of non-payment of rent (*Vermieterpfandrecht*, s. 562 BGB) is unaffected by the opening of insolvency proceedings.[144] Nevertheless, the use of this self-help remedy is limited by the insolvency procedure rules. The landlord may not employ the

---

140 Priority of *Masseverbindlichkeiten* over ordinary claims is regulated in s. 53 InsO and the term is defined in s. 55 InsO. Apart from the costs of the insolvency proceedings, all liabilities arising from obligations or contracts entered into by the receiver are *Masseverbindlichkeiten*.

141 Federal Supreme Court, decision of 5 July 2001, IX ZR 327/99, ZMR 2001,792. Also note that it is on the landlord to prove that damages occurred during receivership.

142 ss. 314, 50 InsO.

143 s. 94 InsO.

144 Federal Supreme Court, NJW-RR 2004, 772 (772).

remedy for arrears accruing after the opening of insolvency proceedings.[145] Also excluded is distress for rent for damages because of the receiver's lease termination, and for rents that were due more than one year before the opening of the insolvency proceedings.[146] A landlord can therefore only distress for rent arrears that occurred within a year before the opening of insolvency proceedings.[147] In practice, the use of distress for rent may be limited by secured claims of other creditors on the most valuable property on the tenant's premises (Franken and Dahl, 2006, pp. 105-106). If the landlord seeks to distress for rent that was due before the opening of insolvency proceedings but where proceedings have been opened in the meantime, the right to distress for rent until the opening of insolvency proceedings is converted into a special claim against the receiver.[148]

5.2.5 Evaluation of the landlord's position under German insolvency law

So far, the rules that govern the relationship between landlord and tenant, or rather, landlord and receiver have been illustrated. The above analysis of the economic functions of insolvency law has revealed, however, that negotiations between the parties before formal proceedings are initiated are often beneficial. Moreover, it was stated that an economically efficient insolvency law has to reduce unproductive search and monitoring costs.

German insolvency law does unfortunately not provide much scope for parties to a lease to reduce *ex ante* transaction costs. It has been shown that the landlord's position during insolvency proceedings is fairly weak because of the objective to allow insolvent businesses to continue their operations.

Hax (1985, p. 81) suggests that insolvent businesses should be allowed to continue their operations if the expectation value of continuation less the costs of continuation is higher than the expected inflows in case of winding-up the firm. It would thus be wrong to criticise the law for its objective but it remains questionable whether the German rules set efficient *ex ante* incentives because of their mandatory character. The mandatory nature of the rules may cause inefficiencies.

---

145 s. 91 (1) InsO.

146 s. 50 (2) 1 InsO.

147 As explained by Hörndler in Lindner-Figura (2006, p. 795) because of s. 91 I InsO and s. 50 I 1 InsO; note also that general restrictions on distress also apply, in particular the prohibition of seizure of goods used for the conduct of the tenant's business activities, s. 811 No. 9 German civil procedure rules.

148 s. 166 (1) InsO with a fiduciary duty of the receiver towards the landlord, s. 60 InsO.

The opening of insolvency proceedings is not a reason for termination of the lease for either party (Franken and Dahl, 2006, p. 44). The opening of the pre-stage of insolvency proceedings sends a negative signal to the landlord. Being aware of his relatively weak position in these proceedings, a landlord would often prefer a termination of the lease. Most German commercial leases therefore contain clauses stipulating a termination of the lease upon opening of insolvency proceedings. Five of the six case study-leases contain clauses that stipulate automatic termination of the lease once the tenant becomes insolvent or insolvency proceedings are opened.

Being against the spirit of the insolvency rules all these clauses are, nonetheless, void.[149] At first sight, the inability to contract-out of this tenant-friendly regime might seem as a desirable protection of tenants, but this is questionable. Many newly-founded or small businesses struggle to find appropriate premises. This is not because of a lack of supply of commercial premises but rather because of the guarantees that businesses find difficult to provide. There is an increasing tendency on the side of businesses to limit liability and thus personal risk. An example is the spread of English limited companies operating in Germany to avoid the fairly high minimum capital required for German limited companies (GmbH, *Gesellschaft mit beschränkter Haftung*). Such potential tenants are then often unattractive to landlords because the probability of default is high and the likelihood to recover rents low; the long period to recover possession is another aspect. All these elements then lead to a rationing of the supply of commercial premises comparable to the rationing taking place on credit markets, as modelled by Stiglitz and Weiss (1981). The effect seems to be that only tenants with a good credit record can occupy desirable premises.

Inability to contract-out of costly clauses also increases the investment by landlords in the search for potential tenants. As illustrated above by reference to Barzel's orange basket example, this information creates only private but no public benefits.

Furthermore, landlords will try to protect their interests by asking tenants for security deposits that should be expected to increase with the barriers to exit imposed by insolvency law. These funds then idle in low-interest accounts and cannot be invested more productively.

It is also worth investigating whether the new insolvency law has helped to secure the continuation of insolvent businesses. Each year, there are around 40,000 insolvencies in Germany. Experts estimate that around 20-30% of insolvent firms would qualify for continuation via an insolvency plan, but there

149 Franken and Dahl (2006, pp. 55-56) summarising the dominant view in the literature.

are only several hundred of these procedures each year. Reasons are thought to be a lack of management skills by administrators and courts and a flawed selection procedure of administrators that is purely based on formal legal qualifications but not on proven management experience. The German Association of Insolvency Courts (*Bundesarbeitskreis Insolvenzgerichte*) currently plans an empirical evaluation of the success of individual insolvency administrators. According to a member of the association, only around 100 of the 1,800 registered insolvency administrators would have the necessary skills and qualifications to successfully manage a large-scale insolvency. Lack of transparency as to administrators' skills is seen as the major reason for the currently low survival rate of insolvent businesses (Dierig, 2009, p. 25).

The new insolvency law has thus been fairly ineffective in increasing the number of firms that "survive" insolvency proceedings. Unquantifiable is the number of potential tenants who fail to find appropriate premises because of the inflexibility of the current regime. One should not overestimate the ability of the receiver to arrange continuation of a business. Most start-ups and small businesses arguably fail because of misjudgements as to the demand for their product or service. For an economy at large it is important that business ideas can be tried out. This should be valued higher than the protection of incumbent businesses.

The probably strongest argument against a prohibition of contracting out from the insolvency regime is in the author's opinion the connection of business success and location. As described in the introduction to the chapter on rent adjustment, for some businesses, e.g. restaurants, retail outlets and so on, there is a strong link between location and success, here called location-dependant goodwill. If a restaurant or retail outlets fails, this should in many instances be due to the inappropriateness of the given business model for a certain location. Protecting the tenancy would not help in these cases as the insolvency administration will not succeed in turning the business around. Where the location of a business is not a determining factor of its success, protecting the location is, on the other hand, not as important as alternative premises could be found should it be thought that the business can otherwise be continued.

Especially start-ups suffer from an insolvency regime that is actually designed to protect them. A recent study conducted by BITKOM[151] finds that the inability to arrange financing is the main reason for failure to launch new businesses (64% of respondents).[152] The study also revealed that two thirds of the potential

---

151 *Bundesverband Informationswirtschaft, Telekommunikation und neue Medien* (Federal Association of the IT, telecoms and new media industries).

152 Perspektive Mittelstand (2008).

start-ups in the IT, telecoms and new media sector would require not more than € 40,000. For such start-ups, security deposits for renting premises that typically amount to two or three monthly rents mean a significant burden. The ability to contract out of the insolvency rules would enable landlords to reduce these deposits and thus assist start-ups while facing less risk to be disadvantaged in insolvency proceedings.

5.3 Forfeiture of leases and debt enforcement in Germany

The previous section discussed the position of a landlord vis-à-vis an insolvent tenant. It was found that in case of tenant insolvency the landlord is in a weak position as he cannot terminate the lease for rent arrears that had accrued before the tenant filed for insolvency. If rent arrears occur while the tenant's business is under receivership, the landlord has to obtain a new court order before evicting the tenant.

Landlords are thus well advised to forfeit a lease before the tenant officially files for insolvency. In any event, obtaining a court order to forfeit a lease is necessary as self-help as known from English land law, such as peaceful re-entry, is not known in German landlord and tenant law.

This section will evaluate the remedies that are available to a German landlord confronted with non-payment of rent.

The principle remedies are:[153]

1. Suing for debt: Either by way of a court judgment or by obtaining a payment order (*Mahnbescheid*[154]); in addition there is the possibility of enforcing the repayment of debt without a court ruling by way of a publicly certified contract;
2. Forfeiture of the lease: Eviction of the tenant and enforcement with a bailiff;
3. Distress for rent (*Vermieterpfandrecht*[155]): Seizure and auctioning of goods belonging to the tenant.

The workings and the economic efficiency of the individual remedies are now discussed.

---

153 Compare e.g. Horst (2003), Neuhaus (2005).

154 s. 688 ff ZPO (German civil procedure rules).

155 s. 562 BGB.

5.3.1 Suing for debt

Suing for debt is an appropriate remedy if a landlord wishes to enforce his financial claim but at the same time continue the lease. A landlord suing for debt therefore anticipates that the tenant will not file for insolvency and that the reason for non-payment is only a temporary shortage of funds or strategic behaviour. Suing for debt can also be an appropriate remedy when there is a dispute as to the payment of service charges or other ancillary obligations.

A landlord can only sue for debt if payments are due. The German civil code regulates that rents have to be paid at the beginning of the period for which the rent is calculated. As rents in Germany are normally calculated on a monthly basis, payments are thus due at the beginning of each month. The rent has to be paid until the third business day of each period.[156] The payment of rent is also recognised as a tenant's primary duty under a lease.[157] After payment is due, the landlord has the right to sue the tenant for payment. Interest on the amounts due is also payable.

5.3.1.1 Debt enforcement by way of payment order

A special feature of German law is the ease with which a creditor can obtain a payment order (*Mahnbescheid*) against a debtor. The creditor can apply for the issue of such an order to the local county court (also on-line) and for payment of a moderate fee the payment order is then sent to the debtor.[158] The court does, at this point, not verify whether the claim is justified. The debtor has the alternative of either objecting to the order, simply by ticking the appropriate box on the form sent to him, or accepting the claim. If the debtor objects to the claim, the creditor has to use the normal court track to enforce his claim. If, on the other hand, the debtor does not object within a specified period, the creditor can obtain an enforcement order (*Vollstreckungsbescheid*), with which a court-appointed bailiff can then enforce the claim.

It is observed that a payment order is best used if objection by the claimant is unlikely and if no further debt will accrue, as the amount on the payment order cannot be modified after issuance (Horst, 2003, p. 485).

---

156 s. 579 (2) BGB referring to s. 556b (1) BGB.

157 s. 535 (2) BGB.

158 The costs for obtaining a payment order for € 10,000 are around € 600 for the payment order and a further 240 € for the enforcement order (excl. VAT).

5.3.1.2 Court track

Particularly where it is likely that the tenant would object to a payment order or where rent arrears continue accruing, it is more appropriate to enforce payment via the court track, either before a county court (*Amtsgericht*) or before the high court (*Landgericht*) where the value of the claim exceeds € 5,000.[159] Similar to the Woolf reforms in England and Wales, the German civil procedure rules have been amended to facilitate pre-trial settlements between the parties.[160] Before the actual trial, negotiations with the aim of reaching a consensual settlement are mandatory.[161] It is feared that this will lead to delays in trials. Horst (2003, p. 489) thus argues that in the case of landlord and tenant disputes these pre-trial negotiations are counter-productive. He claims that in contrast to other trials, e.g. in employment law, where both parties have an interest in timely and cost effective settlements, tenants in particular may be interested in delaying trials.

This claim is particularly valid where the tenant seeks to file for insolvency because then legal proceedings are suspended (see above).

It would exceed the scope of this work to describe in detail the procedural rules for lawsuits. It should be mentioned, however, that leave to appeal is subject to the appealing party paying a deposit on court fees. Only questions of law, not questions of fact, are reviewed in appeal trials (Horst, 2003, p. 490).[162]

Having obtained a favourable court ruling, the landlord can then commence enforcement, which has to be through court appointed bailiffs.

5.3.1.3 Contracts certified by a notary public

As described above, suing for debt by using the standardised court track can lead to considerable delays in enforcement. This may threaten the landlord's position, in particular where insolvency of the tenant is luring.

This threat can be avoided if the tenant agrees in the lease to accept immediate enforcement in case of non-payment of rent without resort to the courts.[163] The lease will then, however, have to be drafted and witnessed by a notary, which is not a necessary condition for creating an otherwise valid lease.

159 s. 1 German civil procedure rules; 23 (1); 71 GVG (German Courts Constitution Act).

160 Civil procedure reform act of 27 July 2001 which came into effect on 1 January 2002.

161 s. 278 (2)-(5) German civil procedure rules.

162 There remains a limited scope to reconsider facts on appeal: s. 513 II, 529 German civil procedure rules.

163 Such clause was held to be valid by the LG Wuppertal, ZMR 2000, 836.

Enforcement would still have to take place through a publicly-appointed bailiff, but in lieu of a court ruling the bailiff has to accept the certified lease as a proof of the claim.[164] Horst (2003, p. 481) points out that this procedure speeds up enforcement and can, in case of insolvency, secure a higher ranking in the creditors' list.

From an economic point of view, this procedure has to be assessed negatively, however. The contracting-out of the judicial enforcement mechanisms creates only private benefits. The parties who are willing to contract out will be those that have in any event a low default probability. Certification by a notary also invokes high costs and requires a formalised procedure. It is therefore likely that only well-informed parties that possess superior information will use this procedure, and that it will only be used when the premises in question possess a high value. In short, it is unlikely that the premises required by small businesses will be the ones that could benefit from contracting out. Landlords and tenants should thus be able to contract out of the judicial enforcement system more easily so that landlords would be more willing to let to tenants with lower credit risks. Clearly though, such contracting out should be limited to non-payment of rent, which can easily be defined. Otherwise, landlords may use the possibility of circumventing the courts to abuse tenants.

5.3.2 Forfeiture of leases

The forfeiture of leases is regulated in the German civil code. The most common ground for forfeiture is non-payment of rent (Oprée in Lindner-Figura et al., 2006, p. 631).

Forfeiture is furthermore a possible remedy for the breach of covenants other than non-payment of rent. The civil code expressly recognises the following breaches as grounds for forfeiture:

1. Risks to health[165];
2. Nuisance[166];
3. Derogation from grant (termination by the tenant)[167].

More general grounds for forfeiture are also given: a "breach of covenant" by the tenant[168], "significant violation of contractual obligations"[169] or, less clearly

164 s. 794 (1) No. 5 German civil procedure rules.
165 s. 569 (1) BGB.
166 ss. 543 (1), 569 (2) BGB.
167 s. 543 (2) No. 1 BGB.
168 s. 543 (2) No. 2 BGB.
169 s. 543 (1) BGB.

defined, an "important reason"[170]. There is seemingly an overlap between these grounds. The reason is that the courts have held that "breach of covenant" only encompasses dereliction or wilful neglect[171] of the premises by the tenant or unauthorised sub-letting or assignment (Orprée in Lindner-Figura, 2006, p. 635). A "significant violation of contractual obligations" is then any other breach that, taking into account all circumstances, would lead to an overburden of the affected party if the lease were to be continued (Orprée in Lindner-Figura, 2006, p. 637).

The ground for forfeiture with the highest commercial significance, however, is non-payment of rent.

The conditions for forfeiture for non-payment of rent are clearly defined. The relevant s. 543 (1) and (2) BGB read:[172]

> Termination for cause without notice for a compelling reason
>
> (1) Each party to the contract may terminate the lease for cause without notice for a compelling reason. A compelling reason is deemed to obtain if the party giving notice, with all circumstances of the individual case taken into account, including without limitation fault of the parties to the contract, and after weighing the interests of the parties, cannot be reasonably expected to continue the lease until the end of the notice period or until the lease ends in another way.
>
> (2) A compelling reason is deemed to obtain in cases including without limitation where:
>
> 1. The lessee is not permitted the use of the leased property in conformity with contract, in whole or in part, in good time, or is deprived of this use,
>
> 2. The lessee violates the rights of the lessor to a substantial degree by substantially endangering the leased property by neglecting to exercise the care incumbent upon him or by allowing a third party to use it without authorisation, or;
>
> 3. The lessee,
>
> a) Is in default, on two successive dates, of payment of the rent or of a portion of the rent that is not insignificant, or
>
> b) In a period of time spanning more than two dates is in default of payment of the rent in an amount that is as much as the amount of rent for two months.

170 s. 242 BGB; forfeiture based on the doctrine of good faith. Treated very restrictively, the courts have established several situations that would not constitute a violation of the rules of good faith (Oprée in Lindner-Figura et al., 2006, pp. 638-639).

171 "Wilful neglect" is widely defined and can also include changes of use (LG Heidelberg, WuM 1992, 190) and other acts not actually affecting the structure of the building.

172 English translation by Langenscheidt, obtained from http://www.gesetze-im-internet.de/englisch_bgb/englisch_bgb.html.

> In the case of sentence 1 no. 3, termination is excluded if the lessor has by then obtained satisfaction. It becomes ineffective if the lessee has succeeded in discharging his debt by set-off and declares set-off without undue delay after notice of termination is given.

The landlord thus has the right to forfeit the lease if rent arrears accrue for more than two consecutive periods (b) or where "substantial arrears" have accrued (a). What constitutes "substantial arrears" is ultimately a question to be decided on the merits of the individual case but it seems to be generally accepted that arrears of more than one monthly rent would suffice (Orprée in Lindner-Figura, 2006, pp. 631-632).[173] In case of forfeiture, there is no notice period but in principle the tenant is obliged to vacate the premises immediately.

Neuhaus (2005, pp. 372-373) observes that in principle parties can individually agree on differing conditions for forfeiture but such clauses must not put one party at an unreasonable disadvantage.[174] Oprée (in Lindner-Figura et al., 2006, p. 635), however, claims that the landlord's rights to forfeit the lease cannot be extended in the light of the law on unfair contract terms. In particular, general terms and conditions may not stipulate forfeiture of the lease when only one monthly payment is paid with delay[175] or seek to establish a general worsening of the tenant's financial circumstances as a ground for forfeiture.

In the light of the above it is certainly less risky not to draft clauses that differ from the default rule provided by the civil code.

It should be noted that even if the criteria for forfeiture are fulfilled, the landlord has no right to resort to self-help. He has to resort to the courts or present a lease certified by a notary to a court-appointed bailiff (see above).

From an efficiency perspective, the German law of forfeiture bears attractive properties: the default rule provided in s. 543 BGB is clearly drafted and does not leave room for many doubts. The clarity of the German rules will become more obvious when the English law of forfeiture is discussed. The author would also claim that the German law maintains a proper balance between the *ex ante* and *ex post* incentives.

German law affords a certain degree of protection to the tenant by effectively tolerating delays in payment of up to two months. This protects the business interests of tenants that experience temporary financial difficulties. Applying the analytical scheme proposed by Hax (1985), one could also say that a firm that

173 The Federal Supreme Court followed the view that the absolute amount of arrears constituted the main criterion for establishing whether it qualified as "substantial" (WuM 1987, 317).

174 s. 307 BGB, regulating unfair contract terms.

175 Grapentin in Bub and Treier (1999, p. 1264): no limitation of tenant's rights in a standard terms and conditions. Forfeiture after one delayed payment may be permissible in an individually negotiated contract.

manages to overcome financial difficulties within two months is surely worth more as a going concern than its assets would be worth if it were liquidated. It could of course be argued that two months are too short a period for a business in financial difficulties to be turned around. One could think of a business with seasonal fluctuations that could e.g. be affected by a rainy summer. Longer periods of tolerated rent arrears would, however, lead to an externalisation of risks from tenants to landlords. Where tenants are aware that long-term delays in payment would not lead to serious consequences for their business, there is little incentive to employ sound financial management. Ultimately, such practices may lead to the continuation of economically non-sustainable businesses.

The *ex ante* effects of a more tenant-friendly law of forfeiture would nonetheless be more significant. First of all, the already above discussed search costs leading only to private rather than public benefits would spiral. Landlords would also try to protect the interest in their reversion by drafting complex ancillary agreements and by demanding high security deposits. This would ultimately lead to a market with rationed supply where only certain groups of good-risk tenants would be able to secure premises while many other business ideas would be foregone for society.

5.3.3 Distress for rent

The final remedy open to landlords is distress for rent (*Vermieterpfandrecht*).[176] Unless excluded in the lease, a landlord has the right to seize goods belonging to the tenant that are kept on the demised premises to satisfy his claims against the tenant.

It is necessary for the goods to be on the premises but goods that are necessary for the conduct of the business are barred from seizure.[177] This means that the only goods that can effectively be seized are stocks or raw materials that the tenant stores on the premises. Problematically, those are often not in the tenant's ownership but are kept on commission for the actual owner such as a bank (Horst, 2003, pp. 401-402).

The landlord must not keep the seized goods for himself but has to dispose of them by way of a public auction.[178]

Another limitation to the practical use of distress for rent is that the right to seize goods is extinguished once the goods are removed from the premises. The landlord's right to employ self-help is limited. He has a theoretical right to

---

176 ss. 562 (1), 578 BGB.
177 s. 811 No. 5 German civil procedure rules.
178 s. 1235 BGB.

prevent the removal of goods when the tenant moves out,[179] but there are practical difficulties. It is also uncertain whether the use of force is permitted in such cases (Horst, 2003, p. 400).

To conclude, the view of Neuhaus (2005, p. 332) should be followed that distress for rent plays only a secondary role in protecting the landlord's interests. The unclear ownership of many goods on a tenant's premises and the requirement for a public auction create high transaction costs.

5.3.4 Penalties

Finally, it should be mentioned that parties can stipulate in the lease that breach of covenant or late payment of rent triggers a penalty (Neuhaus, 2005, pp. 332-333). The freedom of contract to include such clauses in the lease is limited by the law on unfair contract terms[180]. Penalties must not be excessive; the court has the power to reduce excessive penalties[181]. A multiple of the monthly rent is held to be excessive[182].

Penalty clauses could act as a measure to discipline tenants and thus potentially reduce monitoring costs of a lease. However, it does not seem that such penalties would serve to reduce *ex ante* search costs. It would seem that only financially strong tenants would be willing to voluntarily agree on such penalties while high-risk tenants would both be unwilling to agree on such clauses and would, moreover, be unable to credibly commit to them. When faced with financial difficulties of the tenant, the landlord's interest in his reversion is not protected by the existence of penalty clauses. In such a case, the claim may only exist on paper but remain unenforceable.

5.3.5 Evaluation of German remedies for tenant default

The foregoing sections have reviewed the remedies that are available to a German landlord in case of non-payment of rent or breach of other covenants. The evaluation of the law from an efficiency perspective reveals positive and negative elements.

It has to be positively acknowledged that the civil code provides a variety of default rules that help to reduce transaction costs and provide clear guidelines for contracting parties. As a consequence, lease contracts can be significantly

179 s. 563b (1) 2 BGB.
180 s. 307 BGB.
181 s. 343 BGB.
182 OLG Celle (appeal court), decision of 19 May 1995, 2 U 192/92, NJW-RR 1993, 1228: penalty of five times the monthly rent held to be excessive.

shorter than their English counterparts and the reliance on defaults provided by the civil code assures that there is less scope for erroneous drafting of contracts. This surely benefits smaller landlords and tenants, who are as a consequence less dependant on professional (and costly) advice.

The rules of the civil code on forfeiture for non-payment of rent appear particularly efficient because of the clear guidance given and the balance between *ex ante* and *ex post* effects. The positive evaluation is nonetheless tainted by the strong reliance on courts and judicially-appointed bailiffs in cases that are very clear both in points of law and points of fact. As the rules on forfeiture provided in the civil code are fairly clear, it is doubtful whether a full trial in the courts is always necessary.

The weak position of the landlord in insolvency proceedings also ought to be criticised. The ability of the tenant to prolong trials or enforcement measures and have them suspended when insolvency proceedings are opened exacerbates this problem. Once again, a barrier to exit can pose a barrier to entry. It should be possible for landlords and tenants to stipulate that a lease can be terminated when a tenant's business files for insolvency. Renegotiation of the lease could still take place after insolvency proceedings have been opened, but having a right to evict the tenant, the landlord would be in a stronger position to negotiate.

A provision to terminate the lease at the opening of insolvency proceedings would also reduce *ex ante* search costs and limit the ability of the tenant to externalise business risks on the landlord.

The next section now analyses the positions of landlord and tenant under English law.

5.4 English insolvency law and the insolvent tenant

Insolvency law in England and Wales is regulated by the Insolvency Act 1986 and was recently amended by the Enterprise Act 2002 which came into force on 15 September 2003 (Slaughter & May, 2008, p. 1).

A company is insolvent if it is "unable to pay its debts"[183]. Pursuant to the statutory definition, this inability to pay debts occurs where:

- The company is unable to pay its debts as they fall due[184];

183 s. 123 (1) Insolvency Act 1986.
184 s. 123 (1) (e) Insolvency Act 1986.

- The company has not paid a debt exceeding £750 after being served with a court order to pay ("statutory demand")[185];
- An execution or other [enforcement] process issued on a judgment [...] in favour of a creditor of the company is returned unsatisfied in whole or in part[186];
- It is proved to the satisfaction of the court that the value of the company's assets is less than the amount of its liabilities, taking into account its contingent and prospective liabilities[187].

For a company in financial difficulties, five types of proceedings may be invoked, each with different legal ramifications for the landlord.

The five insolvency procedures are (Companies House, 2008):

1. Voluntary arrangements;
2. Schemes of arrangement;
3. Appointment of an administrator;
4. Appointment of an (administrative) receiver; and
5. Liquidation of the company ("winding-up").

5.4.1 Voluntary agreements

A Corporate Voluntary Arrangement (CVA) is an agreement between a company and its creditors.[188] The purpose of a CVA is to prevent liquidation and to secure the continuation of a business. The arrangement may be proposed by the firm's directors or, if under administration or liquidation, by the firm's administrator or liquidator. The proposal is made to shareholders and unsecured creditors and consists of a so-called "composition in satisfaction of the company's debt" or a scheme of arrangement of its affairs.[189] A person authorised to act as a nominee or supervisor evaluates the proposal and reports his evaluation to the court.[190] Following an affirmative evaluation by the nominee or supervisor, meetings of shareholders and creditors are called. The proposal is accepted if a simple majority of shareholders and a majority of three-quarters of creditors (by value of claim) vote in favour of the arrangement (Slaughter and May, 2008, pp. 2-3). The rights of secured creditors are treated differently and usually their agreement is necessary for the arrangement to take effect. There are certain

185 s. 123 (1) (a) Insolvency Act 1986.
186 s. 123 (1) (b) Insolvency Act 1986.
187 s. 123 (2) Insolvency Act 1986.
188 As regulated in s. 1 to 7 of the Insolvency Act 1986.
189 s. 1 (1) Insolvency Act 1986.
190 s. 1 (2); s. 2 (2); s. 390-391 Insolvency Act 1986.

safeguards to prevent arrangements that result in a preferential or prejudiced treatment of a certain shareholder or creditor (Slaughter and May, 2008, p. 2).

For the landlord of a tenant proposing a CVA, two issues are of interest: the treatment of past and future rent arrears and whether the landlord has the right to forfeit the lease.

In Burford Midland Properties Ltd v Marley Extrusions Ltd [1995] 30 EG 89 it was held by Cooke J that only the rent that had accrued by the date at which the CVA was made was subject to the CVA. Future rents were held to be unaffected and could be claimed from the tenant.[192] There are, however, other authorities with greater weight indicating that future rents could be included in a CVA:[193] Doorbar v Alltime Securities Ltd [1994] BCC 994 and Cazaly Irving Holding Ltd v Cancol Ltd [1995] EGCS 146.

Parsons (2006, p. 223) maintains that whether forfeiture is open to the landlord depends on the individual CVA and the landlord's consent to it. Jourdan (2002, pp. 12-14), on the other hand, adopts a different view and suggests that a landlord may challenge a CVA excluding forfeiture on the basis of prejudicial treatment. The case law on the question is far from unambiguous. In Re Naeem [1990] 1 WLR 48 it was held by Hoffmann J that the CVA in question did not affect the landlord's right to forfeit the lease. However, the judgment left open if this is meant to be a general rule or should apply only to the CVA in that case. In a subsequent case, the right to forfeit a lease was interpreted as the enforcement of a security. As secured creditors were not affected by a CVA, the court held that the landlord could still forfeit the lease. The case was appealed but the Court of Appeal held that the landlord's ability to forfeit the lease was not disputed on appeal.[194] In March Estates v Gunmark [1996] 2 BCLC 1 the view was expressed that a CVA could not affect a landlord's right to forfeit a lease if there are rent arrears. This was said, however, as an obiter dictum and furthermore rests on the assumption that the right to forfeit a lease is to be seen as a security in the sense of s. 4 (3) and s. 258 (4) Insolvency Act 1986, preventing approval of a CVA affecting secured creditors' rights.

In a subsequent case, however, Lightman J, who expressed in March Estates that the right to forfeit is to be seen as a security, corrected his views and pronounced that this right was not a security and the landlord thus not a secured

192 More precisely, from the old, insolvent tenant and the new tenant that took over the firm pursuant to the CVA.

193 Quoted by Parsons (2006, p. 223).

194 Doorbar v Alltime Securities (No. 2) [1995] BCLC 513; [1996] 1 WLR 456 (CA).

creditor.[195] Lightman J did not, unfortunately, clarify whether this would affect a landlord's right to forfeiture in case of a CVA.

In Re Lomax Leisure [2000] Ch 502 it was finally decided that the right to forfeit a lease is not to be seen as a "security". Apart from being a first instance judgment only, the case did not decide whether a landlord can forfeit a lease where a CVA is in place. Somewhat ironically, the consequence of finding that the right to forfeit is not a security meant that the landlord in Re Lomax could forfeit the lease because here the tenant was under administration. In this case, the Insolvency Act prescribes that once an application for an administration order has been made no steps may be taken to enforce any security over the company's property.[196]

The cases reveal that the discussion about viewing forfeiture as a form of security is in the first place a way of fitting the landlord's rights within the provided legal definitions. The case of Re Lomax showed that courts aim to protect the landlord's commercial interest. The author would thus speculate that courts would not be unwilling to grant leave to forfeit a lease also where a CVA is in place. Nevertheless, it should be considered that CVAs and administration fulfil different economic functions. A CVA is clearly directed at achieving a continuation of the business and a consensual outcome. Administration, which will be discussed below, also has the aim of continuing the business, but it is an aim amongst others. Winding up of the company is also a possible outcome of a company being under administration. Also, under an administration order more weight is given to the protection of creditors.

If a CVA is agreed on with a view to continuation of the business, forfeiture of the lease would be counter-productive. The CVA is aimed at company rescue and, generally, creditors and shareholders would not agree on a rescue plan where the firm would be worth more if wound-up. Furthermore, there are certain safeguards to monitor the implementation of the CVA: dissenting creditors can challenge the CVA in court on the basis of prejudicial treatment within 28 days after the meeting (see above) and, where the scheme is implemented, the supervisor, who manages the scheme, is subject to court control. Creditors may challenge his decisions in court at any time (Keenan, 1999, pp. 452-454). With these safeguards in place to ensure a controlled continuation of the firm, it would seem counter-intuitive that the landlord should be able to "blow" the whole scheme by forfeiting the lease. A firm under a CVA is very unlikely to be able to obtain another lease and the CVA would thus become obsolete. Where the business is highly location-dependant, because of goodwill and/or business-immobility, there would be little chance of continuation without the lease. Also,

195 Razzaq v Pala [1997] 1 WLR 1336.
196 Bird and Bird (1999, pp. 2-3).

it would be somewhat ironic that, following Cazaly Irving Holding, the landlord's future rents would become part of the CVA but that he should, at the same time be able to forfeit the lease because of previous rent arrears.

5.4.1.1 Position of guarantors under a CVA

A recent case raised issues relating to the treatment of guarantees in the context of CVAs. A guarantee is a form of security provided to a landlord where the guarantor covenants to fulfil the tenant's obligations under a lease in case of the tenant's default. Such guarantees are widely used where a holding owns several subsidiaries that are legally independent companies but economically part of the same entity. Such guarantees are also used in the German lease case studies for the car repair station and the car rental station because these are also "independent" legal entities with weak financial strength that are, however, part of a much larger corporate entity. In Prudential Assurance Co Ltd v PRG Powerhouse Ltd [2007] EWHC 1002 (Ch); [2007] Bus. L. R. 1771 (Ch) the electrical retailer Powerhouse decided to close a number of unprofitable shops. These retail outlets formed a legally independent entity. The CVA proposed by Powerhouse intended that the landlords of these shops should accept surrenders of their leases.[197] The parent company of Powerhouse had acted as a guarantor for many of these leases and the CVA also proposed that Powerhouse would be released from its role as a guarantor. It was decided by Etherton J that this was unfairly prejudicial to the landlords so that the CVA was set aside. Unfortunately, it was not decided in the case whether CVAs could never be used to release guarantors but only that the agreement in this case was unfairly prejudicial.

The problem with this decision is that it casts doubt on the value of guarantors as a security to landlords. While the CVA was in this case set aside, it created no precedence to the effect that future cases would be decided in the same way. Landlords are thus advised to ensure that the tenant himself provides strong covenants rather than relying on a guarantor.[198] From an economic point of view it would not be desirable that guarantors are released. Where landlords cannot be certain that a guarantor would have to meet the guarantee's obligations they would either refuse tenants without sufficiently strong covenants and/or demand additional securities such as higher rent deposits. CVAs are desirable because of their informal nature assisting in the continuation of businesses. Smaller business and start-ups, however, frequently depend on guarantors because of lack of own financial strength. Uncertainty as to the

197 Surrender basically means that the lease prematurely comes to an end and that both parties are released from their obligations under the lease.

198 Property Law Bulletin, 2007, 28 (2), 11.

guarantor's position in case of a CVA may pose a barrier to entry for those tenants.

5.4.1.2 Moratorium for small companies

Parliament's wish to foster continuation of insolvent businesses is also expressed by the recently introduced moratorium for small companies proposing a CVA.[199] These new provisions took effect on 1 January 2003. The definition of "small firms" is found in the Companies Act 2006. A firm is, for the purpose of this Act, considered "small" if two of the following three criteria are fulfilled: turnover below £ 5.6m; balance sheet total below £ 2.8m; number of staff below 50. Therefore, the word "small" is not taken too literally and the vast majority of UK business is covered by the scheme: in 2006, 99.3% of enterprises in the UK private sector were considered as "small" under this definition, providing 47.1% of UK private sector employment and 37.2% of UK private sector turnover.[200]

The moratorium is intended to enable the management of a firm threatened by insolvency to devise a rescue strategy.[201] For the duration of the moratorium no proceedings, executions or other such legal processes may be commenced or continued. Furthermore, no landlord may exercise his right of forfeiture by peaceable entry.[202]

The moratorium provides management with an initial "breathing space" of 28 days; the court may extend the moratorium by a further two months.[203] The Insolvency Act 1986 furthermore provides certain safeguards enabling courts

---

199 The Insolvency Act 2000 inserted a new Schedule A1 into the Insolvency Act 1986.

200 BERR (Department for Business, Enterprise and Regulatory Reform). The definition of "small companies" used by BERR set out at http://www.berr.gov.uk/bbf/financial-reporting/acc-audit-developments/page16361.html, accessed on 1 July 2008, is the same as the definition in s. 382 (3) Companies Act 2006.

201 A political will to extend the benefits of the moratorium to a large part of the business community is also shown by a raising the threshold defining a company as "small". According to the old Companies Act 1985, only firms with two of the following three criteria were considered small: turnover below £ 2.8m; balance sheet total below £ 1.4m; number of staff below 50. The financial limits have thus been doubled.

202 See para 12 (1) (f) Schedule A1 Insolvency Act 1986: [During the period for which a moratorium is in force for a company] no landlord or other person to whom rent is payable may exercise any right of forfeiture by peaceable re-entry in relation to premises let to the company in respect of a failure by the company to comply with any term or condition of its tenancy of such premises, except with the leave of the court and subject to such terms as the court may impose.

203 Paras 8 (3) & 32 (2) Schedule A1 Insolvency Act 1986.

and concerned parties to monitor the conduct of the insolvent firm's management. The Act also excludes certain companies that would otherwise meet the definition of small companies, in particular firms that are engaged in activities involving certain financial instruments.[204]

The introduction of moratoriums should be welcomed. Previously, the effectiveness of CVAs was partly prevented by the creditors' ability to enforce their claims while the firm's management was drawing up a rescue plan. If landlords were allowed to forfeit a lease while a CVA is in place this would, however, mean that attempts to rescue the insolvent firm would be pre-empted. The moratorium is monitored by the courts but administered by the concerned parties themselves. The advantage is thus that it offers safeguards that would not be available where parties negotiated without the background of a legally enforceable framework. Moreover, the outcome would still be close to the parties' interests as creditors and shareholders vote on the CVA and management has an interest in the CVA's approval.[205] Given that the initial duration of the moratorium is only 28 days and extensions are only granted where some progress is shown, the insolvent firm's management is pressed to devise a strategy quickly. This also serves to protect the landlord of the insolvent business. It is an acceptable infringement of the landlord's right to forfeit the lease that he has to wait for a maximum of three months to regain possession of his premises. Where the lease is immediately forfeited but other parties have agreed to a CVA overall welfare is clearly reduced. Where the majority of creditors and debtors have agreed on a CVA there has to be some realistic prospect of a continuation of the business. The value of the business going concern is estimated to be higher than the value of the wound-up business. It does not seem to be the case that the introduction of moratoriums creates an insolvency law that is "too soft" (see e.g. Bigus and Eger, 2004, pp. 195-196): it seems unlikely that the prospect of a three month long moratorium would induce a firm's management to act less diligently or carefully. On the other hand, the gains from a moratorium may be significant if a successful rescue plan can be implemented.

5.4.2 Schemes of Arrangement

A Scheme of Arrangement fulfils a role that is somewhat similar to that of CVAs in the sense that both are aimed at finding some compromise to continue a firm that would otherwise have to be discontinued. As Schemes of Arrangement are regulated by the Companies Act 2006 they are, strictly speaking, not part of

---

204 This would exclude most special purpose vehicles from benefiting from the scheme.

205 As the CVA increases the chances of the present management staying in office.

insolvency law: Any firm could in principle at any time enter a Scheme of Arrangement. The functions of both procedures are, however, largely similar, with the difference that Schemes of Arrangement are often used to implement amalgamations of companies. In contrast to a CVA, a Scheme of Arrangement is less informal and the court is not merely monitoring the scheme but taking a more active role. Unlike a CVA, which is being proposed by the insolvent firm's management, a Scheme of Arrangement is typically advanced by either a major creditor or shareholder.[206] They may, on application of either group, summon a meeting of shareholders and creditors.[207] If a majority in number representing 75% in value of the creditors [...], present and voting either in person or by proxy at the meeting summoned under section 896, agree a compromise or arrangement, the court may, on an application under this section, sanction the compromise or arrangement (s. 899 (1) Companies Act 2006). The effects of such a Scheme can be wide-ranging in terms of re-scheduling debt and re-organising the firm so that they are often used when the (would-be) insolvent firm ultimately merges with another corporate entity (Slaughter and May, 2008, p. 3). The Insolvency Service, a UK government agency, notes on its website that "the format and content of a scheme is not laid down in legislation and is decided by agreement between the company and its creditors and members and is subject to the approval of the court. It cannot, however, authorise anything contrary to general law".[208]

With a view to the Powerhouse litigation (see above) it should be noted that under a Scheme of Arrangement the landlords with guarantees would have been a separate class of creditors and could have vetoed against the Scheme. Furthermore, with a guarantee in place the landlords whose arrears were fully met by the guarantors would not even have been included in the Scheme. The crucial difference between a CVA and a Scheme of Arrangement is thus that all creditors form a single class for the purpose of voting on a CVA.[209] The absence of these class issues is normally seen as one of the main advantages of CVAs compared to Schemes of Arrangement (Baird and Ho, 2007, p. 124). For the landlord with a guarantor, however, the classification of creditors is a clear advantage. Classes of creditors should be homogeneous in that "[membership of a class] must be confined to those persons whose rights are not so dissimilar to

---

206 s. 896 (2) Companies Act 2006. The company itself or an administrator or liquidator may also apply for a Scheme of Arrangement.

207 s. 896 (1) Companies Act 2006.

208 http://www.insolvency.gov.uk/freedomofinformation/technical/TechnicalManual/Ch49-60/Chapter56/Part4/part4.htm, accessed on 2 July 2008.

209 See also memorandum by Allen & Avery (2008), accessed online at http://www.allenovery.com/AOWEB/AreasOfExpertise/Editorial.aspx?contentTypeID=1&contentSubTypeID=7944&itemID=35369&aofeID=308&prefLangID=410, accessed on 2 July 2008.

make it impossible for them to consult together with a view to their common interest".[210] This means that employees normally form one class, unsecured creditors another class, and so on. Because landlords can be sure that they can enjoy the benefit from their guarantees, the law would not seem too "soft" on a firm in difficulties. Landlords would continue to accept tenants with weak covenants as long as a guarantee is provided. It would, however, seem that companies will in future prefer CVAs because they offer certain advantages, e.g. the moratorium that is not offered by Schemes of Arrangement (Baird and Ho, 2007, p. 124).

5.4.3 Administration Order

The appointment of an administrator is another means of continuing a company that is insolvent or threatened by insolvency. Compared to CVAs and Schemes of Arrangement, administration is subject to stricter court control and sanctioning. The firm's management is effectively removed and a qualified insolvency practitioner is appointed by the court as an administrator. The administrator takes over the management of the firm and seeks to devise a rescue strategy. During administration a moratorium is in place, effectively barring the landlord from taking any action against the tenant (Parsons, 2006, p. 221). Recently, the Enterprise Act 2002 further restricted the landlord's rights vis-à-vis a tenant under administration.

The relevant restrictions of the landlord's rights are set out in s. 43 of Schedule B1 of the Insolvency Act 1986:

> Moratorium on other legal process
>
> (1) This paragraph applies to a company in administration.
>
> (2) No step may be taken to enforce security over the company's property except—
>
> (a) with the consent of the administrator, or
>
> (b) with the permission of the court.
>
> (3) [...].
>
> (4) A landlord may not exercise a right of forfeiture by peaceable re-entry in relation to premises let to the company except—
>
> (a) with the consent of the administrator, or
>
> (b) with the permission of the court. [...]

---

210 This definition goes back to Bowen LJ in Sovereign Life Ass Co v Dodd [1892] 2KB 573.

(6) No legal process (including legal proceedings, execution, distress and diligence) may be instituted or continued against the company or property of the company except—

(a) with the consent of the administrator, or

(b) with the permission of the court.

The result of a moratorium thus is that the landlord is barred from using all remedies that are normally available against a defaulting tenant. Neither distress for rent, nor forfeiture by peaceable re-entry, nor the enforcement of court judgments may then be employed by the landlord without consent of the administrator or permission of the court. An administrator will agree to a peaceable re-entry where the lease does not contribute to the attempted rescue of the firm, e.g. because the firm has rented too much office space and needs to downsize its corporate overheads in order to stay in business. In some instances, the administrator will very much welcome such a request from the landlord: Unlike a liquidator, the administrator has no right to terminate the lease.[211]

The more likely scenario, however, would seem to be that the administrator not consent to any of the above measures and the landlord instead seek permission of the court.

The issues to be considered by the court when deciding on such an application were set out in Re Atlantic Computer Systems plc (No 1) [1992] 2 WLR 367. Atlantic Computer Systems was a provider of IT services that was funded by several financial institutions that were at the same time its main clients. The leases in question were for computer equipment that was let to these financial institutions. The reasoning of the case nevertheless also applies to leases of real property. Nicholls LJ gave some general guidance as to the treatment of such applications, at the same time warning that "Parliament has left at large the discretion given to the court, and it is not for us to cut down that discretion or, as it was put in argument, to confine it within a straightjacket" (p. 543). Following the judgment, the landlord seeking to forfeit a lease of a tenant in administration has to show the following:

1. In general, the landlord needs to show that leave should be given;
2. Leave should only be granted if the purpose for which the administration order was made would not be impeded;

---

211 The technical term is to "disclaim" the lease (s. 178 Insolvency Act 1986). The effect of a disclaimer is that the tenant is released from liability. The landlord can claim his losses arising from the disclaimer. Rent arrears can be claimed in full, but future rents are discounted because of the accelerated receipt: Re Park Air Services plc (1999) The Times, 5 February.

3. The court has to balance the interests of lessors/landlords and the interests of other creditors;[212]

4. When balancing creditors' interests the court should give weight to the landlord's proprietary interests. It was noted that the interests' of secured creditors have to be particularly protected where the administration order was made in lieu of the insolvent firm's liquidation.[213] Equally, the protection of creditors with a proprietary interest has to be warranted except where infringements are unavoidable;

5. Leave should not be refused where the landlord would suffer a significant loss because of refusal. Loss includes any direct or indirect financial loss and may also include non-financial losses.[214] Nicholls LJ employs a reasoning that is based on the economic effects of granting or refusing leave by stating: "[I]f substantially greater loss would be caused to others by the grant of the leave, or loss which is out of all proportion to the benefit which leave would confer on the lessor, that may outweigh the loss to the lessor caused by a refusal" (p. 543). The court is therefore called to conduct an economic analysis of benefits and costs of granting leave. In assessing the losses the court will consider the company's financial position, its ability to pay rental arrears, details of the administration order and the administrator's proposals. Furthermore, the court will consider the perceived effects of leave on the administration's prospects of success. The court is hence asked to attach probabilities to the different possible outcomes.

Nicholls LJ stresses that the above list is not exhaustive and that courts may develop additional criteria in the future.

It is quite remarkable that in assessing whether to grant leave to initiate legal proceedings against a tenant in administration the court does not merely call

---

212 Nicholls LJ notes that the purpose of the statutory rules has to be kept in mind when balancing these interests. The prohibition of forfeiture and other legal processes is intended to enable the company to achieve the purposes for which the administration order was made. Nicholls LJ concludes that leave should be granted where the prohibition would lead to "inequitable" results (see p. 542). The author would suggest, however, that Nicholls LJ actually meant that the court should look into the economic function that the lease(s) play for the business and thus for the administration order's prospects of success. The word "inequitable" should thus be read as "economically inefficient".

213 Bristol Airport plc v Powdrill [1990] Ch 744 per Sir Nicolas Browne-Wilkinson V-C.

214 The judgment does not describe further what is to be seen as a non-financial loss, but it would seem that loss of reputation, image, and so on would be meant.

upon vague concepts such as "inequity". Instead, the court is required to assess the economic impact of either granting or not granting leave. The court essentially determines the relevance that the lease(s) have to the business. Where a turnaround seems possible without the leases, leave will be granted. At the same time, the court also tries to protect the interests of secured creditors. This is important in so far as otherwise the value of guarantees for weak-covenant tenants as a security would decrease; landlords would then either ask for higher deposits or refuse such tenants.

The law therefore equips the court with a wide degree of discretion as to the treatment of application for leave to initiate legal proceedings. The author would propose that such wide-ranging powers are only acceptable because of the special nature of the English legal system: judges are appointed from within the legal community and have served as senior lawyers (mostly barristers) before becoming judges (Slapper and Kelly, 2004, pp. 238-240). There is no "career judiciary" as found on the Continent. Because of their experience with commercial work as practicing lawyers, English judges are probably better equipped to handle case-by-case decisions based on commercial and economic arguments than judges in other jurisdictions.

5.4.4 Administrative Receivership and Receivership

Administrative Receivership and Receivership are procedures by which secured creditors can enforce their rights vis-à-vis a defaulting debtor.[215] Because of limited impact on the landlord-tenant relationship the topic will be discussed in outline only.

A distinction has to be drawn between Receivership and Administrative Receivership. Receivership may be used where property has been used as a security for a loan under a fixed charge[216] (Keenan, 1999, p. 464). Typically, the receiver would collect income from a property used to secure a loan or would sell the property. The receiver is not involved in actively managing the secured property. This type of receiver is also referred to as an LPA Receiver as his powers are set out in the Law of Property Act 1925.

An Administrative Receiver, on the other hand, is appointed where the security is under a floating charge; not a single asset is used as a security but a

---

215 (Administrative) Receivership is comparable to the German *Zwangsverwaltung* that enables mortgagees to enforce their claims against defaulting mortgagors.

216 Fixed charge: a specific asset has been used as a security. Fixed charges are to be distinguished from floating charges. Under a floating charge a pool of assets is used as a security; this pool is transformed ("crystallised") into a fixed charge at the occurrence of certain events, in particular creditor's default including insolvency.

pool of assets whose composition may vary over time. Such floating charges are mostly used where banks seek to secure debentures.[217] The Administrative Receiver is appointed where the prospects of repayment are better if the company is continued for some time and sold on a going concern basis. The Administrative Receiver may be appointed by the court on application of the secured creditor (Keenan, 1999, pp. 464-465).

Since the coming into force of the Enterprise Act 2002 the use of administrative receivers has been restricted (Parsons, 2006, p. 224). While the old law remains valid for creditors under a floating charge created before 15 September 2003, all holders of such charges created after this date can no longer appoint Administrative Receivers. Instead, they can now appoint administrators without leave of the court (Parsons, 2006, pp. 6-7). The law was changed because of an increasing perception that holders of a floating charge benefit from wide-ranging powers to enforce their claims at the expense of unsecured creditors.

Receivership and Administrative Receivership have little effect on the landlord's remedies. In particular, there is no bar on forfeiture either by court action or peaceable re-entry (Jourdan, 2002, p. 7). An exception is that execution of a judgment is not possible against goods which are the subject of a crystallised floating charge (Parsons, 2006, p. 204).

5.4.5 Liquidation

A company may be liquidated by a process known as winding-up. There are two forms of winding-up a company, compulsory winding-up and (rarer) voluntary winding-up. Here only compulsory winding-up is considered. It occurs where a company is unable to pay its debts[218] and all attempts to rescue the company have failed or would fail.[219]

Compulsory winding-up commences by an application to the court, known as presentation of a petition. This petition may be presented by the company, its directors or by its creditors.[220] The court is not obliged to follow the

---

217 Debenture: UK terminology for a corporate bond.

218 s. 122 (1) (f) Insolvency Act 1986.

219 Voluntary winding-up can be further distinguished into two categories: member's voluntary winding-up: the members (owners) of the firm seek to wind-up a solvent company, e.g. because the business carried on by the firm becomes obsolete; creditor's voluntary liquidation: the company is insolvent and its members pass a winding-up resolution and appoint a liquidator. In a subsequent meeting of creditors the appointment of the liquidator is approved or another liquidator is appointed (Keenan, 1999, pp. 488-504).

220 s. 124 (1) Insolvency Act 1986.

application.[221] If the court follows the application, a winding-up order is made and a liquidator appointed.[222]

Once an order is made all actions for debt against the company stop[223]; the company discontinues its business activities unless continuation for a limited time enhances the prospects of realising the firm's assets; the powers of the company's directors are removed[224] and all employees are automatically laid off[225].

The process of winding-up a company is then carried out by the liquidator. His duties are as follows (Keenan, 1999, p. 480):

1. Production of the list of contributories;
2. Collection of the company's assets;
3. Discharging the company's liabilities to its creditors;
4. Redistribution of the surplus to the contributories according to the rights attaching to their shares of the company capital.

When the company is fully wound-up, the court will issue an order dissolving the company.

Issuance of a winding-up order by the court has significant consequences for the landlord of an insolvent tenant. The effects of winding-up on the landlord's remedies are now discussed.

5.4.5.1 Effects of liquidation on distress for rent

Distress attempted or carried out after a winding-up petition is presented is void.[226] The landlord may theoretically apply to the court for leave to carry out the distress.[227] It is, however, unlikely that leave is granted for distress relating to rent arrears that have accrued before the winding-up order has been made. The court is likely to permit distress for rents that fell due after the petition had been presented (Parsons, 2006, p. 77). The courts are thus willing to protect the

---

221 The court may not issue an order e.g. where a small creditor's debt is not paid by the company but a substantial group of other creditors oppose liquidation. The court may then find that it is reasonable to follow the wishes of the majority and continue the company: Re ABC Coupler & Engineering Ltd [1961] 1 All ER 354.

222 The Official Receiver, a public official, will automatically become the liquidator until another liquidator is appointed (s. 136 Insolvency Act 1986).

223 s. 130 Insolvency Act 1986.

224 Fowlers v Broads Patent Night Light Co [1893] 1 Ch 724.

225 Chapman's Case (1866) LR 1 Eq 346.

226 s. 128 (1) Insolvency Act 1986.

227 s. 130 Insolvency Act 1986.

landlord's position to the extent that he should be no worse off than other creditors. While his rent arrears from the time before the petition had been presented are treated like the claims of other creditors, the courts recognise the landlord's vulnerable position after the presentation of the petition.

5.4.5.2 Effects of liquidation on the enforcement of judgments

Where a judgment for payment of, for example, rent arrears has been obtained against the tenant, enforcement will not be possible after a petition for winding-up has been presented.[228] This is a general rule and applies to all creditors of the insolvent company. As already discussed, the way of enforcing a claim against a tenant by obtaining a court judgment is unattractive for many other reasons, too. Landlords would thus either seek distress or forfeiture as more convenient remedies.

5.4.5.3 Effects of liquidation on forfeiture

Liquidation also impacts on the landlord's ability to forfeit a lease. A distinction needs to be made between forfeiture by peaceable re-entry and forfeiture by court action.

First of all, it should be underlined that the lease expressly needs to reserve the right to forfeit the lease in case of insolvency. The common law does not imply the right to forfeit the lease (see also the section on remedies in general). It is therefore essential that the forfeiture clause is not omitted and that the wording is sufficiently clear to describe the situations where forfeiture is permissible (Parsons, 2006, p. 39).

A landlord seeking forfeiture after a winding-up petition has been presented will require the court's leave to commence proceedings. As in case of forfeiture of a solvent tenant's lease it is also necessary that a notice in accordance with s. 146 of the Law of Property Act 1925 is served.[229] The notice has to refer to the reasons for forfeiture specified in the lease. If the lease does not state insolvency as a ground of forfeiture then the notice is void. It is advised that the landlord seeks an order for possession, a so-called "Blue Jeans Order"[230] (Parsons, 2006, p. 221). The Insolvency Service advises that such applications are likely to be

---

228 s. 128 (1) Insolvency Act 1986.

229 While s. 146 LPA 1925 lists some exceptions where a notice is not required, notices are mandatory for virtually all business leases.

230 Named after the case Re Blue Jeans Sales Ltd [1979] 1 WLR 362.

granted where a third party occupies the premises without the landlords consent.[231]

The landlord's right to forfeit a lease by peaceable re-entry where the tenant is insolvent has been clarified by the Insolvency Act 2000.[232] Pursuant to s. 128 of the Insolvency Act 1986 the landlord requires the court's consent for re-entry.

5.4.5.4 Disclaimer

An insolvent company remains liable to perform its obligations under a lease, e.g. to pay rents and service charges. The liquidator is, however, authorised to terminate leases and to discharge the insolvent company from its obligations under the lease.[233] The law permits the liquidator to disclaim "onerous property" which, for the purpose of the Insolvency Act, is defined as property that is unsaleable and gives rise to liabilities to pay money.[234] The liquidator is required to obtain leave from the court to disclaim a lease. Several other procedural safeguards have to be observed to protect mortgagees and under-lessees; the landlord is given the opportunity to object to the disclaimer.[235]

While it seems at a first glance counter-intuitive that the landlord would seek to object disclaimer in certain cases, it has to be noted that disclaimer may disadvantage him: Where the tenant is discharged from liability, the landlord may prove the losses arising from disclaimer. In Re Park Air Services plc (1999) The Times, 5 February it was held that losses of future rents had to be discounted to reflect for the time value of money and because the landlord regains control over his reversion earlier. While the landlord would be unlikely to receive his full debts, a high claim puts him in a better position in the liquidation procedure. The decision in Re Park Air Services gives insolvent tenants the possibility to avoid full liability for future rents by disclaiming the lease. The landlord may thus consider releasing the tenant from liability and negotiating this release without resort to the courts (Parsons, 2006, p. 211).[236]

---

231 http://www.insolvency.gov.uk/freedomofinformation/technical/TechnicalManual/Ch25-36/Chapter31/part3/part4/part_4.htm, accessed on 17 July 2008.

232 The Insolvency Act 2000 made several amendments to the 1986 Act.

233 s. 178 Insolvency Act 1986.

234 s. 178 (2); (3) (b) Insolvency Act 1986. It should be noted that long-leases with a low rent can sometimes be sold (comparable to the sale of a long-term building right, or *Erbbaurecht*, under German law). Leases are therefore not automatically disclaimed.

235 s. 178-182 Insolvency Act 1986.

236 A voluntary release from obligations is known as "surrender of the lease".

5.4.5.5 Security deposits

Deposits are a common safeguard against financial difficulties of the tenant. Nevertheless, there was until recently no authority in English law as to how such deposits should be treated in case of the tenant's insolvency. The particular question was whether the landlord could deduct rent arrears from the deposits or whether the deposit was part of the tenant's assets to be distributed among creditors. The issue was clarified in Re Greenport Ltd (in liquidation) [2000] All ER (D) 2083. As a result of this case, landlords should be able to deduct rents of insolvent tenants from deposits provided that the deed is properly worded (Jourdan, 2002, p. 10). Meticulous attention to the wording is required. In her judgment, Williamson QC quotes the lease contract, giving illustrating insights into the excessive verbiage that characterises common law contracts. In the author's opinion it is particularly unfortunate that terms such as "default", that should have a clear and unanimous meaning, are defined in the individual contracts. As a consequence, the meaning of the word "default", or other such terms, differs from contract to contract.[237] The lack of a coherent codification of property law thus reveals two potential sources of excessive transactions costs: 1) The need to draft lengthy contracts enunciating, in principle, every possible state of the world that may occur in future (see the quotation from the contract in Re Greenport) and 2) uncertainties that exists upon contracting as many legal issues will only clarify once they are brought before the courts. The common law is thus reacting to actual contracts rather than taking a law-creating approach as codification achieves.

5.5 Forfeiture and debt enforcement in England and Wales

The English landlord has a number of available remedies against a tenant failing to comply with his obligations under a lease. At first sight, these remedies are very much the same as the remedies provided by German law. The differences, which are indeed significant, are to be found in the detailed regulation of the remedies.

---

237 For the contract in Re Greenport Ltd, "default" was defined as "any failure by the tenant to pay (whether or not any formal demand has been made) the whole or any part of the rent reserved by the lease or any monies (including interest) payable pursuant to the lease ort his deed or any expense incurred by the landlord or due to the landlord in consequence of any failure by the tenant to observe and perform the covenants and obligations of and the conditions binding the tenant contained in the lease ort his deed, or the determination of the lease before the expiration of the term by forfeiture or by the disclaimer of any liquidator or trustee in bankruptcy of the estate of the tenant or otherwise than by agreement".

The landlord's remedies against a tenant in breach of covenant are (Gray and Gray, 2006, p. 523):

1. Actions for arrears of rent:
2. Forfeiture of the lease;
3. Distress for unpaid rent;
4. Damages for breach of covenant;
5. Injunction and specific performance.

5.5.1 Actions for arrears of rent

A landlord obviously has the right to sue a tenant for payment of rent arrears. English law does not have an equivalent to the German type of payment order (see above) so that the landlord must always resort to the court track.[238] The civil process underwent reforms following the Woolf Inquiry which was set up in 1994 to investigate why litigation was very costly and time consuming and raised so many uncertainties (Slapper and Kelly, 2004, p. 295)[239]. The Inquiry and a subsequent report resulted in the Civil Procedure Act 1997 and the Civil Procedure Rules 1998. The key features of the reformed civil process are (1) the monitoring of case progress by an IT system, (2) the allocation of claims to county and high courts on the small claims track, fast track or multi-track, depending on the value and perceived complexity of the case and (3) documentation by questionnaires to allocate claims (Slapper and Kelly, 2004, p. 300).

The landlord's right to sue is limited to a maximum of six years of arrears.[240] Traditionally, there is no duty to mitigate losses in English law. Therefore, if a tenant abandons the premises and fails to pay the rent, the landlord is under no obligation to re-let the premises but can instead sue the tenant for the accruing arrears.[241] The Law Commission has proposed to reduce the limitation period for the recovery of rent to three years from the landlord's actual or constructive

---

238 There is, however, a small claims procedure for claims below £ 5,000 (Slapper and Kelly, 2004, p. 298).

239 Lord Woolf expressed his view of the civil justice system as follows: [...] the key problems facing civil justice today are cost, delay, and complexity. These three are interrelated and stem from the uncontrolled nature of the litigation process. In particular, there is no clear judicial responsibility for managing individual cases or for the overall administration of the civil courts (Lord Woolf, Access to Justice, Final Report, 1996).

240 s. 19 Limitation Act 1980.

241 Boyer v Warbey [1953] 1 QB 234, CA.

knowledge of the default or 10 years from the date of this default, whichever period expires first.[242]

The assessment of English actions for rent to provide efficient incentives has to come to a negative conclusion. First of all, the lack of transparency of the costs and time of court proceedings deter landlords from going to court. The most likely outcome of starting a case will be that some form of settlement will be reached. The landlord will thus normally not be able to recover the full amount actually owed to him. The non-standardised fees of solicitors and barristers furthermore add to the spiralling costs of court proceedings. The relative ineffectiveness of actions for rent compared to other remedies (e.g. forfeiture, see below) could result in a too early termination of leases. To recall Hax (1985, p. 81), business should be continued if the expectation value of continuation is higher than the expectation value of winding-up the business (net of costs). Where the legal system does not provide the landlord with an appropriate remedy to protect his commercial interests that would at the same time allow the tenant's business to continue, other remedies may be resorted to unnecessarily often. It is suggested that where a landlord does not have other remedies than terminating the lease this will lead to a situation where business tenants that are only in temporary difficulties will also be subject to eviction even though continuation would lead to higher expectation values.

In that sense, the English landlord and tenant law is contradicting the objectives of English insolvency law (see above). While the insolvency law's primary objective is the continuation of businesses, the remedies available to a commercial landlord often leave little alternatives but to terminate the lease.

Another deficiency of the English law is that a landlord cannot sue for "payment and forfeiture" but that the remedies of action for rent arrears and forfeiture work independently based on their individual rules.

5.5.2 Forfeiture of leases

Forfeiture of the lease is the unilateral termination of the lease by the landlord for failure to pay rent or comply with other covenants.

Compared to German law, the main differences are:

1. The extra-judicial nature of the remedy;
2. The possibility of relying on self help;
3. The lack of statutory default rules.

242 Law Com No. 270 (2001), cited in Gray and Gray (2006, p. 535).

Forfeiture is also called the "right of re-entry" because the remedy gives the landlord the right to "re-enter" the premises of a tenant in breach of covenant (Gray and Gray, 2006, p. 524).

The function of forfeiture has been characterised by Arden J as the landlord's ultimate security against the non-payment of rent and his ultimate insurance in respect of the commercial investment represented by the lease.[243]

A major difference to German law is that the landlord's right to forfeit the lease has to be expressly reserved in the lease. The courts will not imply a right of re-entry in a lease.[244] There is thus no default rule comparable to s. 543 of the German civil code that would by default give any landlord the right to terminate the lease without notice upon the occurrence of certain breaches of covenant. The financial consequences for a landlord not entering the right to forfeit in the lease can be severe. In the worst case, the landlord would have to bear the defaulting tenant until the lease comes to its contractually stipulated end. It is needless to say that small landlords in particular are vulnerable to omit entering the right in their leases.

Another major difference to German law is the enforcement mechanism. In German law, enforcement will always be by way of legal proceedings (or exceptionally a lease certified by a notary) and a court-appointed bailiff. English law, in quite sharp contrast, gives the landlord the right to enforce forfeiture by physical entry upon the premises. Possession proceedings are also an alternative but not mandatory.[245] This means that a landlord wishing to enforce his right to forfeit a lease is not obliged to resort to the courts at all. The landlords can equally resort to self-help. This illustrates why forfeiture of a lease is an attractive remedy compared to costly and lengthy actions for rent arrears.

Further differences between the English and German law of forfeiture are the English doctrine of waiver and the rules on remediable breaches.

5.5.2.1 Doctrine of waiver

The doctrine of waiver demands that in order to forfeit a lease the landlord must not, before re-entry, treat the tenant in a "tenant-like" manner.[246] Treating the tenant in a "tenant-like" manner encompasses all interactions that normally

243 Inntrepreneur Pub Co (CPC) Ltd v Langton [2000] 1 EGLR 34.

244 Except in the commercially irrelevant case of equitable leases that arise when the lease lacks certain formalities to be classified as a legal lease; Chester v Buckingham Travel Ltd [1981] 1 WLR 96.

245 Billson v Residential Apartments Ltd [1992] 1 AC 494, CA; reversed [1992] 1 AC 494, HL.

246 Grimwood v Moss (1871-72) LR 7 CP 360.

characterise the relationship between landlord and tenant. To put it differently, the doctrine of waiver would waive the landlord's right to re-entry if, with notice of the tenant's breach, the landlord deals with the tenant on the basis that the tenancy is continuing.[247] This would especially be the case where the landlord makes a demand for payment of rent (in many older leases, rent does not become due automatically but has to be expressly demanded) or where the landlord accepts the rent.[248] The effect of the doctrine is illustrated in Central Estates (Belgravia) Ltd v Woolgar (No 2) [1972] 1 WLR 1048: The landlord, Central Estates, decided to forfeit the lease for breach of covenant. A memo was circulated among the landlord's property agents not to make a demand for rent or accept the rent. One of the employees did not take notice of this memo and made a demand for rent. The tenant, when paying the rent, knew that the landlord had the intention to forfeit the lease and that this intention was unchanged. The court nevertheless ruled that the right to forfeiture had been waived. The doctrine of waiver can thus become a trap to landlords. Whether they intend to continue the lease or forfeit it is irrelevant. One could imagine that historically the doctrine of waiver was developed to protect ill-informed tenants from landlords who would otherwise have the lease forfeited after the tenant has actually complied with other covenants (e.g. forfeiture of the lease for breach of repair covenant while the tenant has continued to pay rent). Today, however, the doctrine of waiver does seem outdated: Breach of covenant is easily made known to the tenant by serving a notice and especially with regard to non-payment of rent there is usually no lack of clarity as to the nature of the breach.

5.5.2.2 Self-help and court orders

Considering the length and costliness of a lawsuit in England, forfeiture is an attractive remedy to commercial landlords because it does not require the landlord to go to court. With the exception of forfeiture for breach of a repairing covenant, the landlord of business premises can recover possession without a court order.[249]

---

247 Law Com No 303 1.10.

248 It should by the way be noticed that bank transfers directly from one account to another are fairly uncommon in the UK. Payments are either made by cheque or by direct debit, whereby the creditor is given the authority to withdraw the outstanding amount from the debtor's account.

249 s. 1 Leasehold Property (Repairs) Act 1938.

As long as the landlord does not fail to serve a statutory notice that may be required (see below), the so-called "peaceable re-entry" is an option.[250]

There remains a risk of criminal liability pursuant to s. 6 (1) of the Criminal Law Act 1977.[251] The re-entry by the landlord has to be "peaceable" so that it cannot be effected when the premises are occupied by the tenant or its employees. Gray and Gray (2006, p. 526) thus suggest that the risk of criminal liability can be circumvented if re-entry takes place outside business hours or at weekends when the premises are unoccupied. Conversely, peaceable re-entry would thus never be possible if the tenant has some security service or receptionist on the premises who guards the property around the clock.

Being able to circumvent criminal liability by re-entry upon the premises at night or on a Sunday again highlights the unfortunate nature of the English law of forfeiture: It encourages a form of behaviour that, while being perfectly lawful in a strictly legal sense, still has a certain rogue nature to it. It furthermore creates uncertainty and highlights the archaic nature of English land law.

Peaceable re-entry was reviewed by the House of Lords in Billson v Residential Apartments Ltd. [1992] 1 AC 494. The Lords affirmed that a landlord's re-entry without the tenant's knowledge remained possible. The facts of the case highlight the legal uncertainty created by a landlord's re-entry: After serving a notice on the tenant that the lease was to be forfeited, the landlord peaceably re-entered the premises at 6 a.m. about 12 days after the notice was served. The landlord changed the locks on the doors and fixed notices to the doors informing that the lease had been forfeited. Later that day, however, builders working for the tenant broke into the premises to continue their construction works. The question that came up before the House of Lords was whether the temporary possession by the landlord sufficed to forfeit the lease or whether the action by the builders defeated re-entry. Further questions arose as

250 For example confirmed in Kataria v Safeland plc (1997) 75 P & CR D30, CA: in this case the Court of Appeal confirmed the validity of re-entry without a court order. At first instance, the behaviour of the landlord regarding the conduct of forfeiture has been described as "monstrous". In the CA, Brooke LJ, however, explained: "[...] whatever view might be taken of the landlord's conduct in a court of morals, in this court we are bound to hold that the landlord's conduct was lawful".

251 Violence for securing entry: s. 6 (1) reads: Subject to the following provisions of this section, any person who, without lawful authority, uses or threatens violence for the purpose of securing entry into any premises for himself or for any other person is guilty of an offence, provided that (a) there is someone present on those premises at the time who is opposed to the entry which the violence is intended to secure; and (b) the person using or threatening violence knows that that is the case.

to the remedies available to the tenant. It was held that the temporary possession sufficed but the Lords also expressed their disliking for such surreptitious methods of re-entry.

5.5.2.3 *Pre-conditions for forfeiture*

Before a landlord can forfeit a lease for breach of covenant, he has to observe certain formalities. These formalities particularly include the serving of notices informing the tenant of the breach and giving the tenant the opportunity to rectify the breach where possible.

These necessary formalities depend on the nature of the breach. The formalities required for forfeiture because of non-payment of rent differ from the formalities for forfeiture for breach of other covenants. The approach taken by the courts to grant relief from forfeiture also depends on the grounds for which forfeiture is sought.

5.5.2.4 *Non-payment of rent: formalities*

It is a common law requirement that re-entry must be preceded by a "formal demand" for rent, unless this requirement is waived in the lease. Furthermore, there is a statutory waiver of the formal demand that applies in certain circumstances.[252] Today, almost all commercial leases exclude the need for a formal demand. The Law Commission thus holds the law concerning formal demands as "obsolete".[253]

One should thus notice that in order to create a commercially attractive lease, it is necessary to include the right to re-enter in the lease and then also to exclude the need for a formal demand of rent. The lack of clear default rules in the law thus creates unnecessary transaction costs and risks to landlords who fail to include or exclude certain provisions in the lease.

The German civil code is in that sense more effective in reducing transaction costs as a lease can actually be a fairly short document because of the various default rules in the code. As these defaults (particularly with regard to breach of covenant) are also maintaining a relatively fair balance between landlord and tenant the risk stemming from failure to include certain provisions in the lease is not as high as in English law.

---

252 s. 210 Common Law Procedure Act 1852.

253 Law Com No 303, 1.12 (6).

The bodies representing solicitors and barristers both publicly declare that the law on forfeiture is in urgent need of reform.[254] However, it should not be forgotten that each additional provision that needs to be included in a lease gives solicitors the opportunity to charge for it. A fairly efficient regime of default rules would significantly reduce the need to include substantial verbiage in lease contracts. The common law, on the other hand, provides an attractive job machine for lawyers.

5.5.2.5 Relief from forfeiture for non-payment of rent

Another issue is the willingness of the courts to grant relief from forfeiture. In contrast to the German law which defines "tenant default" in a fairly clear manner, the English law is fairly opaque regarding the rent arrears that need to have accrued to justify forfeiture of the lease.

Gray and Gray (2006, pp. 530-531) observe a general tendency by the courts to restrict the exercise of forfeiture for non-payment of rent. The result is that re-entry will be refused where the tenant pays off all rent arrears and accrued costs (Howard v Fanshawe) [1895] 2 Ch 581. The right to forfeit a lease is seen as a "security" for the rent, to use the wording employed in the old case of Wadman v Calcraft (1804) 10 Ves 67 (also Sanders v Pope (1806) 12 Ves 282, 289). This function of forfeiture as an ultimate security is thus a very old principle. As a result, courts will always grant relief, save in the most exceptional circumstances (Gill v Lewis [1956] 2 QB 1). Newer cases have shown some willingness not to grant relief where the tenant seems to use the granting of relief strategically by using procedural rules to delay payment.[255]

Because of the ancient nature of the rules, the approach taken by courts to grant relief is not suitable for modern times and economically inefficient. In particular, no account is taken of the time value of money. The judges deciding the cases on forfeiture in the 19th century did not consider the fact that money paid today may be worth more than money paid later. This is not surprising because by that time interest bearing accounts were rare and most people probably had their wealth in physical assets rather than money. Furthermore, mortgages and thus the need to meet re-payment plans were very rare. To wait for a payment did thus not lead to so severe consequences.

Today, however, with highly leveraged real estate investments and the need to meet financial commitments, this view of relief to forfeiture can no longer be

254 Law Com No 303.

255 Somers Mews Investments v Miller (unreported), 29 January 1982, CA; see also the principle of equity that those who come to a court of equity need to do so with clean hands.

supported. It has to be recognised that delayed payments should also give rise to forfeiture because of their potential interference with the landlord's business activities and the relevance of the time value of money.

The procedural rules governing relief from forfeiture put the landlord at a further disadvantage. If possession proceedings are brought against the tenant in court, the court will, as stated above, grant relief if all owed rent and arrears are paid before the date of the trial.[256] Granting relief is mandatory in this case.

Even after this date, however, courts have discretion to grant relief from forfeiture where costs and rent arrears are paid after a court order for possession has been issued but before the premises have been re-let to another tenant.[257] Furthermore, if the landlord has already recovered possession by peaceable re-entry, the court may grant relief within six months after the landlord's re-entry.[258]

Even if grounds for relief are not statutorily defined, the court may still grant relief out of its equitable jurisdiction. This leads Gray and Gray (2006, p.531) to conclude that "relief against forfeiture tends to be withheld only in the most exceptional circumstances."

The point is illustrated by Public Trustee v Westbrook [1965] 1 WLR 1160, CA: The circumstances of the case are difficult to grasp because the lease in question was a long-lease of land upon which the houses had been bombed out in 1940 and had not been rebuilt. The situation was further complicated by the presence of sub-tenancies and sub-sub-tenancies. As a result, no rent was paid for twenty-two years. The Court of Appeal held that in these exceptional circumstances no relief from forfeiture could be granted.

The case is clearly surprising to (Continental-) European observers. How can it be that no rent has been paid for twenty-two years and still the court does not find it easy to declare that no relief from forfeiture could be granted? The answer to this question is found by examining the role that leases play in English land law. There are the typical short-leases for offices or flats that are similar in their function to the types of contractual leases that are typically found in Germany. Then, again, English lease law also regulates the long-leases that are not comparable to German leases. These long-leases are often granted for land for surprisingly long terms. They are comparable, to some extent, to what in Germany would be an *Erbbaurecht* (long-term heritable building right). In England, unlike in Germany, these long-leases are very common. Historically,

---

256 s. 212 Common Law Procedure Act 1852; s. 138(2) County Courts Act 1984.

257 s. 210 Common Law Procedure Act 1852; s. 138(3)-(5), (9A) County Courts Act 1984.

258 s. 139(2) County Courts Act 1984.

they have allowed the owner of the freehold, often an aristocrat, to grant rights out of his land while retaining ultimate control over it.[259]

Considering the facts of the case, the twenty-two years in Westbrook do then not seem so outrageously long. Lord Denning summarised the facts as follows:

> Before the war the site was covered by about 15 houses. The freeholder was the Earl of Derby. A head lease for 999 years had been granted from 1853 of this site of 15 houses at a rent of £22 5s a year. The head lease is now vested in the Public Trustee who has, from the beginning until now, always paid his rent of £22 5s to the Earl of Derby's estate. Out of that head lease there was granted a sub-lease of five of the sites of the houses for 990 years from 1853 at £15 a year. The holder of that sub-lease is unknown: he has disappeared. Out of that sub-lease, in 1897, there was granted a sub-sub-lease of two of the houses covering a site of 195 square yards at a ground rent of £8 a year. Until recently, that sub-sub-lease was vested in a brewery company. I expect that before the war the brewery company let the houses to occupiers who held sub-sub-sub-leases of the houses.

Lord Denning's description of the ownership structure highlights the often fairly convoluted nature of leases, sub-leases, and yet more leases created out of the sub-leases. The facts of the case also describe a concept of leases alien to the Continental reader. Remarkable is also the length of the leases: the closest German equivalent, the long-term building rights, are granted for a maximum period of 99 years and are not treated as leases but rather as freehold ownership.[260] For the holder of an English long-lease there is, in effect, little difference to holding as a freeholder.

While these cases could be seen as curiosities of English land law that have little impact upon modern commercial leases, the following has to be noted: Under English land law, a lease is treated the same whether it is for nine or 900 years. This means that the law of forfeiture also is the same for either lease. This multi-applicability to two types of leases that fulfil very different economic functions is highly undesirable. It is the reason why the laws governing forfeiture have to be fairly imprecise and give the courts so much discretion. The rules cannot, under the current treatment of leases under English law, be more precise because then the "one-size fits all"-approach to the law of leases could no longer be maintained. The fairly ambiguous rules on forfeiture give judges the ability to effectively consider each case on its individual merits.

Another issue may be surprising to the European reader: it is normally thought on the Continent that English law is particularly investor-friendly and tends to protect the rights of capital owners much stronger than in Continental

---

259 Many dwellings in England are built on land which is held on a long-lease. The lease has to be purchased like a freehold and the rent is typically very low.

260 See for example s. 21 Erbbau VO (old version): ability to mortgage long-term building rights.

legal systems. England is often used as an example of de-regulation and the freedom of markets. These developments are, however, fairly recent if compared to the long history of English land law. While the economic opening and reforms in the United Kingdom began with the coming into power of Mrs. Thatcher, English land law has a much longer history.

The economic incentives caused by this historically developed law are, however, far from efficient.

From an *ex ante* perspective, the wide discretion given to judges and the uncertainties created by the ambiguous rules could cause landlords to be overly restrictive in the selection of tenants.

5.5.2.6 Breach of covenants other than non-payment of rent: formalities

The formal requirement for forfeiture for a breach of covenant other than non-payment of rent is regulated in the Law of Property Act 1925 (LPA 1925). Such other breaches most typically relate to the tenant's failure to comply with repairing obligations, but can also include non-monetary issues such as nuisance or other unacceptable behaviour.

Under s. 146 of the LPA 1925 the landlord has to serve a notice on the tenant informing him of the nature of the breach. This notice is commonly referred to as a "section 146 notice". Unless such a notice is validly served and the tenant is given a reasonable time to rectify his breach, the lease cannot be forfeited. The section 146 notice has to contain the following:

1. Specification of the breach of covenant;

2. Request that the tenant rectifies the breach if it is "capable of remedy";

3. Typically a demand for compensation in money for the breach.

The purpose of the section 146 notice is to provide basic procedural safeguards for the tenant. Slade LJ described the notice's role as "to give even tenants who have hitherto lacked the will or the means to comply with their obligations one last chance to summon up that will or find the necessary means before the landlord re-enters".[261]

261 Expert Clothing Service & Sales Ltd v Hillgate House Ltd [1986] Ch 340, CA.

5.5.2.7 Breach of a repairing covenant

If the section 146 notice is served for breach of a repairing covenant it has, in addition to the above stated elements, to inform the tenant that he may benefit from certain rights under the Leasehold Property (Repairs) Act 1938. This Act prescribes that forfeiture by re-entry is not possible for breach of a repairing covenant if the lease meets certain conditions.[262] It is then mandatory for the landlord to obtain a court order.[263] This limitation of the use of extra-judicial remedies was introduced to limit the vulnerability of tenants to unwarranted claims of failure to comply with repair obligations: as repair works are, because of their very nature, often a subject of dispute, there would otherwise be the risk that a landlord uses a spurious claim to forfeit the lease perhaps because another tenant would be willing to pay a higher rent.

5.5.2.8 Remediability of the breach

An important question in determining whether the lease can be forfeited is whether the breach is capable of remedy. This quite sharply distinguishes the English from the German rules as under German law the question is rather whether it would be reasonable to accept a continuation of the current lease.[264] Whether the breach as such can be remedied is not a major issue under German lease law. For forfeiture under English law, however, the remediability of the breach is the "ultimate question".[265] Slade LJ in Expert Clothing explained that a breach was capable of remedy where the landlord could be restored within reasonable time to the position in which he would have been had there been no breach. It was also pointed out that forfeiture will be rare because the breach can normally be remedied (Gray and Gray, 2006, p. 529).

A distinction is drawn between breaches of positive and negative covenants. A positive covenant requires a certain action or activity (e.g. repair) while a negative covenant stipulates that something ought not to be done (e.g. no noise between 8 p.m.-6 a.m.). Breach of positive covenants is normally always remediable because performance, albeit belated, cures the breach. Belated performance may be compensated for by adequate money compensation in

262 This rule applies to leases for a term of seven or more years, three or more of which have to remain unexpired at the time of expiry of the lease; ss. 1(1), 7(1) Leasehold Property (Repairs) Act 1938.

263 s. 1(3) Leasehold Property (Repairs) Act 1938.

264 s. 543 (1) BGB.

265 Slade LJ in Expert Clothing Service & Sales Ltd v Hillgate House Ltd [1986] Ch 340, CA.

addition to performance.[266] The courts have nowadays adopted the approach to also view negative covenants as remediable provided that "the mischief caused by the tenant can be removed" if the tenant fulfils his obligations.[267] Only the gravest breaches are seen as non-remediable.[268] In most cases, however, late compliance with the covenant and additional money compensation suffice to avoid forfeiture.[269] There are a few cases where the court held forfeiture to be inevitable; these cases, however, had to be decided on the basis of rather unusual facts so that the normal rule is that tenants can protect their lease by late compliance and the payment of money compensation.[270]

In addition to the common law rules on remedial breaches, the court is also given discretion to grant relief from forfeiture under s. 146(2) LPA 1925. Again, the court is given wide ranging powers to grant relief. After receiving a section 146 notice the tenant can apply to the court for relief. The tenant's right to apply for relief is finally extinguished only when the landlord has obtained a judgment against the tenant and has already entered into possession, or where the landlord peaceably re-entered and the tenant failed within a reasonable time to apply for relief (Gray and Gray, 2006, pp. 531-532). In deciding whether to grant relief, the court will consider the severity of the breach, the relation of the value of the property and the monetary value of the breach, and the extent of the damage caused by the breach. The landlord's position must not have been "irrevocably damaged".[271] The courts will therefore normally grant relief whenever the breach is either comparatively small or was committed unintentionally or where a remediable breach has been cured. Relief is normally not granted where the breach is not remediable, but these cases will be exceptional (Gray and Gray, 2006, pp. 532-533).[272]

The law of forfeiture for breach of a covenant other than non-payment of rent is again surprisingly ambiguous and fairly tenant-friendly. Forfeiture is only possible in the most exceptional circumstances.

---

266 Expert Clothing Service & Sales Ltd v Hillgate House Ltd [1986] Ch 340, CA.

267 Staughton LJ in Savva and Savva v Hussein (1996) 73 P & CR 150, CA.

268 E.g. assignment of a lease without consent as the negative covenant not to assign cannot be remedied by "re-assigning" the lease; Scala House and District Property Co Ltd v Forbes [1974] QB 575, CA.

269 Bingham LJ in Bass Holdings Ltd v Morton Music Ltd [1988] Ch 493, CA.

270 Such unusual cases include: Rugby School (Governors) v Tannahill [1935] 1 KB 87, CA (tenant used premises as brothel; court found a permanent "stigma" attached to the lease) and Van Haarlam v Kasner (1992) 64 P & CR 214 (tenant was a convicted foreign spy and carried out his operations from the premises).

271 Clark (WG) (Properties) Ltd v Dupre Properties Ltd [1992] Ch 297.

272 An example of an irremediable breach was Duraven Securities Ltd v Holloway (1982) 264 Estates Gazette 709, CA: use of the premises as a "sex shop".

Compared to German law, it is particularly interesting that there is no instrument to evict a tenant on the basis that a continuation of the tenancy is unreasonable because of a continuous breach of covenants. English law allows forfeiture only where there is a definite and major breach. The scenario that would appear to be more common, that a tenant is somewhat "notoriously difficult" and is constantly sub-performing his obligations, e.g. to repair, is quite problematic for the landlord as in such case there would be little chance to obtain a forfeiture order. This sub-performance would, however, be a typical result of moral hazard exacerbated by situations where the tenant feels that his contractual rent is excessive and he tries to reduce expenses by a reduced performance of obligations under the lease covenants. This demonstrates a link between the rent adjustment mechanisms and the enforcement mechanisms: If rent adjustment is organised so that it preserves economic incentives, it is not so necessary to have remedies against the "small" breaches of covenants. If rent adjustment mechanisms fail to maintain these incentives, however, the landlord will have to rely on a system of enforcement that is also effective in sanctioning such smaller breaches.

As for forfeiture for non-payment of rent, it should be noted that the rules discussed here apply to both short leases and long leases: to the 15-year office lease as well as the 150-year long lease for a parcel of land. The discretion afforded to the court is thus necessary to accommodate these different agreements under a common legal rule. More desirable, however, would be a lease code regulating short leases in a similar fashion as the German civil code.

5.5.2.9 Position of tenant where forfeiture is granted

Once a lease is forfeited, the position of the English tenant is comparatively weaker than in Germany: when the landlord re-enters the premises the tenant becomes a trespasser and the landlord may use reasonable force to evict him (Gray and Gray, 2006, p. 533). The English landlord has thus much wider powers than his German counterpart who always has to rely on a court-appointed bailiff to enforce his rights.

The forfeiture of a lease also destroys all subleases that were created out of the head lease.[273] It should be recalled that such subleases are very common in England so that this is not merely a theoretical problem. Subtenants thus have an independent right to apply for relief to the court. The court may grant relief on such terms as it thinks fit.[274] The court can even award a new tenancy to the

273 Great Western Railway Co v Smith (1876) 2 Ch D 235.
274 s. 146(4) LPA 1925.

former sub-tenant, which may not, however, be for a longer term than the tenant had under the sublease.[275]

5.5.3 Distress for unpaid rent

Distress for rent is a self-help remedy comparable to the German *Vermieterpfandrecht*. The landlord is entitled to seize goods belonging to the tenant and sell them. The detailed rules are governed by ancient statutes and there have been repeated calls to abolish the remedy.[276] Because of the extra-judicial nature of the remedy – it is not necessary to obtain a court order – the remedy may also violate human rights under the European Convention on Human Rights (Gray and Gray, 2006, p. 535).[277]

5.5.4 Damages for breach of covenant

Damages for breaches other than non-payment of rent may be awarded and are calculated on the usual contractual basis, i.e. to put the landlord in the position in which he would have been if there had been no breach (Gray and Gray, 2006, pp. 535-536).[278]

5.5.5 Injunction and specific performance

Finally, the court may in exceptional circumstances also award the equitable remedies of injunction and specific performance.[279] Gray and Gray (2006, p. 536) point out that courts do not award the remedy where money compensation is also appropriate. In some cases specific performance to comply with repairing covenants has been ordered by the court where the lease did not contain a forfeiture clause (as stated above, forfeiture is not a default rule but has to be entered into the contract).[280]

---

275 s. 138(9) County Courts Act 1984.

276 Statute of Marlborough from the 12th century.

277 The ECHR is incorporated into English law under the Human Rights Act 1998. Distress for rent may violate Art. 6 (right to a fair and public hearing) and Art. 1, Protocol 1 (right to peaceful enjoyment of possessions).

278 An exception applies to damages for non-compliance with a repairing covenant. In this case the damages may not exceed the reduction in property value caused by the breach: s. 18(1) Landlord and Tenant Act 1927.

279 The award of equitable remedies is at the court's discretion while common law remedies (damages) have to be awarded if the necessary grounds for award are met.

280 Rainbow Estates v Tokenhold Ltd [1999] Ch 64.

5.5.6 Evaluation of the remedies and suggestions for reform

Comparing English and German insolvency law and the remedies available to the landlord of a tenant in default leads to two principle findings: The remedies available to a German landlord are characterised by clear rules provided by the Civil Code. The meaning of "default" is defined in the Code and there is little ambiguity as to when default occurs at least regarding rent arrears. Both landlord and tenant can therefore easily identify situations that are likely to lead to forfeiture. Once the conditions prescribed by the Civil Code are met, there is little, if any, scope for judicial discretion.

English remedies, on the other hand, allow for a high degree of judicial discretion and thus create uncertainty. It was described that this uncertainty is partly due to the applicability of the law to several forms of leases that fulfil economically distinct roles. The introduction of a landlord and tenant code as recommended by the Law Commission would thus be highly advisable.[281]

281 Law Com No 303.

6 Summary, concluding remarks and outlook

The purpose of this study is to assess the efficiency of the regulation of commercial property leases in England and Germany from the perspective of a property investor or landlord. The introduction established that investment in real estate is increasing and that there is particular growth in cross-border investments. The surge of new financial instruments that increase liquidity of property investments is a further observation. The financial crisis and following recession have caused turmoil on the markets and particularly affected the UK market and investors from the UK and US. The internationalisation of real estate investments will surely continue and therefore there is a need to compare contractual structures. The author believes that the current discussion surrounding inflation risks following the expansive monetary policy of central banks will again bring investors' attention to real estate as a hedge against inflation.

The UK and Germany are Europe's most important property markets but differ significantly in terms of market structure, market participants and legal framework.

The English real estate market is characterised by a high degree of professionalism, a strong concentration of investment activities on the Greater London area, and a strong valuation profession. This profession, the Chartered Surveyors, is characterised by self-regulation, a setting of own professional standards, and a valuation practice that closely reflects actual market prices.

The German property market, on the other hand, is fragmented because of the country's federal structure, and until recently there have been only few nationwide investors. There is no strong valuation profession compared to UK Chartered Surveyors. German valuers tend to focus on construction-related issues and valuation is often not meant to reflect market prices but rather construction costs. There are comparatively few German valuers and their professional education is not uniformly regulated. German valuers are not often involved in property transactions and are confined to a relatively limited scope of tasks.

As a result of these institutional and structural differences, the international real estate consultancy Jones Lang LaSalle (2006, p. 10) found that the UK property market is one of the most transparent worldwide while the German market is not ranked in the group of the most transparent markets.

In order to reduce the overwhelming scope of real estate regulation, the author decided to limit his analysis to two issues that are particularly relevant to investors' cash flows: The adjustment of rents over the term of the lease and the position of the landlord in case of tenant default or tenant insolvency. Both topics are particularly relevant to a landlord, be he an institutional investor or a "small" landlord, as they ultimately determine the influence of legal regulation on the value of a property. It was shown that market prices for commercial property are quoted in the form of a required yield, which is determined by the market and the annual rent of a property. The mechanism by which the contractual rent is adjusted therefore has a direct impact on a property's market value. The adjustment mechanism becomes particularly important in volatile markets where market rents fluctuate. The landlord's remedies against tenant default also secure the property's value as a property with defaulting tenants, i.e. a reduced rental cash flow, would generate a lower market price. Rent adjustment and remedies against defaulting tenants thus secure the landlord's current rental cash flows as well as the property value. The outcome of the analysis of these two topics is thus thought to serve as a proxy to characterise the overall nature of the countries' regulations of commercial real estate leases.

In order to analyse these topics, two methodologies are employed: the economic analysis of long-term contracts and the economic analysis of insolvency law.

The analysis of the first topic, rent adjustment, revealed that the methods by which contractual rents are adjusted over the term of the lease differ significantly between England and Germany.

The preferred rent adjustment mechanism in England is rent review, the adjustment of rent according to a rent appraisal by a third party, most commonly a Chartered Surveyor. In terms of economic efficiency, this system theoretically offers a number of advantages: as rents are determined by the third party with reference to market comparables, incentive problems would be reduced to a minimum. In practice, however, contracts generally stipulate that rents can only go up so that a tenant is not protected in a falling market. Behavioural studies also indicate that third-party valuers may not always act objectively. A major disadvantage of rent review clauses is the high transaction cost associated both with drafting such clauses and implementing rent reviews. While some guidance is provided by the British property industry's voluntary Code of Practice, there are no legal defaults available that would aid in drafting these clauses. As a consequence, each rent review clause is individually drafted and these clauses have thus caused substantial litigation. Rent review clauses are therefore efficient for big landlords who have professional property managers and where drafting and management costs are not so significant because of the large size of transactions. In Germany, rent review is virtually unused. This has two reasons:

Firstly, the German valuation profession would, by numbers and qualification, not be able to implement rent reviews for a large number of leases. Secondly, legal restrictions make the use of rent review in Germany infeasible.

In Germany, most commercial leases are adjusted by indexation. Rents are linked to the German consumer price index. The advantages of this method are transparency and low transaction costs. Assistance of a third party, such as a Chartered Surveyor, is not necessary to operate this mechanism. The consumer price index does, however, not reflect changes in market rents of commercial property: While rents fluctuate, the CPI normally shows a steady, moderate increase. As a consequence, the rents that sitting tenants pay may differ significantly from current market rents. Some institutional investors view indexation as a very positive feature of German real estate: It essentially combines stable cash flows with the chance that the property will appreciate in value. Indexation is not used in the UK, which may largely be due to a different inflationary environment particularly in the 1960s/70s and a more volatile property market.

Turnover rents are frequently used for retail properties in Germany but rarely used in the UK. This may largely be due to the drafting of these clauses in UK leases and a negative effect on property valuation where such clauses are in place. Turnover clauses nevertheless offer a wide-range of advantages, in particular an alignment of the landlord's and the tenant's interests. In order to operate a turnover clause, there needs to be a close link between the success of the tenant's business and the business premises. This effectively reduces the application of turnover rents to retail premises.

Graduated and fixed rents are used in both countries for rather short and small leases, while graduated rents are sometimes also used in larger German leases, which virtually never happens in the UK.

The second aspect that is analysed is the position of landlord and tenant in case of tenant default. The economic analysis of insolvency law is employed to scrutinise the regulations in both countries. Two issues are discussed: the general remedies available to the landlord of a defaulting tenant and the special position of the landlord of an insolvent tenant. Insolvency law, and also the general remedies available to the landlord, have to strive for a balance between being too "hard" and too "soft". If the law is too hard on the defaulting party, businesses that may still be viable could be discontinued. If regulation is too soft, an unsound financial management of the would-be defaulting party is encouraged *ex ante*. Another factor that is taken into consideration for the analysis is the clarity of (default) rules and their impact on transaction costs.

The German law on remedies available against a defaulting tenant deserves a positive appraisal. In particular, the German law of forfeiture provides clear legal rules and parties do not need to draft costly arrangements. The balance between too hard and too soft rules is attained by providing the defaulting tenant with a period of up to two months within which he can default on rents without risking forfeiture.

English law of forfeiture, on the other hand, could be criticised for a perceived lack of clarity and the need for parties to observe cumbersome procedural elements. Legal defaults are largely not provided so that parties are required to explicitly define in their agreements all such events that may qualify as default. On the other hand, English law gives the parties a wide discretion to negotiate their individual clauses which may be advantageous where both parties are well informed about the implications of their decisions.

It is also found that the rules on forfeiture are ambiguous as a result of the twofold nature of English leases. The English lease may either be used for short-term commercial leases as is the case in Germany, but the same law of leases also applies to leases constituting the quasi-ownership of land via very long leases with low ground rents. It would be highly desirable if a tenant default bill was enacted that separated these two economically very different functions of the English lease. As a result of the current legislation, it is extremely difficult for parties to a lease to assess whether their acts or omissions are likely to lead to forfeiture of the lease. The English law furthermore does provide little remedy against tenants who permanently sub-perform on their obligations under a lease, giving ample opportunities for moral hazard.

A further advantage of German law is the procedural ability to combine an action for payment with an action for forfeiture and to obtain a payment order at relatively low costs.

In many cases, tenant default and insolvency of the tenant coincide. It is therefore also important to analyse the position of the landlord of an insolvent tenant as corporate insolvency typically entails a (partial) suspension of actions against the insolvent company.

German insolvency law again offers the advantage of a clear structure but the position of the landlord of an insolvent tenant is fairly weak. The insolvency administrator may disclaim leases but the landlord has no right to terminate the lease because of an opening of insolvency proceedings. This rule is meant to protect insolvent businesses as it is the aim of the reformed German insolvency law to promote turnarounds and continuation of companies in crisis. Statistics show, however, that the new law has not been overly successful in achieving this aim.

The weak position of the German landlord in case of insolvency may, on the other hand, serve as a barrier to entry where potential tenants are e.g. start-ups.

Landlords may request high security deposits from such tenants which may pose an excessive burden on small or newly-founded companies. It is furthermore doubtful whether the protection of business premises has the relevance that the law affords to it: Businesses that depend on a certain location for their success, e.g. restaurants, may have been in the wrong location in the first place. For other businesses where location plays a secondary role the protection of the old premises may not be so relevant either. It therefore seems that parties to a lease should be able to stipulate termination of the lease in case of tenant insolvency.

While both German and English insolvency law promote the continuation of companies experiencing financial difficulties, English insolvency law provides a wider set of procedures by which (would-be) insolvent companies can be rescued. The landlord's position depends on the scheme under which his tenant was put.

The table below summarises the landlord's position under the different schemes:

Table 6-1: Position of landlord under English insolvency /rescue schemes

Schemes	Position of landlord	Appraisal
CVAs	- CVA are voluntary agreements and are freely negotiated between debtor and creditors - General view is that position of landlord depends on individual CVA - Creditors vote on acceptance of CVA - Case law ambiguous, some commentators claim that landlord may challenge CVAs excluding forfeiture as prejudicial towards landlord - "Small" companies (99.3% of all UK enterprises) may apply for two months moratorium within which no legal action may take place	- CVA may put landlord in disadvantaged position where his claim and thus voting rights are low - As it is a recently developed scheme, there is little case law and position of land law is unclear - It seems likely that new lease contracts will have a section on CVAs included
Schemes of Arrangement	- These are also voluntary schemes that may in future largely be replaced by CVAs, which offer certain further advantages - Position of landlord better than under CVA as landlords would form a class of creditors that may veto the scheme - Also, there is no moratorium under a Scheme of Arrangement	- More advantageous for landlord than CVAs but scheme likely to disappear in future

Schemes	Position of landlord	Appraisal
Administration Order	- Administration similar to German insolvency procedures: court-appointed administrator takes over management and assesses scope for continuation - Landlord is barred from all remedies that are normally available against defaulting tenant (moratorium) - But landlord may challenge refusal of re-entry by administrator in court - The court has to carry out an economic analysis of benefits and costs of forfeiture (Re Atlantic Computer Systems)	- Best in terms of protecting landlord's and tenant's interests - Protection of insolvent tenant's business but court may grant leave to forfeit lease if economically justified - Effectiveness of protection of landlord's interest depends on judge's capacity to assess economic impact of granting forfeiture and quality of landlord's legal representatives
Administrative Receivership	- Procedure to enable secured creditors to enforce their rights - Little impact on landlord-tenant relationship: no bar on remedies	- Landlord may still enforce his rights but potential problems with distress for rent as goods may be collateral of secured creditor
Liquidation	- Winding-up of the company - All actions against insolvent company stop - Forfeiture possible if court grants leave - Liquidator may disclaim (i.e. terminate) leases - Landlord normally able to deduct rent arrears from security deposit	- Court may grant leave for forfeiture but insolvency has to be reserved as a ground of forfeiture in the lease - Disclaimer: landlord may also claim discounted value of future rents - Security deposits caused litigation: in principle, landlord may deduct rent arrears from security deposit but it depends on the wording in the individual lease (Re Greenport Ltd) - Therefore: liquidation carries with it a number of uncertainties for the landlord

As each procedure causes different consequences for the landlord it is difficult to come to a general conclusion on English insolvency law. Certainly, the different positions of the landlord under each scheme cause uncertainties. Further uncertainties are caused by the strong reliance of courts on the actual wording in contracts as enunciated in Re Greenport. Especially for the more recent schemes such as the CVA, further litigation should be expected in the future to clarify the relationship of landlord and tenant under these special circumstances. From a law and economics perspective, the most desirable scheme is surely the appointment of an administrator as the court's decision whether to grant leave for forfeiture depends on an assessment of the economic consequences of exercising the remedy.

A general appraisal of the two systems leads to the conclusion that both are efficient for the types of landlord-tenant relationships that dominate the countries' real estate markets.

The German regulation of business leases is suitable for a business environment with many small and medium-sized enterprises, known as *Mittelstand*, with an overall absence of large, professional landlords. Real estate is largely viewed as a production factor, rather than an investment. Large real estate portfolios are owned by non-property companies.[282] The law provides a large number of default and mandatory rules that cover the majority of real estate disputes. In general, lease contracts refer to the relevant provisions of the civil code and there is relatively little scope for contracting-out of the *BGB*'s provisions.

Inefficiencies may be caused by indexation, the dominant rent adjustment mechanism, as the comparison of market rents and consumer price inflation shows little correlation. On the other hand, indexation is easy to operate without the need to resort to third parties for rent determination. This caters for the needs of small landlords that require a cost-effective adjustment mechanism.

The German real estate market has been undergoing a period of change and, as discussed in the introduction, an influx of foreign investors leads to an increased pressure to act in compliance with international standards. As a consequence, the German market may in future show higher volatility and indexation may no longer be acceptable for larger investment properties.

The English regulation of business leases is also largely efficient, but for a very different group of landlords. The English system serves the needs of large property investors. The class system, which has dominated British society for centuries, and the stability and protection of capital investments in Britain, have let to a concentration of real estate ownership in the hands of professional investors. There is a long tradition of property companies that are listed in the FTSE 100 at the London Stock Exchange and there are also large private property companies such as Grosvenor, which is owned by the Duke of Westminster and holds substantial real estate in Central London and the Regions.

---

282 See also the chart with real estate ownership as a percentage of total assets of German DAX companies. For comparison: GE, the world's largest manufacturer of electronic goods, does not own any real estate but rents its complete portfolio.

In comparison to the relatively detailed regulation provided by the German civil code, drafting of English business leases is almost entirely left to the parties. This means that professional landlords can draft agreements that are customised to meet their individual requirements. When there is equal bargaining power between the contracting parties, this is clearly beneficial, but small tenants may often be disadvantaged.

It will be interesting to see whether the future will bring a convergence of real estate market practices and regulations or whether markets will retain their idiosyncrasies even as internationalisation of investments and asset management increases. Today it is impossible to predict which impact the recession and crisis of financial markets and the financial system at large is going to have on the development of real estate regulation.

It is imaginable that the crisis, which started with the collapse of overheated property markets in the United States but also in the UK, will also question the often alleged supremacy of UK property practice. Investors may in future view national differences in real estate regulation as a further method to diversify risks.

It seems equally likely, however, that the English system, as so often in its long history, uses the current crisis and recession as an opportunity to renew itself. For Germany, this could mean that in a few years strengthened Anglo-American investors may re-discover the German market. Associated with this there may be further pressure to harmonise real estate regulation on a pan-European level. Either development would have its merits.

References

Abitz, E., 2004, *Die Kündigung des Mietvertrages,* Hamburg: Hammonia

Adair, A., Berry, J., and McGreal, S., 1996, Valuation of residential property: analysis of participant behaviour, *Journal of Property Valuation & Investment*, 14(1), 20-35

Adams, M.,1980, *Ökonomische Analyse der Sicherungsrechte,* Königstein/Ts: Athenäum

Addae-Dapaah, K.A., and Yeo, C.,1999, Percentage lease agreement as a shopping centre management tool: a panacea for Singapore's retail industry woes?, *Property Management,* 17, 24-36

Allen, D. and Lueck, D., 1992, Contract choice in modern agriculture: cash rent versus cropshare, *Journal of Law and Economics*, 35(2), 397-426

Allen, M.T., Buttimer, R.J. and Waller, N.G., 1995, An examination of the role of security clauses and deposits in residential lease contracts, *Journal of real estate finance and economics,* 10(3), 271-283

Allen & Overy, 2008, *Powerhouse CVA: how secure is your guarantee?,* London: Allen & Overy

Anon., 2006, Zweiter offener Immobilienfonds wird geschlossen, *Frankfurter Allgemeine Zeitung*, 18 January, no. 15, p. 19,

Ayres, I., and Gertner, R.H., 1989, Filling gaps in incomplete contracts: an economic theory of default rules, *The Yale Law Journal,* 99, 87-130

Baird, D.G., 1990, Self-interest and cooperation in long-term contracts, *Journal of Legal Studies,* 19, 583-596

Baird, K, and Ho, L.C., 2007, Company Voluntary Arrangement: the restructuring trends, *Insolvency Intelligence,* 20(8), 124-126

Barzel, Y., 1985, Are transaction costs just costs?, *Zeitschrift für die gesamte Staatswissenschaft,* 141(1), 4-16

Barzel, Y., 1989, *Economic analysis of property rights,* Cambridge: CUP

Benjamin, J.D., Lusht, K.M., and Shilling, J.D., 1992a, Housing rent differentials among renters who pay higher security deposits: a separating equilibrium, *Unpublished Working Paper*

Benjamin, J.D., Shilling, J.D., and Sirmans, C.F., 1992b, Security deposits, adverse selection and office leases, *Journal of the American Real Estate and Urban Economics Association,* 20(2), 259-272

Bigus, J., and Eger, T., 2004, Insolvenzrecht zwischen privatautonomer Gestaltung und öffentlicher Regulierung, *Perspektiven der Wirtschaftspolitik,* 5(2), 193-209

Bird & Bird, 1999, *Property Update*, Issue 24, London: Bird & Bird Solicitors

Bobka, G., 2009, Indizes – wie praxistauglich sind sie wirklich?, *Immobilienwirtschaft*, 11, 19-27

Bright, S., and Gilbert, G., 1995, *Landlord and Tenant Law: The Nature of Tenancies,* Oxford: OUP

Bub, W.-R., and Treier (ed.), 1999, *Handbuch der Geschäfts- und Wohnraummiete,* 3rd ed., München: Beck

BulwienGesa AG, 2009, *RIWIS – Regionales immobilienwirtschaftliches Informationssystem*, München: BulwienGesa AG

Cheung, S.N.S., 1969a, *The theory of share tenancy : with special application to Asian agriculture and the first phase of Taiwan land reform*, Chicago: University of Chicago Press

Cheung, S.N.S., 1969b, Transaction costs, risk aversion and the choice of contractual arrangements, *Journal of Law and Economics*, 12(1), 23-42

Cock, R., and French, N., 2001, Internal rents and corporate property management – a study into the use of internal rents in UK corporate organisations, *Working Papers in Land Management and Development*, 08/01, The University of Reading: Reading

Companies House, 2008, *Liquidation and insolvency (GBW 1)*, Version 7, January 2008, Cardiff, Edinburgh, London: Companies House

CorpusSireo, 2007, *Portfoliotransaktionen in Deutschland: Trends am Immobilienmarkt Nr. 1,* Frankfurt/Main: Sireo Real Estate GmbH

Crosby, H., Hughes, C. and Murdoch, S., 2005, *Monitoring the 2002 Code of Practice for commercial leases,* London: ODPM

Crosby, N., and Murdoch, S., 1997, *Cutting Edge 1997: the influence of procedure on rent determination in the commercial property market of England and Wales,* London: Royal Institution of Chartered Surveyors

Crosby, N., Murdoch, J., and Lavers, A., 2002, Expert valuation witnesses in the UK - problems and solutions, *Journal of property investment & finance*, 20(4), 316-353

DETR, 2000, *Action plan agreed on rent review clauses (communiqué)*, London: DETR, No. COI2728

Diaz, J., 1990a, How Appraisers Do Their Work: A Test of the Appraisal Process and the Development of a Descriptive Model, *The Journal of Real Estate Research*, 5(1)

Diaz, J., 1990b, The Process of Selecting Comparable Sales, *The Appraisal Journal*, October 1990

Diaz, J., 1997, An investigation into the impact of previous expert estimates on appraisal judgement, *Journal of Real Estate Research*, 13(1), 57-66

Diaz, J., and Hansz, J.A., 1997, How valuers use the value opinions of others, *Journal of property valuation & investment*, 15(3), 256-260

Diaz, J., and Wolverton, M.L., 1998, A longitudinal examination of the appraisal smoothing process, *Real Estate Economics*, 26(2), 349-356

Diaz, J., 1999, The first decade of behavioral research in the discipline of property, *Journal of property investment & finance*, 17(4), 326-332

Dierig, C., 2009, *Gerichte wollen Insolvenzverwaltern in die Karten schauen*, Welt am Sonntag No. 31, 2 August 2009, p. 25

Edwards, C., and Krendel, P., 2007, *Institutional leases in the 21st century*, London: EG Books

Eger, T., 1995, *Eine ökonomische Analyse von Langzeitverträgen*, Marburg: Metropolis

Eger, T., 2001, Bankruptcy regulations and the new German insolvency law from an economic point of view, *European Journal of Law* & Economics, 11(1), 29-46

Eppli, M.J., Hendershott, P.H., Meija, L.C. and Shilling, J.D., 2000, Lease overage rent clauses: motivation and use, American Real Estate Society Conference, Santa Barbara, CA

Ernst & Young Real Estate, 2010, *Real Estate Trends Ausgabe 40, August 2010,* Eschborn/ Frankfurt am Main: Ernst & Young Real Estate

Fama, E.F., and Jensen, M.C., 1983, Agency problems and residual claims, *The journal of law and economics*, 26(2), 327-349

Flath, D., 1980, The economics of short-term leasing, *Economic Inquiry*, 18, 247-259

Franken, T. and Dahl, M., 2006, *Mietverhältnisse in der Insolvenz*, 2nd ed., München: C.H. Beck

Friedemann, J., 2008, *Deutschland ist der Favorit 2008*, Frankfurter Allgemeine Zeitung, 29 February, no. 51, p. 45

Gallimore, P., 1994, Aspects of Information Processing and Value Judgement and Choice, *Journal of Property Research*, 11(2), 97-110

Gallimore, P., 1996, Confirmation Bias in the Valuation process: A Test for Corroborating Evidence, *Journal of Property Research*, 13(4), 261-273

Gallimore, P. and Wolverton, M., 1997, Price-Knowledge Induce Bias: A Cross-Cultural Comparison, *Journal of Property Valuation and Investment*, 15, 261-273

Geltner, D., and Miller, N.G., 2001, *Commercial Real Estate Analysis and Investments*, Mason, OH: Thomson Learning

Goldberg, V.P., 1976, Regulation and administered contracts, *The Bell Journal of Economics*, 7(2), 426-448

Goldberg, V.P., 1985, Economic aspects of bankruptcy law - comment, *Zeitschrift für die gesamte Staatswissenschaft*, 141(1), 99-103

Gondring, H.-P., 2009, *Immobilienwirtschaft*, 2nd ed., München: Franz Vahlen

Goode, R., 2005, *Principles of corporate insolvency law*, 3rd ed., London: Sweet & Maxwell

Gray, K., and Gray, S.F., 2006, *Land law*, 4th ed., Oxford: OUP

Hart, O.D., 1995, *Firms, contracts and financial structure*, Oxford: Clarendon

Hart, O.D., and Holmström, B., 1987, The theory of contracts, in Bewley, T. (ed.), *Advances in economic theory: fifth world congress*, Cambridge: CUP

Havard, T., 1999, Do valuers have a greater tendency to adjust a previous valuation upwards or downwards?, *Journal of property investment & finance*, 17(4), 365-373

Hawkings, H.W., 1990, Shopping centres: turnover rents on the increase, *Estates Gazette*, 22 September, 28-29

Hax, H., 1985, Economic aspects of bankruptcy law, *Zeitschrift für die gesamte Staatswissenschaft*, 141, 80-98

Hendershott, P.H., 2002, A comparison of upward-only and turnover leases, *Journal of property investment & finance,* 20(6), 513-524

Horst, H.R., 2003, *Praxis des Mietrechts*, München: C.H. Beck

House of Commons Library, 1999, *Inflation: the Value of the Pound 1750-1998*, Research Paper 99/20, London: House of Commons Library

Hviid, M., 2000, Long-Term Contracts and Relational contracts, in Bouckaert, B., and De Geest, G. (eds.), *The Encyclopaedia of Law and Economics vol III*, Cheltenham: Elgar, 46-72

Industrie- und Handelskammer Frankfurt/Main, 2007, *Mietvertrag für Gewerberaum*, Frankfurt am Main: http://www.frankfurt-main.ihk.de/recht/mustervertrag/mietvertrag_gewerbe/index.html#bem

Industrie- und Handelskammer Nürnberg für Mittelfranken, 2002, *Leitfaden für den Abschluss eines Gewerbemietvertrages*, Schriften und Arbeitspapiere Nr. 109/02, Nürnberg: IHK Nürnberg für Mittelfranken

Investment Property Forum, 2005, *The size and structure of the UK property market*, London: IPF

Investment Property Forum, 2007a, *Risk management in UK property portfolios: a survey of current practice*, London: IPF

Investment Property Forum, 2007b, *The Use of Periodic Valuations in Indirect Property Investment*, London: IPF

Jensen, M.C., and Meckling, W.H., 1976, Theory of the firm: managerial behaviour, agency costs and ownership structure, *Journal of Financial Economics*, 3(4), 305-360

Johnson, G., and Scholes, K., 2006, *Exploring Corporate Strategy*, 7th ed., London: Financial Times/Prentice Hall

Jones Lang LaSalle, 2006, *Real estate transparency index*, Chicago, IL: Jones Lang LaSalle Research

Jones Lang LaSalle, 2007, *City profile Hamburg Q3 2007*, Hamburg: Jones Lang LaSalle Research

Jones Lang LaSalle, 2008, *Investmentmarktüberblick Q1 2008*, Frankfurt/Hamburg: Jones Lang LaSalle Research

Jones Lang LaSalle, 2008, *Key market indicators Q3 2008*, London: Jones Lang LaSalle Research

Jones Lang LaSalle, 2009, *City profile Hamburg Q2 2009*, Hamburg: Jones Lang LaSalle Research

Jourdan, S., 2002, *Leases and insolvency*, London: Falcon Chambers

Keenan, D., 1999, *Smith & Keenan's Company Law for students*, 11th ed., London: Financial Times/Pitman

Key, T., and Almond, N., 2004, *The impact of banning upward only rent reviews*, report to the British Property Federation, Cass Business School & Jones Lang LaSalle

Kinnard, W.N., Lenk, M.M., and Worzala, E.M., 1997, Client pressure on commercial appraisal industry: how prevalent is it?, *Journal of Property Valuation and Investment*, 15(3), 233-244

Kirchhof, H.-P. (ed.), 2008, *Münchener Kommentar zur Insolvenzordnung – Band 2*, 2nd ed., München: C.H. Beck

Klug, W., 2008, *Künftige Haus-Aufgaben*, Euro am Sonntag, 17 August, p. 12

Law Commission, 2001, *Limitation of actions (LC 270)*, London: Law Commission

Law Commission, 2006, *Termination of tenancies for tenant default (LC 303)*, London: Law Commission

Lewellen, W.G., Long, M.S., and McConnell, J.J., 1976, Asset leasing in competitive capital markets, *The journal of finance*, 31(3), 787-798

Lewis, P., 1989, Retailing: importing the American style, *Estates Gazette*, 7 January, 20-21

Lindner-Figura, J. (ed.), 2006, *Geschäftsraummiete*, München: Beck

Lofstedt, C., and Baum, A., 1993, *International Leasing Structures*, London: Royal Institution of Chartered Surveyors

Ludwig, H., 2005, *Prognose von Gewerbemieten in Deutschland: Methodik und Umsetzung von Mietprognosemodellen für unterschiedliche Marktcharakteristika bei Gewerbeimmobilien,* TU München (dissertation): http://deposit.d-nb.de/cgi-bin/dokserv?idn=978862716

Luebeck Business Development Corporation, 2006, *Guide to commercial rents in Lübeck,* Luebeck: Luebeck Business Development Corporation

Maier, K.M., 1999, *Risikomanagement im Immobilienwesen*, Frankfurt am Main: Fritz Knapp

Masten, S.E., 2000, Contractual choice, in Bouckaert, B. and De Geest, G. (eds.), *The Encyclopaedia of Law and Economics vol III*, Cheltenham: Elgar, 25-45

Maxted, B., and Porter, T., 2003, *Impact of Banning Upward-only Rent Reviews on UK Commercial Property Lending – Research Findings*, Report to the British Property Federation, De Montfort University

McAllister, P., 1996, Turnover rents: comparative valuation issues, *Journal of property valuation & investment*, 14(2), 6-23

McParland, C., Adair, A., and McGreal, S., 2002, Valuation standards - a comparison of four European countries, *Journal of property investment & finance,* 20(2), 127-141

Morgan, J.F.W., 1998, The natural history of professionalisation and its effects on valuation theory and practice in the UK and Germany, *Journal of property valuation & investment*, 16(2), 185-206

Murdoch, S., and Crosby, N., 1994, The legal implications of rent-free periods at rent review, *Journal of property valuation & investment*, 12(2), 43-50

Nagel, B., and Eger, T., 2003, *Wirtschaftsrecht 2 - Eigentum, Delikt und Vertrag,* 4th ed., München, Wien: Oldenbourg

Neuhaus, K.-J., 2005, *Handbuch der Geschäftsraummiete*, 2nd ed. , Recklinghausen: ZAP

Newell, A., and H. A. Simon, 1972, *Human problem solving,* Englewood Cliffs, NJ: Prentice Hall

Nobes, C., 1989, *Pocket accounting (The Economist)*, London: Profile Books

ODPM (Office of the Deputy Prime Minister), 2004, *Business tenancies: new procedures under the Landlord and Tenant Act 1954, Part 2*, London: ODPM

ODPM (Office of the Deputy Prime Minister), The Parliamentary Under-Secretary of State Yvette Cooper, 2005, *Commercial property leases (statement dated 15 March 2005)*, London: ODPM

Parsons, A.E., 2006, *Tenant default under commercial leases*, 4th ed., Welwyn Garden City: xpl law

Pashigian, B.P., and Gould, E.D., 1998, Contracts, externalities, and incentives in shopping malls: an empirical analysis, *Stigler Centre for Study of the State of the Economy Working Paper Series*, No 143

Perspektive Mittelstand, 2008, *Studie: Existenzgründer scheitern am häufigsten an der Finanzierung,* Unterdießen: Perspektive Mittelstand,

Posner, K.A., 1992, Hedging against changes in market rent levels, *Real estate review*, 22(3), 21-27

Pretorius, F., Walker, A. and Chau, K.W., 2003, Exploitation, expropriation and capital assets: the economics of commercial real estate leases, *Journal of real estate literature*, 11(1), 3-34

Property Industry Alliance, 2009, *Property Data Report 2009*, London: Property Industry Alliance

Rao, C.H.H., 1971, Uncertainty, entrepreneurship and sharecropping in India, *Journal of Political Economy*, 79(3), 578-595

Reichel, R., 2008, *Vorwürfe gegen Immobilienbranche - Analysten beklagen fehlenden Durchblick*, Handelsblatt, 16 July: http://www.handelsblatt.com/finanzen/immobilien/analysten-beklagen-fehlenden-durchblick;2012194

Reid, J.D., 1977, The theory of the share tenancy revisited once again, *Journal of Political Economy*, 85(2), 403-407

Salanié, B., 1997, *The economics of contracts*, London: MIT Press

Sanders, A.B., Pagliari, J.L. jr., and Webb, J.R., 1995, Portfolio management concepts and their application to real estate, in Pagliari, J.L. jr. (ed.), *The Handbook of Real Estate Portfolio Management*, Chicago: Irwin Professional

Schreiber, M., 2008, *Mangelware Asset Management*, Financial Times Deutschland (online edition), 23 June

Schulte, K-W, and Schäfers, W. (eds.), 1998, *Handbuch Corporate Real Estate Management*, Köln: Verlagsgesellschaft Rudolf Müller

Schulte, K-W, Rottke, N., and Pitschke, C., 2005, Transparency in the German real estate market, *Journal of property investment & finance*, 23(1), 90-108

Schwartz, A., and Scott, R.E., 2003, Contract theory and the limits of contract law, *Yale Law Journal,* 113

Simon, H.A., 1978, Rationality as Process and as Product of Thought, *American Economic Review*, 68(2), 1-16

Slapper, G., and Kelly, D., 2004, *The English legal system*, 7th ed., London: Cavendish

Slaughter & May, 2008, *An introduction to English insolvency law*, London: Slaughter & May

Smales, B.J., 1981, *Economic history*, 2nd ed., London: Heinemann

Smith jr., C.W., and Wakeman, L.M., 1985, Determinants of corporate leasing policy, *The journal of finance*, 40(3), 895-908

Sparkes, P., 2001, *A new landlord and tenant*, London: Hart

Statistisches Bundesamt, 2006, *Preise in Deutschland 2006,* Wiesbaden: Statistisches Bundesamt

Stiglitz, J.E., and Weiss, A.M., 1981, Credit rationing in markets with imperfect information, *American Economic Review*, 71(3), 393-410

The Joint Working Group on Commercial Leases, 2007, *The code for leasing business premises in England and Wales 2007*, London, http://www.leasingbusinesspremises.co.uk

Thomas, M., 1995, The performance of the German property market between 1989 and 1994, *Journal of property valuation & investment*, 13(5), 67-84

Turner, N., and Thomas, M., 2001a, Property market indices and lease structures – the impact on investment return delivery in the UK and Germany: Part 1, *Journal of property investment and finance*, 19 (2), 175-187

Turner, N., and Thomas, M., 2001b, Property market indices and lease structures – the impact on investment return delivery in the UK and Germany: Part 2, *Journal of property investment and finance*, 19 (3), 296-321

Walsh, B.P., 1988, Shopping centres: why are turnover rents not more popular, *Estates Gazette*, 2 April, 20-24

Weise, P., Brandes, W., Eger, T., and Kraft, M., 2002, *Neue Mikroökonomie*, 4th ed., Heidelberg: Physica

Williamson, O.E., 1971, The vertical integration of production: market failure considerations, *American Economic Review*, LXII, December, 777-795

Wolverton, M., 1996, *"Diaz, J."*, Royal Institution of Chartered Surveyors, London, paper presented at the Cutting Edge Conference

Wolverton, M.L. and Gallimore, P., 1999, Client feedback and the role of the appraiser, *Journal of Real Estate Research*, 18(3), 415-432

Woolf (Lord), 1996, *Access to Justice – Final Report*, London: Department for Constitutional Affairs, http://www.dca.gov.uk/civil/final/contents.htm

Wüstefeld, H., 2000, *Risiko und Rendite von Immobilieninvestments*, Frankfurt am Main: Fritz Knapp

Sebastian Michael Gläsner

Return Patterns of German Open-End Real Estate Funds

An Empirical Explanation of Smooth Fund Returns

Frankfurt am Main, Berlin, Bern, Bruxelles, New York, Oxford, Wien, 2010.
XII, 111 pp., num. tab. and graph.
Corporate Finance and Governance. Edited by Dirk Schiereck. Vol. 1
ISBN 978-3-631-60406-9 · hardback € 27,80*

The aim of this study is to better understand stable capital growth of German properties and to contribute to the explanation of stable fund returns. In the course of the investigation, evidence is found that both phenomena are interrelated. All analyses are based on publicly available data; therefore they are not limited by client interests. Results show three different pieces of evidence on return smoothing, namely the influence on valuation, the timing of valuations, and the influence on returns resulting in return differences by calendar months. Together with the notion of internationally uniquely stable returns, it seems impossible to extract true asset volatility from the observed appraisal-based time series.

Content: Appraisal Smoothing · Client Influence · German vs. UK Concept of Market Values

Frankfurt am Main · Berlin · Bern · Bruxelles · New York · Oxford · Wien
Distribution: Verlag Peter Lang AG
Moosstr. 1, CH-2542 Pieterlen
Telefax 00 41 (0) 32 / 376 17 27

*The €-price includes German tax rate
Prices are subject to change without notice

Homepage http://www.peterlang.de